growing up
in public

growing up in public

Coming of Age in a Digital World

Devorah Heitner, PhD

A TarcherPerigee Book

tarcherperigee
an imprint of Penguin Random House LLC
penguinrandomhouse.com

ISBN 9780593420966
Ebook ISBN 9780593420973

Printed in the United States of America
1st Printing

Book design by Laura K. Corless

This book is for Harold, who has excellent boundaries, and for Dan, who tells important stories.

contents

There's pressure to share more of ourselves than we want. We often feel we have no other choice. To be relevant. To fit in. To get ahead. To be trusted and liked. Accepted and understood. This new compulsion toward self-exposure is possibly the biggest social experiment in history. We're making life-altering decisions about our personal boundaries with no guidance and no precedent. Fortunately, there is a blueprint. Anyone who's lived in the public eye as an athlete, a politician, or an entertainer has navigated a version of this . . .

Before I share, I ask myself: Why? What's the purpose?

And most importantly, how does it serve the people I love?

—Bryce Dallas Howard, TED Talk, April 2022

Kids growing up are immersed in digital communities, from Minecraft to Discord, from group texts to social media . . . even Google Docs and classroom apps are places where they hang out. With all this networked connection, a large proportion of their lives is lived in public. So unless you were a child celebrity, your children likely have far less privacy than you did.

Things were different when I was a teenager. When I was fourteen and enjoying time away from my parents at summer camp, my cabin thought it would be so rebellious, feminist, and just plain fun if we took our "cabin portrait" in our bras. I was all in with this idea. To my thinking at the time, posing in our bras didn't look that dissimilar than being in bikini tops. I wasn't worried about the photo moving beyond our little camp world into wide circulation. Especially since our camp zine was a low-tech affair, photocopied in black and white like a good 1990s zine. Indeed, nobody made a fuss about the photo. A few other cabins copied our brilliant idea. But I'm thankful I was born in the pre–digital age, because if I'd done that as a teen today, the repercussions could have been serious. What if that picture had been posted online? What would the wider community have thought about me and my friends? Would we have gotten into big trouble legally? Would parents and other adults have passed judgment on us for agreeing to pose for that picture?

Today, we can track our kids' every move with apps, see their grades within minutes of being posted, or fixate on their digital footprint, anxious that a misstep could cause them to be "canceled." But how can they figure out who they really are when they have zero privacy and constant judgment? For over a decade, and especially since writing my book *Screenwise: Helping Kids Thrive (and Survive) in Their Digital World* (2016), my mission has been to bridge the gap between adults, parents, educators, and young people, helping adults understand young people's experiences growing up in our digital age. I've consulted on digital citizenship curricula at large and innovative school districts, as well as at independent schools, to help them adopt a more positive, less fear-based approach to mentoring kids on growing up in the digital world. In every community, parents are seeking actionable information about the implications of their children's online sharing, as well as their own.

Breaking down misunderstandings about the ways we live and

relate in the digital age has been the focus of my work for the past decade. At my student workshops, young people confide that they feel like their parents are paparazzi they need to hide from. Meanwhile, parents confidently say to me, "Kids don't care about privacy!"

A fellow mother called me saying, "My son just posted a stupid video on TikTok where he is trying to be funny but sounds really offensive. I'm afraid this will be following him around forever. People who don't know him and his quirky sense of humor will definitely get the wrong idea. I already told him to take it down, but the thought of dealing with this for the next few years is giving me nightmares. What do we do?"

Other parents have come up to me after a public talk at their kid's school with questions like: "My daughter just posted a 'thirst trap' photo on Instagram; how will this affect her reputation and her mental health if she perceives she doesn't get enough positive feedback?"

Or, "My kid saw a post where all the other boys in his class were invited to a party, and he wasn't. What can I do?"

After the "Facebook whistleblower" came forward in 2021 with evidence that Meta, Instagram's parent company, had internal research showing that using their product was potentially harming children and teenagers, parents' alarm only grew. Hearing so many questions from parents worried about both how their kids' digital selves are perceived *and* how that perception affects a kid's self-image made me curious: How many parents are losing sleep over their kids' "permanent records" or reputations online? What are they worried about in terms of pressures to be famous or to get likes? I sent a survey to the parents on my email list to ask:

What do you worry about most in terms of your children growing up in public?

Hundreds of parents responded within twenty-four hours, sharing their concerns and filling me in on their worst fears. Most of their worries involved:

- What kids post publicly.

- Confusion about privacy settings and who can see their kid's posts.

- Oversight ("Should I read their texts?").

- Reputation: they wanted to learn about the impact of their kid's digital profile on their college admissions prospects.

- The constant pressure to earn "likes" and to present a digital façade of their life.

- The possibility that their kid's friends could take a picture or video of them doing something embarrassing and share it widely, shaming their kid and possibly even foreclosing future opportunities.

- Vulnerability of online data even if it is supposedly "locked down," for example, school data breaches, cloud hacking, a Snapchat hack, private messages on Facebook being used to prosecute individuals, etc. Even if you know how to use privacy settings, Snapchat and other online apps have been hacked. (This is how Jennifer Lawrence had her nude photos leaked, leading her to forsake social media.)

One parent wrote:

> *I worry that [adolescents'] developing brains will lower their inhibitions and that they will post something or text something that will come back to them later in life.*

I am 100 percent positive that I would have made really bad choices when I was a kid if I'd had access to social media and texting. I am glad that nothing exists from that time period. My own kids won't be so lucky.

I wrote *Growing Up in Public* to bridge the communication gap between generations by helping parents understand and empathize with their kids' digital experiences in new ways. As a parent and former college professor with tremendous affection and admiration for young people, I want to help build more empathy for adolescents doing all their messy, chaotic, and stressful growing up in public. Online, they, their friends, and even we—their well-meaning parents—can share their photos and news in ways that may feel constraining, embarrassing, or worse.

Growing Up in Public tackles the "What if my kid goes viral for the wrong reason" question *and* the deeper questions that most parents *aren't* asking themselves about how surveilling our kids can undermine our children's journeys to independence and figuring out who they are.

Everyone tells parents we should worry about our kids' "digital footprint," but what about tracking our kids on location apps? Or sharing about them ourselves? We're all navigating privacy and boundaries questions. We get worried about reputation, but we need to think about the bigger picture of what it means for our kids to grow up so searchable and with so much surveillance. We need to be sure we're not adding the problems that can come with this superconnected life our kids are living. The coming-of-age journey toward a grown-up identity is messy. No amount of parental monitoring, Life360, or perfectly curated family social media sharing can be guaranteed to keep that messiness from getting real. Very real.

In the chapters that follow, I offer pragmatic ways that parents can support their kids who are coming of age in public because young people should not have to hide or go underground to preserve their privacy. *Growing Up in Public* **makes the case that parents should shift their focus from consequences to building character, helping their kids figure out who they really are, and teaching them to respect their own privacy and reputation by modeling that respect for them.** This modeling sets them up for accountability and authenticity, which are crucial for adulthood.

Parents feel like they can never win with kids in the digital world: too much oversight and their child may resent the hovering and actively try to hide or "fake it"; too little, and they may be in the dark about their child's progress, or their child may post something they regret on social media that could cause stress and alienation, potentially impacting their future.

As the parent of a middle schooler, I understand how deep the desire is to protect our children in this crazy world—to try to scare them toward making "good choices" by sounding the alarm about dire consequences should they make a wrong move, or to figure out how to "scrub" their mistake. (And on that note, I only mention that I have a middle schooler, but will not share extensive details about him out of respect for his privacy.) In our quest to be caring, involved parents, we have been encouraged to surveil our kids: tracking their location, checking up on grades, and scanning their communications with friends. We do this to "keep our kids safe" without realizing we're interrupting their process of becoming independent.

What I've observed through interacting with thousands of parents and kids is that a fear-based approach—i.e., a *consequences-based* approach—can breed more secrecy and distrust. It makes our kids feel like they are being watched but not *seen*; monitored but not *understood*. Instead, we can focus on helping our children build character (who they are) over threatening consequences (the bad things that can happen to them) to enable them to independently and reliably navigate their own boundaries, privacy, and reputation. We can mentor our kids in digital spaces by focusing on empathy and thoughtfulness, by being accountable, and repairing when things go wrong. We can also refuse to participate in gleefully amplifying the mistakes that other people's kids make.

As parents and role models, we need to hold *ourselves* accountable for the behaviors we may be unconsciously modeling for our kids, like using the very tech we complain about to monitor them, or sharing photos of them without their consent.

This book explores the key milestones of navigating privacy and online reputation that are part of growing up today. Each chapter includes insights from teens, tweens, and parents, as well as research-based data about how our children grow up in public. These chapters address the ways schools can use technology to surveil kids, parental "sharenting," the ways kids are rewriting the rules on what is okay to share about identity, sexting, the dreaded "What if my kid goes viral for the wrong reason?" question, and more.

While there will always be new threats to consider, new laws to navigate, and new social media platforms to adapt to, the truth remains that our kids need us to make the space for them to figure out who they are. To that end, *Growing Up in Public* explores these central questions:

- How can young people navigate their unfolding identities in a world where social media keeps a record of what they share online, and even what their friends and others share about them?

- What does it mean for kids to grow up in public, with everyone knowing about their bed-wetting or academic difficulties from their parents and other family members sharing on social media?

- Once tweens and teens join the digital world with their own social media accounts and gaming avatars, how will the public nature of this world affect their evolving identities and sense of self?

- What does it feel like for a child to have their number of followers constantly on display, and how does this affect their personality and self-esteem?

- What are the stresses and pressures on kids growing up with a high level of surveillance from parents, school, and peers as kids start to share information about themselves?

- Do colleges really stalk applicants online?

- How can we as parents move from monitoring (using tech to surveil our kids) to mentoring (teaching our children how to move through this world)?

- How can parents help young adults manage their own privacy, digital footprints, and even health records during their digital launch into adulthood?

Since I believe families should make their own choices about rules, access, and oversight of digital tools based on their own child's personality and self-regulation—and I want to empower parents to do this—each chapter lays out the information needed to guide parenting decisions around a particular area of concern. By mentoring and not just monitoring, and by modeling thoughtful uses of tech ourselves, we can help our tweens and teens to develop as responsible caretakers of their own identity and reputation for years to come.

We need to build in more respect for kids' privacy, help them focus on grappling with their identities away from the public eye, and allow them to be comfortable with complexity in their reputations. After all, they are not brands, they are our children, and they are human beings. *Growing Up in Public* lays out ways we can help transform the culture to make it better for ourselves and our kids, and provides crucial steps we can take to help our children stay safe in our current digital world. We can do better. It's up to us.

Tracking Our Kids in a World Where Kids Can Go Viral . . . for All the Wrong Reasons

When a school principal calls me at 7:00 a.m. with an urgent invitation to speak to their community as soon as possible, they are typically dealing with a situation where students have shared something they shouldn't have, and their community has been engulfed by scandal. Recently, one of these calls came from the principal of a middle school where some boys had shared an explicit video of two classmates engaged in a sexual act. It went viral around the school, and even at neighboring schools, in a matter of hours. Classes were disrupted, and everyone was talking and conjecturing. In situations like these, everyone panics—especially parents. *Did their own student see the video? Are their children implicated in some way*?

To the parents of the students who were recorded and the students who shared or posted the video, we can talk about damage control in a private meeting (more on this in chapter 7). Even the parents who are relieved that their kids were not directly involved still want to know how to avoid this kind of trouble for their own children. They want my recommendations on the best software to track, surveil, and mirror their teenager's every text, click, and post to their own phones. My answer is always this: we need to ask different questions. I urge parents to take a mentoring approach rather than monitor in fear.

> **Mentoring is better than monitoring if we want to set our kids up for success. We want our kids to make good decisions, even when we are not right there.**

At my talk to this community, I emphasized, "We want to teach kids to do the right thing, not catch them doing the wrong thing." We need to mentor our kids and teach them how to live in a world with lightning-fast digital sharing, including how to repair their mistakes. At first, some of the parents in the room continued to ask about monitoring software. They were all eager to get a handle on their children's technology use and avoid any lurking land mines.

This is understandable—our kids' digital landscape is overwhelming. Parents can see how much trouble their children can get into, and we want to protect them.

While I encouraged the parents in this community to mentor their children, model good behavior, and teach them how to make thoughtful choices from a place of empathy, some parents still seemed anxious. Perhaps they were mulling over mistakes from their own adolescence, mistakes that, if repeated by their children in the digital age, would be harder to leave behind, given social media's ability to amplify and preserve what we'd like to forget.

"Before you start reading all of their texts, ask yourselves what you are looking for," I advised. "Can you withstand living through middle school again by getting a play-by-play of each interaction your child encounters? If you plan to monitor their phone covertly, what will you do if you see something concerning? In most cases, being in conversation with your kids will give you more insights than reading their texts."

During another Q&A period, a father who appeared to be in his late fifties stood up and shared that he wasn't taking any chances: he tracked his son's and daughter's locations on their phones. In fact, he still tracked his eldest, nineteen, who was away at college in another state. If the "find my phone" tracking app suggested she wasn't in class, he would text her, demanding an explanation. Some other parents nodded their heads, while others grimaced at the casual invasion of this young woman's privacy. As a privacy-loving Generation Xer, I was taken aback, too.

Having talked to families about their lives in the digital age over the past ten years, I can confirm that parents and their offspring hold different notions of privacy. Our children are growing up "in public." Family members, peers, and even strangers follow their comings and goings on social media posts by them and others. Parents, in fact, frequently record and share their children's lives on social media, in addition to tracking where they are with geo-location apps; monitoring their texts, emails, and online activity; and constantly checking their performance with online school portals and behavior-monitoring apps like ClassDojo.

While you might not geo-track your children, read their texts, or post about them, we live in a society where doing so is possible, accepted, and even expected, so that affects our culture.

While speaking with tweens and teens at schools all over the country, I've found that while they consider this type of tech-enabled oversight from their parents and school to be overbearing and stressful, they have also become used to everyone knowing their business, including their friends' seeing their locations.

When I was young, there were no cell phones, no tracking devices. My parents couldn't just call me—I had a quarter to call them on the pay phone when I was ready for them to pick me up from the mall. When I left high school early to go to college at age sixteen, I learned later that rumors followed. *Where has she gone? Is Devorah pregnant? Is she in rehab?* A few close friends knew I was off to a funky little college for young students, but there was no place to make a public announcement, and so my leaving in the middle of junior year surely left some classmates with questions. But I was free to start over in a new space and to reinvent myself. No one from home could see me online, and I only kept in touch with my closest friends.

In contrast, teens today are observed all the time, even if they change settings. They don't have the same kind of privacy and space to experiment and figure themselves out that we enjoyed at their age. Living under "surveillance," with their parents, peers, and even school observing them at all times and the internet cataloging their every move, is the only life many of our children have ever known.

While the ability to maintain contact with our loved ones can be a good thing, our ability to constantly "check in," especially when it isn't mutually chosen, undermines our trust in our kids and their trust in us. This can lead to young people's boundaries and sense of privacy getting eroded. We don't intend to deny them independence or interrupt their development, but it can happen. When we say we're keeping an eye on our kids because they "make bad choices," we are robbing them of opportunities to develop good judgment and boundaries—and to think for themselves.

How Parents Surveil Kids

Parents have been snooping on their children forever. While their sons or daughters were at school, parents would go into their rooms looking for evidence of wrongdoing. They read notes written by classmates and even their private diaries.

The rules of parental surveillance have changed drastically now that tweens and teens live their social lives mostly online. Paradoxically, the very same technology that allowed kids to make their lives more private than ever (e.g., no one can listen to your conversations or come across a note a friend wrote to you via texts and Snapchat) has also made it exceedingly easy for parents to increase their level of monitoring.

This can start early, when a child is still using a shared family device like a tablet. Some parents set time limits or block adult content on streaming services that kids might otherwise come across inadvertently, like an ad for a violent movie that pops up after an episode of *Spidey and His Amazing Friends*. As kids grow older and have more control of connected devices like tablets and smartphones—often from third to eighth grade—some parents start monitoring more carefully the websites their kids visit, reading their emails or text messages, and checking the phone call log as part of an agreement for the child to gain access to a phone. The age when kids first get a phone continues to drop, and even younger children who don't yet have their own phone are often doing a lot of connecting online with other devices at a young age. This means young people need different kinds of direct instruction on how to responsibly use digital tools when interacting with peers depending on their age—a fifth grader is going to run into different texting issues than an eighth grader. For example, potty humor or "spam texting" comes up more often with younger kids, whereas sexting or more sophisticated kinds of exclusion can come up with older kids.

But teaching our children how to interact via tech does not have to mean surveillance. Looking at some of your tween's texts *with them* as part of their first year as a phone user is different from covertly spying, for example.

Surveillance becomes more problematic when parents covertly monitor or, frankly, spy on their teenager's online activity. Consider the following statistics from a study on parental online monitoring[1]:

- 61 percent of parents reported checking their teen's web browsing history.
- 48 percent reported looking at their teen's phone call log or text messages.
- 48 percent reported having access to their teen's email account.
- 43 percent reported having access to their teen's phone password.
- 39 percent reported using parental control apps to monitor their teen's online activity.
- 16 percent reported using monitoring apps to track their teen's location through their phone.

These findings were first reported in 2016. Since then—and especially since the pandemic, when teens everywhere were forced to conduct most of their social life online—there's no doubt that these numbers have increased.

Parents who engage in this kind of surveillance don't always do it with their kids' consent—or awareness. Even when teenagers are in-formed about and consent to having their online life surveilled, the power dynamic and most kids' economic reality make their "opt-in" not actually a true "choice." In some families, young people grudg-ingly accept being monitored and tracked as a condition of having their own phone or even access to a car—which, except for families who live in major urban areas with good public transit, can mean ac-cess to everything: friends, events, independence.

Tracking Our Kids So We Can Stop Worrying

When I ask parents why they feel compelled to monitor and track their kids, the most common response is "to protect my kid." Over the years, media stories have created a persistent sense of danger both online and offline. This fear is founded on real dangers—e.g., kids do get bullied online—as well as high-profile but unusual situations, like the child who is groomed and abducted by someone she met online. But most kids who play games on public servers, use social media, and browse the internet are not ever exposed to that kind of danger or trauma.

However, once these fears are stoked in parents' hearts, we feel like we should do something more to protect our kids. We would feel terrible if something bad happened to our kid online because we weren't keeping an eye out. Since we *can* surveil our kids, we feel that we *should*, that doing so is simply good parenting. In fact, so many parents are doing it that we are socialized to see monitoring and tracking our sons and daughters as a parenting "win."

Tracking our kids' whereabouts via an app, especially, seems to fend off worry and fulfill an obvious parenting desire to know that our kids are safe at all times. In a study of 695 public four-year and com-munity college students recruited from psychology classes, close to

32 percent reported that their parent currently uses location-tracking apps like Apple's Find My or Life360 to keep track of their teens' locations.[2] These were college students, so the majority were at least eighteen years old. The vast majority (82.6 percent) of the students reporting parental tracking explained that "safety" was the primary reason their parents offered for this kind of digital geo-location surveillance.

Long gone are the days when the TV commercial asked us, "It's 10:00 p.m., do you know where your children are?" Today, we can find out with the click of a button. Even without geo-tracking, our ability to "check in" easily via text, phone, or apps has shifted how much we worry and focus on our kids. Yet it's hard to say if tracking technology relieves our anxiety or just keeps it on a low boil. As emerging adolescents become more autonomous—when they start driving or have the freedom to use their after-school time at their discretion—geo-tracking makes parents feel like they are *doing* something to keep our children safe, when really the best thing our kids have going for them when they are out and about is their independent good judgment and, ideally, friends who will watch out for them.

Marisol, a mom from the South Side of Chicago, generally lets her teenagers travel independently; the kids take the El or a bus by themselves wherever they need to go. They have volunteer jobs and lots of extracurricular activities that they get to on their own. They know they can always call their mom if they are in a jam, but they're usually self-sufficient. Prom night, though, was different. While her daughter, Josie, was out with her friends, Marisol spent the evening with another mom, watching their two dots move on a map on their phones. They were making sure their daughters stuck together and were going to places that made sense—a donut shop, a friend's house, the prom venue.

Marisol told me later that she knew she'd be less worried if she followed "the dots." She said she wasn't worried about Josie, who had a history of making good choices. Marisol was worried about "other kids" and the world out there at large. If the technology to track her daughter didn't exist, Marisol acknowledged, she would have been just fine. But since it was there, she used it.

Our parents also worried about us going to prom, driving places, or not being home before our curfew when we were teenagers. Since they didn't have technology to help them check on us, many found other ways to calm their fears: they made sure their children were prepared for any eventuality and had the good judgment to make wise decisions. They helped us stay safe *and* become independent.

When I left home for college, my parents were terrified to send their seventeen-year-old one state over, driving a twenty-year-old car. So the week before I left home, my dad made me drive up Route 7 from Stamford, Connecticut, to Great Barrington, Massachusetts, and back again with him in the car so he could be sure I wouldn't get lost on the semirural route and perish from hunger or thirst in the old Plymouth I'd inherited from my grandfather. My dad is not the chattiest, and there was no tape deck in the car. That very long, boring four-hour practice trip was every bit as much about preparing me for the long drive as it was about giving him the sense that he had done the best he could as I left for college. At the time, I was annoyed. Now I get it. Perhaps a geo-tracker would have been a more painless way to assuage anxiety, but it may also create *more* anxiety than it is worth.

Tracking our kids' whereabouts may make us feel like we're keeping them safe. The truth is, making them install an app on their phone so we can pinpoint exactly where they are is easier than having tough conversations about what we expect from them. It's easier than developing mutual trust. And it's easier than making sure that they know what to do if they find themselves on the side of the road with a flat tire at 10:00 p.m.

Monitoring our kids can give us a false sense of security. We trust that by surveilling their every move, we can step in to prevent harm. But if we are constantly there to catch, fix, and prevent every mistake, it's very likely that our children will keep repeating them. And in the end, constant vigilance may harm our relationships without any guarantee we can keep our kids safe from all harm, mistakes, and danger.

Tracking Our Kids So We Can Stay in Their Lives

For tweens, nothing signifies freedom and maturity like getting their own phone. Finally, they can chat and text to their hearts' content and check social media a gazillion times a day.

Phones tend to come into tweens' lives at a period of their development when they are more likely to prioritize confiding in and connecting with their peer group over hanging out with us parents. Although parents would be loath to admit it, those who are reading their kids' texts or emails or checking up on their social media are simply hungry for the kind of insight into their kids' lives that parents had back when their kids told them everything.

The mother of a thirteen-year-old told me that it was precisely this desire to reconnect with her son that drove her to monitor his messages. When her son started spending less time talking with her and lots of time texting with friends from school and Scouts, and—more worrisome to her—a few that he met on Discord, the mom became curious. Since her son hadn't shared much with her in a long time, she wanted to find out what he was talking about with his friends. She pulled up his messages while he was at school and found, to her surprise, that he had come out to his friends as pansexual. Why was he telling his friends and not her? She and her husband considered themselves accepting and open-minded. "Why would he hide this from us?" she wondered.

Monitoring her child's texts might have satisfied her curiosity, but it failed to achieve her more pressing goal: to connect with her child. She was confused and hurt by him not sharing his feelings about his sexuality, and his text messages only raised more questions than they answered. More important, her snooping robbed her child of the opportunity to come out to her when he was ready, and potentially damaged a chance for genuine connection.

Many parents also resort to reading kids' texts when they are behaving incomprehensibly. As psychologist Lisa Damour points out, behavior that would be potentially diagnosable in an adult can be typical and non-pathological for a teenager, such as door slamming, eye rolling, and secretiveness. But while these behaviors can be hard to deal with, they are typical developmental turns and should not send you rushing to read your teenagers' texts. Doing so will send you back emotionally to middle school or high school to relive those challenging times socially—without necessarily giving you special insight into your kids or helping you get any closer to them.

Kids' Backlash against Surveillance

After interviewing a significant number of young people, I've noticed that their responses to parents' surveillance range from intense frustration and feelings of mistrust to mild annoyance and acceptance.

For the most part, teenagers despise having their online activity monitored. This may seem ironic to parents who often quip that "kids these days don't care about privacy—look at all the selfies and personal things they post on their social media accounts!" Because tweens and teens are growing up "in public," they want to protect whatever privacy they *do* have. They are particularly offended that their parents are reading their texts or emails—and consider it an invasion not only of their privacy, but of their friends' privacy. "If you read my texts, that's personal, not just for me, but for the person that I'm texting with," said Jayden, a student at a suburban public high school. "If it was just my thoughts displayed on the screen, that would be okay, maybe that's different . . . It's such an *invasive* thing to do."

While most kids hate being surveilled, many told me they don't mind being geo-tracked via their phones. "I know some of my friends' parents have found them when they weren't supposed to be out," Tevan admitted to me at a student workshop. "But [in] my personal experience, it's not really a big deal." Some young people admitted that they use geo-tracking on their parents, too. "I check it more than they do," Niahla shared. "If my parents are gone and I want to see if they are driving home, then I'll check it and see where they are." A mother told me that her daughter will yell at her if she sees that she stopped at her favorite bakery and didn't bring her a treat. Many kids who resisted being geo-tracked at first eventually became used to it. "I have Life360 [installed in my phone]," Shannon told me. "When I first got it, I didn't want to have it. But my parents don't really check it that much. They just have it in case something happens."

Most kids understand why parents monitor their online activities and track their whereabouts when they are young. When Adele got her first phone as a twelve-year-old sixth grader, she accepted that her parents would be monitoring her activity on it. Even though she understood her parents wanted to protect her, it felt intrusive. Still it was worth it to Adele to have a phone. Importantly, they did so with her knowledge. Her parents created their own accounts on Instagram and Snapchat (with her help, since they didn't know how) so they could follow her, had password access to her account and phone, and insisted that she adjust the privacy settings of her social media accounts and apps to "private." Three years later, when Adele spoke to me as an older, wiser ninth grader, she had a different view about her parents' monitoring. "I think it definitely helped," she acknowledged. "I was so young. And it's really easy for unsafe or gross things to occur [online]. But when they saw I wasn't doing anything crazy, they backed off . . . After a few months, I think they trusted me to tell them if something was weird or off."

What if kids say they "don't mind" if you monitor them? You still may want to limit your tracking. The fact that so many kids don't mind being monitored constantly is concerning. Either we're getting them a little too used to "Big Brother," or they are not bothered because they are finding other ways to get privacy online, a space to express themselves and test boundaries without their parents' surveillance. Teenagers have always done this.

When I was a teenager, norms were very different, and parents were (mostly) hands-off. During my senior year in high school, my friend Jenna lived with her father and his wife after having been sent there by her mother, who felt her behavior was out of control. Her father and stepmother were not exactly enthusiastic about the situation. When they found a house with a somewhat habitable barn in the back, they bought it, insulated the barn, and essentially let Jenna have her own place. Of course, other friends and I hung out there all year. *Everything* happened at Jenna's barn. One of the few rules my parents had when I was a teen was forbidding me to travel to the next town over to watch the midnight screening of *The Rocky Horror Picture Show*. To do it (because of course I did), all I had to do was tell my parents that I was going to sleep over at Jenna's house.

Now, as a parent who's worked with families in many communities, I can say that sometimes teens seek out spaces away from adult supervision to just be themselves—and sometimes they may have plans that are more problematic (using alcohol or other drugs, for example). Whether it's a studio apartment in a barn, a house so large that the teen has their own wing, or just a home where the parents are rarely around, teens will always find these places to assert and own their privacy. Rural teens might have a spot in the woods. Urban teens can hang out at a certain park or semipublic space. Adolescents will *always* seek out space away from prying adults. How much that should concern you depends on your child's age, their judgment, their friend group, their mental health, and your relationship with them.

When Adele was in eighth grade, her parents, who occasionally still looked at her posts, noticed that her Instagram account was far less active than it had been. As Adele grew older, so did her need for privacy. So she created a "spam" Instagram account (previously known as a "Finsta" for "fake Insta") dedicated to sharing personal photographs and posts with her "inner circle." Many high school girls and some boys that I've talked to have spam accounts on social media to connect with a smaller and more intimate group of friends. In many ways, their "main" account is their public online presence. It is for anyone—even "someone you just met," as one girl explained. When parents hear their kids have two accounts, they are often disconcerted. If, like Adele's parents, they have been monitoring a main account, they might even feel like the child is being sneaky. But kids are simply doing what kids have always done (and should do): sharing some things with their closest friends, other things with family, and more public things with everyone else. This understanding of privacy is a sign of an evolving and more sophisticated sense of self and of social norms for different kinds of relationships. It doesn't mean that the spam account holder is doing something bad or sneaky.

Just because our tools for monitoring our kids got better doesn't mean that most kids will react any differently than we did when we were growing up. As tenth grader McKenna said, "[Life360] definitely makes breaking the rules more appealing because [my parents] shouldn't have put it on my phone in the first place."[3] Had geotracking existed when I was growing up, I would have simply left my phone at Jenna's and headed to the *Rocky Horror Picture Show* without it—and my parents would have been none the wiser. But if I had done that, I would have left behind a powerful safety device: a phone from which to call my parents or someone else for help if I needed it.

The Downsides of Monitoring and Tracking

Brandi, a mother from Texas, told me that she *sometimes* checked on her seventeen-year-old son on the Life360 app. At one point, she noticed that he was going to the same house quite a lot. She looked up the address and found out who lived there: a girl. A girl he had not mentioned to her. He would usually go for short visits, but she could see that he was sometimes there for hours. She was troubled that he didn't say anything to her about the girl. If he wasn't hiding anything, why hadn't he talked about this girl with her?

There are many valid reasons why a seventeen-year-old might want to keep a love interest or even a relationship quiet in the beginning. True, maybe he is up to no good—buying or selling drugs at this girl's house. Or maybe he is being tutored by this girl. Or maybe he is dating this girl and doesn't know yet whether it is going to work out.

Knowing he was going to her house may be deeply meaningful—or not. Unless dating is not allowed in the family, the fact that he didn't share this piece of his private life with his parents does not mean he was doing anything wrong. He was fitting these visits to the girl's house in between school, work, and his extracurricular activities, so he wasn't missing school. He hadn't turned off the geo-tracking app on his phone, so he wasn't hiding his movements, either. It was his mother's use of the app—watching where he went during the day—that introduced doubt and potential conflict into their relationship. Brandi had no reason to mistrust her son until she tracked him, but now found herself questioning everything.

I hear stories like Brandi's all the time. A parent starts tracking their teenager and, suddenly, they are suspicious—even if nothing warrants it. Geo-tracking can also give us data that is very easy to misinterpret. A *New York Times* technology reporter, Kashmir Hill, geo-tracked her husband (with his permission), but the experience showed that at almost every juncture, the tracking provided misleading or confusing information that had multiple possible interpretations.[4] One photo showed him leaving a place that looked like a bar—but it was where he ate breakfast. Other geographic notes indicated he was at a specific business, but it was a building with multiple stories with different functions within—he was on another floor doing something else.

That dot on the geo-tracking app doesn't always tell us much. Kids can be at the library studying with friends, or in the study room goofing off with friends, or *behind* the library vaping. The app will show them . . . at the library in all these instances.

While it is tempting to think we can know where our kids are at all times, do we really want to habituate them to this kind of tracking? It can be upsetting if you don't recognize the place where your child appears to be on the app, but the tracking can be wildly off. One dad in Charlotte, North Carolina, shared that "a woman knocked on our door, wanting to know where her son was. I said I didn't know her son, but she kept telling me she tracked him down to our house. She was very upset, but the location was off and she left in a huff." If the idea of your child's romantic partner tracking them seems creepy, abusive, or stalker-ish, then we should ask ourselves if our tracking is similarly problematic.

What About When They Talk About You?

I was walking home with my friend Rupa one day in seventh grade, and she said she hated her mother. I couldn't believe she'd said that out loud, but I realized that I, too, sometimes had that feeling about my own mother. It would not have been helpful for either of our mothers to hear that conversation. But by reading our kids' texts and seeing their (perhaps momentary) feelings and statements about us, we can be "inside their heads" in ways that are entirely unhelpful—just as they might feel hurt or violated if they heard everything we said about them. (Ask me why I password protect my journal on my laptop now!)

So many parents who surreptitiously read their teenagers' texts come across unflattering comments their teenagers write about them. One mother told me she was deeply offended when she read that her daughter, Emily, had criticized her cooking in a text to her boyfriend. A dad was hurt when he read his son Jordan's texts complaining about a family vacation Jordan had seemed to be enjoying.

Tracking our children's locations or snooping on their texts and emails can quickly undermine the parent-child relationship and add unnecessary conflict to the family. The problem is that the information we glean from surveilling our kids can be misleading, confusing, make us worry more than we should, and lead us to distrust our kids when there is no reason. It often raises more questions than it answers.

While the words in a teenager's texts may seem clear, their actual intent often isn't. Maybe it's true that Emily doesn't like her mom's food and Jordan wasn't enjoying the family vacation, but both are simply showing kindness to their parents by being good sports about it (a healthier way of looking at their deception than being hurt by it). Or maybe Emily likes her mom's cooking just fine, but was flexing for her boyfriend. Maybe Jordan enjoyed his vacation, but thought he would look cooler if he told his teen crew that he was bored. What they wrote in texts to their friends wasn't for their parents' eyes. Kids wear different hats when talking to their peers and parents. They represent themselves differently to their friends—and that's okay. Having the space to be able to do that, to test their personas and independence from their parents, is critical at their age.

If you ever told your friend following a fight at home when you were a kid, "I hate my parents!" or something along those lines—then you know what I'm talking about. In front of your friends, you felt safe blurting out all your feelings, even exaggerating them. But later, you might have felt guilty for saying that out loud to your friends, because, well, you didn't *really* mean it, or at least not in a totalizing way. You didn't hate your parents; you were just mad at them. That kind of processing of feelings requires space to bloom—and is a process that parents are not meant to have a front-row seat for. But back when we vented about our families, peers, or school with our friends, we did it over the phone or in person. Now kids do it via texts and apps that don't provide the same privacy. Just because technology allows us to read those messages—to take that front-row seat—doesn't mean we should.

Just as monitoring our kids can drive our children to be even more secretive than they might have been *without* our surveillance, it can also drive them further away by undermining their trust in us. I've seen it over and over: kids who find out their parents read their texts or track them feel violated and not trusted.

To some degree, being transparent with our teenagers and letting them know we are monitoring or tracking them—and why—can preserve some of the trust in the parent-child relationship. There's a big difference between reading every one of our kids' text messages and tracking their location when we are concerned for their safety. If you check the geo-tracking app when they fail to come home when they said they would, for example, it might not feel to your teenager like trust was broken, but reading a text message meant for one of his friends might. One mom told me, "Before we had the tracking app, I was constantly checking in. Now I don't have to, and it feels like it actually has made some space in our relationship and decreased anxiety and conflict. But if I ask a question that makes it seem like I've been 'tailing her,' she gets annoyed!"

Ultimately, checking our offspring's every move and keeping tabs on what they are writing to their friends might be antithetical to building a relationship of trust, one that shows we have confidence in them and believe them to be honest and reliable. Not using the technology available to us to track our children requires a leap of faith, a belief that we've armed our kids with enough tools to start facing the world on their own, in preparation of adulthood.

For us parents who do track, doing so openly and in communication with our kids can be part of mentoring, especially if we have a plan and criteria for backing off as they get older and we see they are just fine. Angie Aker, a member of the early team at Upworthy, so an early adopter of social media, allowed her kids to get accounts on

Twitter and Facebook as younger teens. At the time, most of her kids' friends' parents knew little about social media. With her teenage son's and daughter's knowledge she "set it up so that I would get a notification anytime one of them posted. I would see it right away," she explained. "If I saw something that was questionable or in poor taste, I would be like, 'Hey, here's why I would not put that out there.' And I would strongly recommend that he either edit it or take it down." Angie found that, most of the time, her kids were open to following her suggestions. Other times, it would lead to meaningful discussions about the posts and whether they merited a revision or should be taken down. "For the first couple years, they had social media [accounts] that were subject to random checks from me. I didn't want to fully invade their privacy—I wanted them to know I'd be looking," Angie said. "But then at a certain point, I just stopped checking completely, because I trusted them."

Here's another scenario—one where content checking and reading texts led a family to impose additional monitoring in the form of Life360. Jonah is a boy who lives in a large city and attends a private prep school. Seventeen-year-old Jonah's mother tracks him using the Life360 app, a practice she initiated after he threw an unauthorized party. She found out about the party because she read his texts. When I met Jonah, he shrugged and rolled his eyes about it, mentioning that he'd had a few kids over when his parents were away. Jonah's father had told him that he could have friends over when they were away, just "not too many girls." And "don't tell Mom."

Jonah's mother has a bigger problem than her son having a party that he knows she wouldn't approve of—she has a double agent in the house undermining her authority. Maybe at some level, she sensed this, which led to overreaching with the intrusive text checking. Having different rules from different parents (who are still together and in the same home) is setting this family up to have an overall trust issue. Jonah said he doesn't mind the Life360 app "too much" and it's not like he's "doing anything wrong." Yet how will Jonah learn to make good decisions independently? While it is clear that this family has some work to do on building trust, surveilling one another on Life360 is unlikely to help them get there.

Parents who limit or avoid tracking and monitoring their teenagers often find that the kids' awareness that their parents trust them enough to *not* surveil is sufficient to foster two-way trust: "I know you can surveil me, but I appreciate that you don't, so I will honor your trust by not doing things we've agreed I'm not supposed to."

That seems to be the case with Alexei, a public school student at a big suburban high school. Both of Alexei's parents are immigrants who came to the US to go to college and became citizens. Alexei realizes that his parents were not that much older than he is now when they moved away from their parents and their home country. "My parents don't track me; we don't have Life360," he explains. "But whenever I go somewhere, I text both my parents and let them know, 'Hey, I'm leaving the house to go to this place right now.' They feel a lot better about it because they at least know that I'm safe. As long as I do that, then we have mutual trust. And I know that if I ever break that trust, they would probably not let me drive or whatever. As long as we just communicate with each other, it's pretty good."

When It May Make Sense to Track Kids Online

There are certain situations where tracking or monitoring your child may be necessary. If you have an elementary or middle school kid who has been the target of cruel behavior online and their safety and mental health are at stake, then being on top of their social media can be a good idea. Sometimes kids will not share or repeat the things people say. Ideally, if they can take a break from the app where bullying is happening without feeling like they are being punished by the "time-out," that can be helpful. But if they feel like they need to "know what people are saying" or that time away will cut them off from crucial support, then they may need access to the app, but in a supported context. Some parents opt to use apps to monitor the messages and posts their child sends and receives. These apps can scan your child's emails, texts, other apps, and social media accounts and flag anything that might appear to be bullying or threats of violence, among other things. The problem with these apps is that they will pick up derogatory language but not comments that don't use nasty language but still can be hurtful. Cyberbullying experts Sameer Hinduja and Justin W. Patchin agree with me that we should be using these apps with our kids' knowledge—not covertly. And they also acknowledge that it is not hard for tech-savvy kids to subvert or go around many of these apps by hopping to a different device or network. In addition, if your teenager is older—but is being harassed or trolled—then you can offer support, but tread lightly. Often, if a teen or tween is being harassed, they might agree to have their social media monitored by someone invested in keeping them safe, or possibly shut down and create new accounts, but it is better to ask.

There are apps that flag other content, including language that might indicate your child is having suicidal ideations. If your child is experiencing mental health issues, has attempted suicide or hurt themselves, or is in treatment, you could make a plan with them, and possibly with their therapist as a mediator of the extent of the agreement, to monitor and track their social media use through such apps—but with their knowledge. And the reality is, no app is omniscient or can offer a totally accurate window into another person's mind.

Further, while no parent *wants* to think of themselves as the source of their kids' mental health struggles, some level of conflict with parents is part of the growing-up process. For some teenagers, their relationship with their parents or their parents' behavior—being controlling, not trusting, overly protective, not empathetic or compassionate, etc.—may indeed be contributing to their mental health issues. In these cases, if parents install software to monitor their kid's private conversations and thoughts in an effort to keep them safe, it might actually do more harm than good. If your child cannot express how they really feel to you, but reaches out to friends about mental health issues, monitoring them too closely might be cutting them off from their support system. In fact, in reviews of one popular parental app feature, kid after kid commented on how such surveillance was making them hide more and undermining their relationship with their parents.

One college woman spoke to Tulane University's newspaper anonymously, and she reported that "Life360 was extending a troubled childhood with controlling parents" and that "her parents insist she has Life360 turned on at all times at college as a condition of paying for her to go."[5]

Proceed with caution.

Understandably, sometimes, after a young person in their community dies by suicide, parents are tempted to "spy" on their children more to "spot the signs" of potential trouble. It might be tempting to read all their messages, but these don't necessarily yield answers. Tragically, at least sometimes, suicide is an impulse that text messages do not forewarn. Texts may show a paradox: a young person who has recently made plans with someone for the next day. There is often little that a parent could have done to prevent a suicide. Certainly if a child has not demonstrated any mental health issues or signs of suicidal ideation, intrusively monitoring them may cause more family conflict and lead the child to hide their digital tracks, which will then increase parental anxiety, forming a vicious cycle. Experts advise parents to be open with their children about their worries, demonstrate authentic interest in who they are and how they feel, and hope they will talk to their parents if they are hurting.

The Problem When Kids Stumble Upon or Seek Pornography Online

Access to adult content is one of those areas that many parents want to and *should* stay on top of, especially when it comes to younger kids. Marie, a mother of a teenage boy, found out through one of these monitoring apps that her son, Todd, was looking at pornographic images. She wasn't shocked that her kid was interested in sexual images. She understood his interest as a normal part of puberty and maturing sexually. But she still didn't want him exposed to the full range of pornography that the internet offers—and many porn sites offer graphic videos and images on their landing pages or as pop-ups, allowing kids to look at even blocked sites.

If you are monitoring your teenager's online activity because you are curious if they have seen pornography, I'd look at the stats: assume they probably have seen something you might wish they hadn't—and understand that it's common for people to be curious about such things at some point in the growing-up years. If you are monitoring them because you don't want them to access any adult content, then installing an app that scans their texts, emails, and web browsing might not be the best way. After all, you don't want to catch them *after* the fact. A determined teen will find a way around these apps: they will use a friend's computer or go on a VPN to keep their browsing secret. **The best offense here is preparing them for a world where porn is highly accessible.** Explain why you don't want them to access it, and have a frank conversation about the values you believe for yourself and your family. You can certainly take the step of **blocking pornography on their devices and on the family router—(even if doing so is not fully effective, it is *something*), but talking with them about why pornography is concerning to you is important, too.** If you suspect or know that your child's interest in adult content has morphed from a teenager's curiosity to an addiction or compulsion, then you may want to help set them up with an addiction counselor, and heavier monitoring and tracking may be in order—but it's important, again, to be transparent about it with your child. Some teens have even asked their parents to help them block pornography, a wish that I would take very seriously and respectfully.

After carefully considering her options, Marie decided to follow the advice of Culture Reframed, a nonprofit aimed at building resistance and resilience in young people to hypersexualized media and pornography. She used their "COMPOSE Yourself!" model for starting a conversation about pornography.[6] She also made sure her son had access to several well-written books about puberty and sexuality. The COMPOSE model is an acronym.

C is for Calm: Start with a calm response. If you are visibly anxious and angry, it will be harder for your child to receive your support. Culture Reframed suggests giving a child or teen "time to compose themselves, as they may feel ashamed or even scared." One idea they suggest: "Ask them to tell you when, in the next 24–48 hours, they're ready to talk about it."

O is for Ownership: Try not to blame; attempt to learn more about what happened. Keep this as private as possible (i.e., discuss it with a co-parent or a therapist, but don't tell your other friends, etc.).

M is for Mood: How are they feeling, how are you feeling? Remember to stay regulated when talking with your child.

P is for Parent: As a parent, you can help your child feel safe and offer a nonjudgmental place to ask questions. "Let them know that you provide a calm, safe, and accepting place for them to come home to."

O is for Override: We "override" what Culture Reframed calls "the power of the porn industry" by providing information about sex that centers on consent. "An important element is to help them consider how they can be part of the solution, rather than be manipulated by the porn industry. Young people hate feeling that they have been brainwashed, and they can be incredible agents of change. Tap into that 'defiance' as a way of motivating changes in attitudes and behaviors.

"Discuss the alternative with them. If they and their peers were to believe everything the porn industry wants them to believe, what would the personal, relational, social, and cultural consequences be? Talk about how things could look if people mobilized to fight back and resist the harms of a pornified culture. Talk about how you will problem-solve together if they lose sight of this goal. Punishment is not the answer, as this will cultivate shame and shut down further discussions."

S is for Strategy: Stay calm and focus on a long-term plan. Don't act impulsively in the moment. What does Culture Reframed say about filters and monitoring apps? They point out that these apps "can assist in reducing access to pornography while your young person is learning to develop self-discipline." They also state: "If you think your child is habituated or addicted to pornography, this will require a different strategy and, often, more support and accountability. Don't be shy about getting help! Professional intervention can equip you with a targeted strategy and provide much-needed reinforcements."

E is for Evaluate: Stay in an ongoing conversation with your child about this issue (and seek professional help if there are deeper concerns).

Active Parenting in a 24/7-Access World

Even if you decide *not* to monitor and track your child, all families would do well to have a conversation to set expectations for when monitoring and tracking might be necessary and acceptable. For example, you might define what constitutes a *Code Red* situation—a situation that requires you to use their passwords to access their emails, social media, or texts to find urgent information or their whereabouts in the face of some threat or danger. You can make it clear that you respect their privacy, but if life and limb are at stake or criminal consequences might be a reality, then you will always put their safety first.

As parents, we have the right to be concerned about our tweens and teens. It's natural to want to know where they are and what they are up to. Of course we want to know how they are behaving out in the world. **But surveillance only gives us one parenting tool: catching them in the act after they've done whatever it is we don't want them to do. It doesn't give us the chance to mentor and guide them, or to help them develop good judgment and make safe choices before they make a mistake and get caught.**

Tracking kids' movements or monitoring what they are texting to their friends can undermine crucial adult skills. Kids need to learn how to set their own boundaries and gain the skills for self-regulation. Ultimately, our tweens and adolescents will need to find their own agency, work out conflicts, self-advocate, and find their way home when they get lost.

chapter 2

Growing Up in the Public Eye

When I work with tweens and teens, I often ask them if they know someone who has an online public image that doesn't match their true personality and behavior. Almost every hand in the room usually goes up.

Posting about oneself is performative for both kids and adults and, to a certain degree, that is savvy and self-protective. **What worries me is when a child appears to be crowdsourcing their personality.** After one of my public talks, a father shared with me his concerns that his son's online persona was eclipsing his real personality. Rahul, an eighth grader, seemed to be overly focused on his public image and trying to keep up with the often over-the-top materialism of his wealthier classmates. The father was worried that Rahul's peers' showing off and bragging were having an overwhelming influence on him. The person in Rahul's posts wasn't the Rahul he knew—the *real* Rahul.

Kids experience the jarring differences between their peers' public personas and the *real* people. When I talk to middle and high schoolers about this, they share stories of classmates who are wild and funny online but reserved in person; friends who swear constantly in person but who are squeaky clean online; or peers who seem "normal and chill" in person but come across as "kinda egotistical" in their posts.

A big part of growing up is figuring out who you are. In the process of maturing, young people may try on and sometimes settle into various identities, depending on the social context. For example, a kid might identify as Irish, Black, Latinx, or Assyrian. They might identify in relation to their gender or sexuality: girl, guy, transgender, gay, pansexual. Within their families, their identity might form around being the middle child, the "smart one," or the rebellious one. Among peers, their identity might form around being one of the "popular kids," one of the "weird kids," the kid with divorced parents, or the only biracial student in the class. They might also define their identity based on their interests, passions, or political inclinations: athlete, music lover, gamer, anime fan, liberal, or conservative. Or they might form identities based on their body perceptions: the big kid or the skinny one, the tallest kid in the class, etc.

For teens, a certain amount of persona shifting between environments is a typical and expected part of their development. Kids, like adults, form a social identity that is different from their home identity. Over the years, though, I've met countless parents like Rahul's dad who worry how a life lived in public on social media will affect their child's identity and self-esteem. They are concerned that the reinforcement from peers is leading their kid to "sell their soul" to social media.

For adolescents, connecting online provides instant feedback on their interests, their activities, their friends, their clothes, their life experiences—whatever they choose to share via a post or a comment online—in the form of likes, follows, and comments. For parents, it can be concerning that any ill-advised proclamation their child makes online—like "F school!"—can become a lasting and searchable part of their identity because of the public and permanent nature of digital posts.

Kids stress about this, too, but their concerns are different from ours. Understanding how our kids experience life "in public" and how that affects their identity at such a crucial developmental stage can empower parents to take a more informed, less worried approach to mentoring them through their digital coming of age.

Kids Comparing Themselves with Others

Comparison is an inevitable and huge part of adolescence. There is no denying that when our kids live their lives in public through online platforms, they have more opportunities than ever before to make comparisons with peers. In some communities, schools and parents exacerbate this tendency by posting about kids in ways that invite comparison and competition. Parents often make their kids cringe when they post gymnastic routines and geography-bee wins. It can be hard to resist sharing these triumphs, but as I will discuss in the "Sharenting" chapter, there can be many good reasons to limit our

On social media, kids are constantly aware of what other kids are up to—whether they are on vacation, shopping with a friend, at a birthday party or sleepover, etc. This makes comparing their lives with peers not only incredibly easy but also misleading. Most kids (like adults) share the "highlights reel" of their lives—or, as my friend says, "crop the sadness out of their lives"—on social media posts.

posts. Schools also contribute to this problem by posting where seniors are going to college.

Even though middle schoolers and older teens are aware that everyone posts their best moments, it can still be quite painful for kids to see others having things that they can't have, or having "a better time" than they are having. They might come across photos or posts of an ex-girlfriend or -boyfriend and their new partner. Or of their peers doing something they are not allowed to do, like going to a concert. Or friends going to an event or party that they weren't invited to. When that happens, kids might be at home alone while posts of their friends "having a blast" keep popping up on their phones in real time. Being excluded is a painful experience for anyone, but especially tweens and teens, for whom belonging is such a primary need.

In all my conversations and workshops with young people, the kids that seem the least bothered by social media understand it to be a performance. Many kids can distance themselves from the fiction of having a perfect life or look at the idea of being "social media worthy" in an ironic way. For some of the teens I spoke with, the ability to resist comparison was stronger when they spent less time on social media, or predominantly used social media to text via direct message—a shortcut that doesn't involve needing to ask for someone's phone number. For almost everyone, it is easier to resist comparison when you are feeling pretty good about yourself. But after a breakup; a conflict with a friend; or a setback like not getting a spot on the team, a part in the play, or a desired acceptance to college, looking at what others are posting can be particularly painful—but also hard to resist. Those are the times we can try to nudge our children to take a break; we can also model taking a break ourselves when social comparison is bringing us down.

"No One Wants to Look Bad": Social Media and a Focus on Appearance

Like most teenagers, I wanted to look cute in high school, but in a very specific way. Theater-kid cute, not necessarily "preppy" cute or athlete cute. Hair over one side of my face in a new-wave haircut that once left me with a half sunburn after a concert in Central Park. Definitely *not* the haircut or the outfits my mother thought was "becoming." And this was decades before social media came on the scene. I was attuned to the context—dressing for school was different than dressing for a concert, which was different than dressing to go to Grandma's house or to do a babysitting job. Social media, famously, compresses those contexts. Teens might dress for their friends, but their parent's best friend, their youth pastor, or their Grandma might well see it, too.

I could dress for different contexts, but I could also be invisible. My friends rarely took photos of me. I was the photographer, and I took darkroom photography—I have many brooding black-and-white photos of my high school friends. Sometimes I envied my gorgeous friends and the attention they got, but I was also relieved that I flew under the radar with a body and "image" that were neither scorned nor fawned over. Living in a body that wasn't seen as overweight, I knew enough to recognize my privilege as I watched my friends in larger bodies get targeted for teasing and harassment.

Today our culture continues to emphasize the importance of physical appearance as much as it did back then. Or maybe even more so. But while we grew up looking at beauty and pop culture magazines that celebrated unrealistic body image standards and encouraged unhealthy diets, today's kids deal with seeing their own image right next to those airbrushed and altered images. Except for the occasional photos taken at dances, with friends, or for the school yearbook, most photos taken of me when I was a teen or tween were kept within the family. They were rarely held up for my peers to judge or comment on. When I took photography in high school, I did enjoy a weekend with friends dressing up in thrifted clothes and posing dramatically, and then printing the photos myself in the darkroom. But only a few people in my friend group saw the pictures. Today, even the most casual Snapchat can be seen by thousands of people depending on who posts it and shares it.

Photo-based social media apps expose tweens and teens (and adults) to countless images of idealized bodies—many of which have been edited or altered in some way. These apps also allow kids to read people's comments on these images and witness how others respond to them. This intense focus on physical appearance on social media often leads teens and tweens to constantly compare themselves against traditional beauty standards—and when they fail to meet them (as most people do), they often feel dissatisfied with the way they look.

The constant feedback about physical appearance in photos (e.g., "You look amazing!" "Smokin' hot!" "Took my breath away, girl!" "omg ur gorgeous"), an obsession with likes, and the millions of diet-related (or "health") posts and ads also reinforce negative body image and poor self-esteem, especially among girls. Some studies, in fact, have found links between social media use and body surveillance, self-objectification, body comparison, body shame, and even disordered eating. Some teens are so aware that someone may take and post a picture of them at any time that they try to look good all the time, just in case. A recent study of US college women found that those who have high levels of appearance-related social media consciousness—which the authors describe as "the extent to which individuals' thoughts and behaviors reflect ongoing awareness of whether they might look attractive to a social media audience"—may have more body dissatisfaction and be more depressed.[1]

As the public learned in 2021, when the Facebook whistleblower Frances Haugen went public, Instagram/Facebook's own research showed that (a) the company was concerned enough about harm to look into it, and (b) some kids did identify harm. Other research shows that certain developmental windows make kids more or less vulnerable to emotional harm from using social media. A British study showed that both boys and girls have a period during which they may be especially vulnerable to mental health concerns after a period of intensive social media use. For girls, the ages when they appear most vulnerable is eleven to thirteen, and for boys, it is ages fourteen to fifteen. "Changes within our bodies, such as brain development and puberty, and in our social circumstances appear to make us vulnerable at particular times of our lives," Dr. Amy Orben said to *Forbes* magazine about the study. Study coauthor Dr. Sarah-Jayne Blakemore pointed out, "Adolescence is a time of cognitive, biological and social change, all of which are intertwined, making it difficult to disentangle one factor from another. For example, it is not yet clear what might be due to developmental changes in hormones or the brain and what might be down to how an individual interacts with their peers."[2] So how likely is it that using social media will cause a specific kid emotional harm? The answer is: it depends.

These studies, of course, are not perfect, primarily because it's hard to find a control group of people growing up today who *aren't* using social media. But based on my research, I think of social media as an intensifier. If a kid is already ruminating about their body image or has become focused on weight in ways that are concerning, social media use can amplify these issues. Research, for example, shows that posting a lot of selfies can make some people feel more anxious about their attractiveness. It can be hard to discern cause from effect in the case of body-image issues and heavy social media scrolling and/or posting.

One of the most concerning indicators that girls or boys are focusing too much on body image in social media is how often they alter or edit their photos before posting or sharing them. **One study from the UK found that a third of girls and women won't post unaltered images of themselves.**[3] While girls are more likely to check their photos and alter them before they post, kids of all genders "want to look good" and might subtly or overtly shape their appearance for social media. Even a girl who claims not to care about appearances told me, "Look, no one wants to look bad in pictures; of course you want to look good!"

Sixteen-year-old Jayla, a girl from a suburb of Cleveland, identifies with the body-positive movement online. She also points out that sites that "celebrate Black women" make her feel seen and understood. She personally identifies as being in a bigger body, and she gave me a tour of body-positive Instagram and TikTok, explaining that there are many influencer accounts that are "basically coaching people to love themselves and love their bodies." She was careful to let me know that it is okay to be thin, too, "as long as you're being healthy. If you're just naturally skinny and have a high metabolism so you can't gain weight, you shouldn't feel pressure because everybody will think *you are tiny, you need to eat more*, or that y*ou're not pretty*." In other words, although many influencers seem to be championing one kind of body ideal or another, Jayla felt that ultimately the message is *be yourself*, but she also recognized that thinness and whiteness are often the "self" that is celebrated, and she was careful to curate her social "feed" differently to reinforce positive messages about both Blackness and body-positivity.

Clearly not all teens or adults find that same message from social media. Mainstream media is hardly neutral in presenting beauty ideals that glorify whiteness, thinness, and youth, among other attributes. Jayla is finding her own influencers and has a supportive family and friend group that encourages her to value herself for who she is. I don't share her story to suggest that social media won't exacerbate or reinforce damaging body ideals, but I spoke to enough kids like Jayla to feel it is possible to find other messages out there—you just have to be intentional about it.

Parents and educators typically focus their worries and any protective impulse on girls when it comes to body image. Yet boys tell me that while they are not *supposed* to care how they look, they do, and social posts with photos can exacerbate those pressures, too. Boys are typically careful to avoid leaving any trace of having "tried too hard," or are reluctant to acknowledge having taken down photos where they didn't get likes. The boys I spoke to also said they wouldn't alter their pictures (and a few admitted that if they did, they wouldn't want anyone to know). The very act of editing one's photo is more stigmatized in boys, while for girls the practice is more of an "open secret." One group of ninth-grade boys shared a story of a male classmate who'd photoshopped abs into his photos, but did so as a joke. Had he done it "for real" and not as a joke, it could have backfired, as boys in general tease one another if they appear to be too focused on appearance. Still, for boys, it is important to emphasize that the hyper-muscular ideal propagated in mainstream media and some social channels is unrealistic and not a safe goal for any teenager.

In general, both boys and girls told me that taking silly or ugly photos and using apps where the photos disappear is a good way to get around appearance anxiety. Further, many kids of all genders use social media without posting many selfies. While looking at both celebrity and peer content might still invoke some anxiety, not inserting their own images into the fray is self-protective for some, and simply typical practice in groups who might predominantly use social media for its messaging features.

For kids of any gender, it is important that we counter-message both mainstream media and peer social pressures to look a certain way—especially when it comes to attempting to alter appearance through dieting, extreme exercise, or other dangerous practices.

The dangers of an appearance-focused culture can feel more apparent for our daughters, with trends such as boys comparing images of girls and "rating" them.

Of course, not all kids identify as boys and girls. Nonbinary kids can be especially sensitive to externalized pressure about bodies and society's obsession with the gender binary in general.

Regardless of how they identify, tweens and teens are attuned to social status, and for some of them, social status can be intricately connected with physical appearance. Many of them use social media to show themselves fitting the image—hot, pretty, cute, quirky—most closely associated with those with higher-level social status. Vivian, Neenah, and Nilofar, a group of ambitious, academically successful, first-year high school students laughed out loud when I asked if any of them wanted to be "influencers." One of them said, "Yeah, no . . . I want to be a neuroscientist." All three agreed that "looking good" is not their "main priority in life," but "no one wants to look . . . bad," Neenah acknowledged.

Jayla and many other girls also spontaneously brought up the objectification and sexual harassment they experience online. So many girls described receiving direct messages on social media, often from older men—some offering to pay for "pics" (sexual or nude images). One girl said, "If I show you my inbox, you will see a lot of things . . . including sugar daddy requests, and it's so uncomfortable to me. A random dude might DM you and say, 'I'll give you five hundred dollars weekly just for your company.'" Although girls nonchalantly describe getting friend requests from "dudes I don't know" again and again, few of them talk to their parents about it. "I just block them," said one girl. A few younger girls did acknowledge that DMs from strangers saying they are "pretty" can be flattering . . . at first. But they get "creepy" fast.

Being There for the Likes

One of the most anxiety-inducing consequences of growing up today is having your life measured and quantified with real-time feedback from peers and "the public." From Snapchat to TikTok to Instagram—social media apps have become one of the main vehicles for kids to experiment with their social identity. And almost every one of these apps offers users a way to keep tabs on how many likes their posts, photos, or content have earned. This transparency makes "peer opinion" more quantifiable and, therefore, more influential than ever. These apps also make visible the number of followers users have accumulated, creating an intensely quantified measure of "popularity" that can become preoccupying for some kids.

According to the Pew Research Center, many adolescents do in fact experience "pressure to curate positive and well-liked content." As many as 40 percent of adolescents reported "feeling pressure to post positive and attractive content about themselves."[4] Very few kids will admit that *they're* posting to get likes, but they are very sharp at identifying that behavior in peers. The reality is that kids want some kind of online attention—and feel hurt when they make bids for it and it doesn't come. They begin tailoring themselves according to the reaction they want. **I asked a kid what she would do when other kids posted about events in which she was not included. She responded that she would have other friends over and post to "show she has a life." This girl was eleven.**

The pressure to post content that makes themselves look good also comes from well-meaning educators and parents. Even though they deeply understand that adolescence is a complex time for identity formation, they don't want their kids to undermine future opportunities—social, academic, or professional. The overwhelming message they send their sons and daughters is that "the internet is forever," and therefore they must carefully curate their online persona: "Top-choice colleges won't want you if you don't make yourself look good." "Your friends will judge you [or me as your parent] if you share that!"

Kids are constantly seeking their peers' engagement and strive for "streaks"—a volley of reciprocated Snapchat messages that ends if someone fails to reply within twenty-four hours. Kids who go out of Wi-Fi and data range for trips will pass their log-in information to a trusted friend so they don't break their streaks.

If middle schoolers post something a little outrageous or rebellious on social media and get lots of positive attention, it can fuel a cycle where they feel like they need to step it up each time to continue garnering likes and attention, which can sometimes lead to crossing the line. For example, in seventh grade, Travis posted a video he thought was hilarious about a teacher. Talking to him and his parents later, I really believe that he didn't mean to hurt her. But she considered leaving her job, and did take a two-week leave. His actions had serious consequences that his young adolescent brain had a hard time predicting. He felt terrible, his parents were mortified, and the teacher was shaken and upset. But other "hilarious" videos he had posted got him likes and attention. It was stunning for him to see how quickly everyone turned to judgment and contempt. Some kids' parents didn't want their kids to hang out with Travis after the video. And as much as he regretted the video once he understood the pain it caused, he knows people have it and that he can't undo his actions. The permanence and easy shareability of digital information create a perfect storm at a time when the brain is creative and growing but also extra drawn to novelty and more tuned in to rewards than danger.

As Dr. Eva Telzer from UNC–Chapel Hill said about teenage brains and social media, "The adolescent period is a huge time of brain development, second only to that that we see in infancy. And so not only do we see this heightened sensitivity in terms of reward sensitivity and social sensitivity, but we see that the environment and things that teens are exposed to can shape further brain development. We don't yet know how these digital media platforms might be integrated into their brains."[5]

Certainly we know that young people and *all* humans are sensitive to social approval. The "like" button on many apps provides a reward that is highly motivating to most of us (I'll include myself in this). While most young people I interviewed claimed not to care "too much" about getting likes, comments, or new followers, they could all identify peers who care "a lot." One boy described how his cousin Cleo, an eighth grader, checks obsessively after posting anything to see what kind of response she is getting. "Every time I see her, or she comes over, she'll be lying around and checking on social media," he shared with me. "Last time I saw her was on New Year's Eve. She had posted something about the new year, and the whole night she was kind of just looking at it, seeing who liked it and who commented on it." A school counselor told me about a girl who acquired a large following at her high school and beyond after throwing a huge party. She started checking her phone during class and undermining her relationships with teachers, but when she spoke to her school counselor, she admitted she was feeling more pressure to post. It was a big distraction that she acknowledged was a lot of work—but she felt she couldn't stop.

The documentary *The Social Dilemma* echoes worries that young people are so obsessed with likes, followers, and comments that they are losing touch with themselves. While I found the documentary to be a bit heavy-handed in its portrayal of the manipulative power of social media, it does expose the intricate research involved in designing these apps to be so sticky, so hard to walk away from. We do want to be responded to, noticed, included, and, yes . . . liked. Belonging is a human need, and for adolescents it can feel more important than almost anything else. The movie *#Like* also explored the ways the "like" button in particular offers irresistible human feedback—we crave a response. If you are on social media, you probably check to see who has seen and responded to your posts. Dr. Telzer said, "Social media has really . . . changed the social landscape of what adolescence looks like today, compared to, for example, when I was a teenager and had to see my peers, either in person or talk to them on the phone, in order to interact with them. **There's this around-the-clock ability to engage either synchronously or asynchronously** . . . You can be texting back and forth into the wee hours of the night, you can be scrolling through social media and putting up comments and getting likes and getting feedback on that very quickly."[6]

For adolescents, peer feedback is even more crucial and irresistible. Last year, after one of my talks, fifteen-year-old Beth's parents approached me, concerned their daughter was "being sucked into cultivating positive feedback from all her social media peers." They worried her social media posts didn't reflect who she was—a spiritual, nature-loving, generous young woman. "I don't want her to post things just to create a façade representing someone she's not," Beth's mother told me, describing the way Beth obsessed over which photos to post after a fairly mundane outing.

Stephanie Reich, a researcher at University of California, Irvine, conducted a participatory research project with middle schoolers and found that at least some level of "façade," or emphasizing some parts of self over others, is common behavior for kids online.[7] At one point, she told me, Instagram had a feature, since discontinued, that allowed users to see what their Instagram friends liked. One study participant, a seventh-grade boy, was self-conscious that the posts he liked might not be cool to other seventh-grade boys, so he created a separate account where he could "like and comment on the cartoons and cooking content he enjoyed."

Still, other parents told me they find their kids' photos remarkably creative. One parent who had never seen her kid dance at family events was amazed to see videos of her son dancing with his friends on TikTok, all filmed at the courtyard outside the public library. She was surprised that her son would dance outdoors with his friends to make TikToks, while he was shy about dancing at a recent family quinceañera, for example. Other parents found their kids' new photography and image-making skills to be impressive, again not necessarily correlating with a previous interest in art or design that the parent was aware of. Writing—whether fan fiction or other creative forms adapted to the web—is yet another area where kids may surprise us. A student who finds essay questions to be torture may be publishing poems to a website or fiction to a story site, or collaborating on a Wikipedia page.

The disconnect between online personas and the real person is a great conversation starter for kids. Ask them if there is someone they first encountered online and then later met whose in-person personality seemed markedly different from how they choose to represent themselves online. Even across different apps, the experience can be very distinct—some teens will present themselves one way on TikTok and another way on Discord, for example, because they are sharing in a unique community and specific aspects of their personality are more relevant in one space than the other. I find myself doing this, too. Some media is more personal, where I am speaking to friends, whereas Twitter and LinkedIn are more public and professional. The constraints and structure of each app bring out a different mode of interaction.

But using social media doesn't actually *transform* kids into completely different people—nor does it necessarily affect their self-esteem in lasting ways. In fact, when I talk to teenagers, it seems that social media use exacerbates existing self-esteem issues rather than initiating them. The academic research validates this: for example, a European study of kids' susceptibility to being hurt by social media use shows that kids' vulnerability varies by age, gender, whom they follow, how much time they spend on social media, and which apps they use.[8] It also depends on protective factors, like whether kids have close relationships with peers, parents, or someone they can count on. "Our results suggest that for the majority of adolescents, the momentary effects of social media use are small or negligible," the researchers write. But they also acknowledged that self-esteem is not fixed and can vary day-to-day in adolescents. "All adolescents may occasionally experience social media–induced drops in self-esteem," Patti Valkenburg and her coauthors explain. "Social media [has] become a fixture in adolescents' social life, and the use of [this] media may thus result in negative experiences among all adolescents." Lest we think "just unplug them," it is worth looking at the research. In a recent study, lead researcher Keith N. Hampton and Inyoung Shin found that children whose parents restrictively disconnect them from the internet report lower self-esteem, while children whose parents are media-supportive and instructive report higher self-esteem and spend more time with friends and family.[9]

Keeping Up with the Rules of Engagement

Painstakingly curating a public, online persona, competing for followers, and always angling for more "likes"—while also engaging with other kids' posts—is a complex kind of social labor that can be exhausting and produce anxiety for many kids. But it can be hard to opt out of these networks, especially if that is where your friends are. Belonging is very important to teens. Even if your teen is in a self-described "outsider" or "weird kid" friend group, make no mistake—belonging is important to them, too.

"Adolescence is not a period of being 'crazy' or 'immature.' It is an essential time of emotional intensity, social engagement, and creativity."

—Daniel J. Siegel, MD,
Brainstorm: The Power and Purpose of the Teenage Brain

Whereas adults might rely on the internet more to nurture relationships they've already cultivated, tweens and teens are likely to be initiating at least some friendships there, and dating relationships, too. In a Pew study, more than 57 percent of kids between thirteen and seventeen said they had made a new friend online.[10] Boys were even more likely to do this than girls, possibly because they have fewer perceived safety concerns and probably also because they're more involved in interactive online communities like gaming. The fact that the internet is the site of these new connections means kids develop relationships with their peers in very different ways than we did.

Connecting on social media is less of a big deal than going through the ritual of getting someone's phone number. A group of ninth-grade girls who identified as heterosexual explained that the level of intimacy involved in asking for or giving out their phone number is much higher than sharing or intuiting someone's social media handle in order to get in touch. I asked the girls about meeting new friends (boys or girls) at school.

"They've never asked me for my number. And I've never asked for their number. That's just not a thing anymore," Adrienne told me. "It's just, 'What's your Snapchat?' or 'What's your Insta?' A phone number signifies you [are] on a really, really close level: a friend or someone you're going to text more often." This became especially clear when schools shut down suddenly in 2020 and many kids didn't have each other's numbers. The fortunate ones were still able to contact someone through social media. But giving out their social media handle to someone they meet does not mean that kids today are giving the new acquaintance real access to them. For example, many kids have an official or main Instagram account that is public and another that they share to a select group.

Adrienne's friend Yasmin explained to me that her spam account has only a few close friends that she actually interacts with. "I feel the reason [people] make a spam account or private account is because their main Instagram account is for people who barely know them," she tells me. "Let's say you meet someone, and it's like, 'Hey, what's your Instagram?' You're gonna give them your regular Instagram where [there are] pictures of you and your friends." Most public social media is a non-creepy place to follow someone. But, as she explained, her spam account is more personal. "You're gonna want to really make sure that who you're accepting are people that you like and feel comfortable with," she warns me. In other words, for many adolescents, their main public social media handle is more like their listing in the phone book: it's a directory that is comfortable to share.

In the realm of dating, asking for someone's phone number can imply romantic interest—and may feel like a bold move. Kids are "flirting" or "hanging out" or "talking to each other" on other social apps without necessarily overtly acknowledging romantic interest. But giving someone your phone number? That is a big deal. Finding people on social media can be a low-risk way to connect. But asking for a phone number is a very open bid for friendship or romantic involvement.

The implicit rules of behavior that kids must abide by when "meeting" people on social media are very complicated. I first wrote about this phenomenon in an article for the *New York Times* called "Rules for Social Media, Created by Kids."[11] In it, I break down some of their usually unspoken rules about whom to accept as a friend (e.g., they admitted they weren't too picky about followers because they "boost your numbers"); what's acceptable to post and what constitutes "bragging" (e.g., it's okay to post one or two pictures of an event, but posting "too many" pictures of the event is "obnoxious"); and when it's acceptable to share certain pictures of themselves (e.g., it's okay for middle schoolers to post a photo in a bikini, but only if they are pictured with a family member or friends—never alone). The "rules" are dizzying and ever evolving.

Seeking Popularity and Viral Fame

Social media apps have subtly changed how popularity is measured. A school counselor at an independent Chicago K–8 school shared with me that her students often tell her about some kid who is supposedly "the most popular middle-schooler in Chicago." But it turns out none of her students know that "popular kid" personally; his social media account just has a lot of followers. The mystery kid appeared popular not because of his personal relationships but just based on numbers.

The public nature of our children's lives, in general, intensifies the degree and nuance to which they are able to compare themselves—and react to these comparisons. Sammi, a self-described "weird kid/band crowd" seventh grader, loved her new purple boots. Proud to be part of the nice-kid group, she avoided the "popular" mean-girl group and resisted the "VSCO girl" (previously named for a photo app, and now associated with a certain aesthetic) trend that those girls favored. When one of the popular girls, Julia, posted a picture of herself in the same purple boots on Instagram, Sammi put hers in the back of the closet. "I don't do things that are trendy," she explained. "Now that it is on Julia's post, everyone will get them."

Living in a public world driven by a pursuit of likes and followers also leads some kids to seek not popularity but actual fame. Because of the many online spaces where posts can potentially go viral, fame seems attainable to them. Kids today have all heard countless stories of a YouTube star who hit it big performing a cover song on the piano. Or a "famous" Snapchatter who documents her every waking moment. Or the Instagram influencer who now makes thousands (or even millions) with sponsored content from lifestyle brands. Sharing videos on YouTube and TikTok, or images and words on social media apps like Snapchat and Instagram, can feel like a pathway to recognition beyond their own town or friends. The truth is, going viral is tough to achieve . . . it can't be predicted. For every teen singer discovered on YouTube, there are many other equally talented teens who will not get plucked from the digital haystack and launched into stardom. That said, social media does help people find their niche. One proud dad shared that his son's band got four thousand followers on TikTok. "It's not millions, but that's big for a local band and otherwise unattainable for a garage/backyard type of band." Another young musician in my own family has been able to survive without a "day job" for a time by selling creative material on Etsy—and the social capital from the band (a successful heavy metal band) helps people find his artwork.

Sometimes, You Do Go Viral

For some young people, however, the attention is not a burden, but rather intoxicating. Andy Zhu is a twenty-three-year-old in the real estate business who had a TikTok video about the GameStop investment trend that went viral. It was his third video. After that, things moved fast, and soon he was hosting "lives" four nights a week. It wasn't Andy's first time as a "public person." As a thirteen-year-old, he had a gaming channel on YouTube that was doing very well by the day's standards. He admits that the most motivating reason to keep it up was some of the positive feedback he received. "I remember one comment on one of my videos said, 'Andy, I was having a really bad day today on my birthday, but I saw your video and it made me laugh. And thank you so much for that,'" Andy shared. "Almost ten years later, I haven't forgotten that because it's like, wow, you know, that's the type of influence you can have."

While for some kids and young adults, the pleasures of this experience—"the rush"—can be positive in the moment, it can also be distracting from other pursuits like school, family, and in-person relationships. "It concerns me that [kids] will forever be seeking out-side validation for their lives, from their clothes, to their bodies, to what they wore to prom, where they go to college, and eventually how their homes look," a parent answered in my survey. "Instead of enjoying the moment, person, and place, they are taking pictures to post, thinking what others will think of where they are instead of enjoying it themselves."

Andy acknowledged that the week we were talking, he'd taken a break from making edited "long-form" content and was only focused on his life, and then doing "live" videos that needed less preparation.

> *I haven't made an edited TikTok for the last, like, week and a half, I just swore it off. I haven't checked the notifications. I get on my lives, which I do from Monday to Thursday at night for an hour or so, and then just log off, and I interact with my people who are talking to me there. But I haven't checked any of my other notifications. And my life is so much better for it. Because I [used to get] sucked into the pressures: Oh, I need to make more content, make three videos a day; I need to have continued follower growth. And when it started to slow down,*

I started to be like, why am I not doing as well? And what have I done wrong? Why am I so awful? And it does get to you. It really does. Because I don't particularly care about that outside validation. But you know, I'm still, at the end of the day, a twenty-three-year-old kid. So it definitely influences your brain.

Andy's bosses at his real estate job were interested in utilizing his TikTok experience. Over the course of 2020–2021, Andy's TikTok, @genzrebuilds, explored mostly financial real estate subjects—Andy's passion is to disseminate financial knowledge to empower people. But he also delved into questioning stereotypes about Asians over the course of his channel; one video that challenged stereotypes about Asian men and sexuality got over six hundred thousand views. His follow-up, a more nuanced discussion about stereotypes, had only five thousand views, which reflects how the "channels" of a medium like TikTok *can* work. Sometimes getting the more complex ideas out there doesn't hit the algorithm quite as well as a simple joke. As someone who has tried my hand at author TikTok along with many of my peers, I can say that it isn't easy to have your finger on the pulse. But there was something about Andy's third video that spoke to the zeitgeist and went viral. Later, Andy moved on to a new job in his industry and is thriving. I wonder how he will think about his "viral year" later on—but my take was that it was a good experience, just not a very balanced one in terms of having the kind of full life he wanted, and he moved on.

Young adults like Andy show us that it is possible to "go public" for a time and then move on, not just unscathed, but perhaps enriched by the experience—but it doesn't have to define your entire life. This may be a relief to parents who see public or private as more of a fork in the road.

Becoming an "Influencer"

The desire for fame or fantasies about "going viral" can motivate some kids, and being an "influencer" can become a job. But . . . it is a lot harder than it may appear.

Sophia Pruett started her YouTube channel at the age of thirteen, and over the ensuing years accumulated 446,000 subscribers. She started out making "silly videos with friends, DIY crafts videos, etc." When she started making more how-to content, her site grew popular. "I posted a DIY Mother's Day gift video and then that kind of blew up," she said. Sophia now says she didn't fully acknowledge that people could even see it, especially friends from school and people she knew in person.

"I'm glad I didn't really think about that or else I might not have done it, but I didn't really worry about anyone from school finding out. I was just doing it for fun."

Eventually, Sophia saved her money, got her own MacBook, and subscribed to different software programs to improve her video editing. She planned her video schedule six weeks in advance, which her mom says really helped with her time management.

During our interview, Sophia said that, as a college student, she finds it "cringey" to watch herself in eighth grade, but this was a niche genre that grew very popular, and Sophia had the right combination of savvy editing and charm to make it work.

Once Sophia started spending her lunch period in her mom's car for meetings with sponsors (her mother worked at her school), she realized this was a big deal. Her family helped her find an agent to negotiate brand deals.

Sophia's mother, Natalie, also offered parents a perspective on what they can do to support a child with any level of visibility. "I would watch every video before she hit post; you know, before she published it. And there were a couple of instances where there was our street name or our address; you know, the numbers on our house, but that didn't happen very often.

"She taught herself all the analytics and would spend a lot of time on the titles and the descriptions. We, as her parents, had nothing to do with this other than providing guidance on the security and safety of her identity. Everything was self-taught," Natalie told me, obviously proud of her daughter. She also told Sophia she was free to stop at any time, and that she should not feel pressure to continue if it stopped being fun, even though by this time Sophia was earning significant income from sponsorships.

When Sophia got to college, she found that a few people were familiar with her channel, and it felt good, but a little weird. Her roommates and close friends at college got used to being in her videos. When she discloses personal things, about dating for example, she says it's less weird that hundreds of thousands of people she doesn't know can see it than that her mom and brother can watch. Sophia is very similar to other young entrepreneurs in that she has savings and retirement accounts, and that the highly personal nature of sharing her life as a vlogger is a little hard to separate from her friendships and, ultimately, her identity. At a time in life when most college students have the opportunity to reinvent themselves, Sophia came to college getting paid for being . . . herself. A certain version of herself.

At twenty, Sophia took her first break from being a daily YouTube vlogger with a significant fanbase. In her first vlog after the break, she acknowledged the pressure that can come with having a large and dedicated audience, and having to produce more and more content and manage the sponsorship and advertising deals that come with it, yet feeling like she might want to take her content in a different direction. The COVID-19 pandemic and a greater call to focus on her Christian faith both pulled Sophia away from the ongoing demands of influencing.

She told me, "I've literally grown up on YouTube. I stopped posting [because] . . . no one signed up to hear about my faith. I can share that, but I also don't want to push my faith on others. I want a healthy mix of what I love and what you want to see."

After a month off, she posted a video from her car speaking directly to the viewer about the changes in her life and her feelings about being a public person on YouTube.

"Everyone faces their own insecurities, and everyone struggles with comparing themselves to others. So you really can never win, like, in the world of the internet."

Since that conversation, Sophia, now graduated from college, stopped posting on her channel for a while and started two other businesses. Drawing on both her experiences with videography and her aesthetic and styling experience, she is a wedding videographer, a business she shares with her brother, and she also has an art shop selling handmade art. The tagline for the store on Instagram reads: "a creative expression of hope for the minimal, abstract, & coastal aesthetic. the future is bright."

While Sophia built her following over a period of years, TikTok has the potential to make someone famous overnight or put someone at the center of a negative hatestorm extremely quickly. Take "nintendo.grl," Junna Faylee, who has 9 million followers. She told the *Washington Post* that the work of maintaining that fame is a job that never ends and consumes the creator in ways that are unsustainable.[12]

"There is this power TikTok has: it's just so, so popular, and that can be a scary thing . . . You have to be constantly fighting against other content creators to be seen," she said.

"You don't realize the impact of having so many eyes on you," Faylee told the *Post*. "Those people who've chosen not to like you, they're going to see you, right there on their screen, and nothing you do is going to make a difference. You've got to learn to deal with the hate."

If your teenager wants to embark on a public presence or has dreams of going viral, it could be relevant to watch YouTuber Daniel Howell's "Why I Quit YouTube." In some ways, the challenges that vloggers, TikTokers, and "streamers" face in terms of navigating the tension between being public and maintaining content protection is just an extreme version of what any of us who have an online presence might feel. For example, do I, Devorah, need to hire someone to post on my public social "channels" for me when I'm on vacation, or is it okay to be offline for a week or two? How much do any of us want to maintain a "public presence" or "personal brand"? Where do our in-person relationships with friends and family fit into that public image?

Even on a very small scale, teens sometimes apply the language of fandom to real life. One mother shared with me a story of how girls at her son's middle school started "shipping" (being fans of a relation-ship or hoped-for relationship—usually in a book or movie). In this case, the girls were shipping her son, Jake, and his best friend. While that may seem LGBTQ+-positive, or cute and harmless, the two boys were just friends and were very uncomfortable with all the attention and resulting pressure on their friendship. The shipping drove them apart—they are no longer as close as they were.

Many ambitious teens head to YouTube, TikTok, and other plat-forms intending to become influencers and it doesn't happen. Sophia is one of the eager teens who stumbled into fame and then found it to be a defining (and remunerative) experience for many years. Still, Sophia warns, "Once you gain success, the numbers start to matter. It can become a toxic place in your mind . . . which takes the fun away."

What's next for Sophia? "I think I want to do something completely different, start up a different business or something, helping people with a different topic completely, or do something more artistic and then just leave social media and YouTube," she said to me.

Kids Are Afraid of Getting Canceled or Humiliated

Kids, especially teenagers, tend to have a decent handle on the many rules that dictate what is acceptable behavior in their "public life." They know a racist slur or homophobic slur will be social death in many communities. But kids who are less savvy about reading between the lines often miss the subtler rules—what constitutes "trying too hard" in a medium that is all about vying for attention? What kind of posts constitute bragging? What is appropriately "sexy" and what is too sexual? Because the rules aren't clear, kids may gossip or even ice out a peer if they feel a fellow teen or tween has gone too far.

The notion that a single post or comment that you make about yourself can lead to widespread shunning from your community if someone picks it up and shares it in a new context is scary.

People can also post about you or take pictures at school, for example, without permission. "People can be exposed on the internet . . . There are a lot of mean people . . . They expose you [by posting] weird pictures or inappropriate pictures of you. You probably think to yourself: 'I didn't post this. I want to know how they got it.' They can put it all over the internet," twelve-year-old Nola explained to me. "It's not really okay. I don't care if it's a joke or not."

This level of fear is a lot for a sixth grader to carry around. While Nola enjoys her digital life, especially when it provides a respite from the isolation of remote school, the worry of being "canceled" and the inhibition that comes with it can overwhelm her. Nola is not alone. Therapist Stephanie Zerwas talked to me about the negative impact that watching mean-spirited videos that have gone viral—such as the one of a woman falling into a fountain at the mall—can have on kids. While kids may find these videos funny or entertaining on the surface, the videos also tap into their darkest fears . . . that the world is a nasty place, and that there are eyes everywhere, waiting to catch you picking your nose, falling into a fountain, or pulling your car up to a gas station the wrong way.

The idea that they can be caught unwittingly saying or doing something clumsy or embarrassing, and that their misstep can live forever in perpetuity in the form of a video or photo that will be shared widely, can be hugely stressful for teens and tweens.

When we were in sixth grade, my friend was a star in the play. She was running a fever and feeling really sick the day of the play, but insisted she wanted to go on. To everyone's horror, after she said her first line, she fainted and fell off the small stage in our cafeteria. She ended up being fine, but she sure was embarrassed that an entire auditorium full of people saw her pass out and fall off the stage. I can only imagine how that could affect her now if someone had posted that online.

It could have been a meme. Would she have embraced it like "Side-Eyeing Chloe," whose YouTuber mother made her famous at age two? In a video she made with her mom at age eleven, she said she sometimes forgets that she "is her meme"—"I'm really famous," she laughs in the video. She has over half a million Instagram followers. How will Side-Eyeing Chloe feel when she's twenty-five? Will she put it in her Tinder profile or job applications? What about Star Wars Kid? Or that adorable baby—"Success Kid" Sammy Griner? His family used the famous photo of him from 2007 in their GoFundMe campaign to cover a transplant for Sammy's dad in 2015. Laney Griner threatened to sue Iowa representative Steve King for repurposing the viral meme of her son, Success Kid, in his campaign. In response to her threatened legal action, King stopped using the image. But it brings up huge questions about issues that can arise when images of kids go viral.

It is worth noting that the "default public" privacy setting has contributed to viral memes of kids. David After Dentist's dad posted on YouTube to share with family, and Laney Griner posted Sam Griner to Flickr—both parents initially intended to reach smaller audiences, but the tech defaulted to public sharing.

Rebecca Black certainly didn't intend to be a poster teen for growing up in public. At age thirteen, she recorded a video performing the song "Friday" with her friends—part of a music video production package her mother purchased for her—she couldn't have known that it would end up on YouTube, go viral, and be labeled the worst song in history.[13] And she certainly didn't expect to be ridiculed and bullied at school, and even in the media, where thousands made cruel comments on the video on YouTube, and hundreds of people made videos mocking the song—and Rebecca.

While there were opportunities that came from her sudden fame, like hosting the Teen Choice Awards, there was also a lot of sadness. When it all got too much, she even spent a few years out of school. Nobody wants to feel like the whole world is laughing at them, said

Black, years later about the experience. Today, Rebecca is a musician who has released successful singles and is uber-popular on TikTok. She's also queer. In that way, she's like a lot of people—the thirteen-year-old who makes the cheesy video that people make fun of grows up to be the famous, attractive queer artist who is probably too cool to go to those middle school reunions. So perhaps she has made the best of the situation, which she acknowledges helps to support her current platform. But kids who grow up seeing this kind of take-down, and adults who see that the world was this mean to a thirteen-year-old, are terrified of going through something similar—even on a smaller scale. And why wouldn't they be? None of us would wish Rebecca's experience on our own children.

Trapped Online in Old Narratives

Adolescence is a time of profound identity development. Kids are asking fundamental questions about themselves: Who am I? Am I normal? Do I fit in? And to answer these questions, they try on many different hats. But when they grow up in public, these hats can take the form of those highly curated online personas we discussed earlier. The problem is that anything these kids—or their family or friends— share digitally becomes part of their permanent digital footprint. Once those photos and videos are out in the world, whether they were posted with their consent or even by them, it's hard to pull them back.

The bigger issue is that sometimes these photos or videos tell a story about who they are that no longer matches who they *want* to be. Kids might be ready to try on a new hat, but the old one stubbornly refuses to budge. In those instances, they find themselves trapped in narratives created by them or by others, some of which were created when they were very young and had no control over it. For example, imagine if a dance studio features videos of your daughter's performances on their website. She loved dancing, but perhaps, as she grows older, she no longer wants it to be a prominent part of her social identity because she's moved on to other interests. Yet, when anyone searches her name, her performances from years ago are the first to pop up in the search results. You or your daughter could call the dance studio and ask them to take down the videos. But what if the poster of the videos is you? Will you take them down if asked?

The Story of Zephyrus

Zephyrus was assigned female at birth and became famous as Super Awesome Sylvia, the star of a YouTube STEM channel for girls.[14] This YouTube channel left an extensive digital record of Zephyrus's childhood that is now complicated for Zephyrus, who no longer identifies as a girl. In a Medium article, he wrote about trying to reconcile his present with the past.[15]

"Living as and existing as Super Awesome Sylvia has been very painful for me to attempt. It takes a toll on my mental health since the amount of gender dysphoria I feel reaches unbearable levels when even just attempting to put my mind in her place," he wrote. "I cannot be known as, or work as a girl, character, or person, especially when it's meant to embody who I was. It does not match up with who I actually am. It feels like being trapped."

Zephyrus also wrote about the way fame trapped him in a narrative that no longer applied, even before he came out as transgender. Being promoted and known as a "child genius" at age eleven was a lot of pressure. Super Awesome Sylvia was recorded and photographed doing things like meeting the president and traveling the world to speak (and bringing his family, who wouldn't have otherwise had those opportunities). It was therefore difficult for Zephyrus to say, "Actually, I'm not interested in doing this anymore; this is not who I am."

Our kids' identities are constantly shifting and changing—though perhaps not in such significant ways as Zephyrus, who has a different name and gender identity. When we were growing up, we were free to remake our identities and write our own narratives. While kids born in the digital age seemingly have *more* freedom to explore their identity—a plethora of ways to express themselves—they also have less freedom to get away from the identities they have created and "start over." They are both freer to experiment and less free to reinvent themselves with all traces of that experiment left behind. Kids growing up in public experience this tension between freedom and constraint.

The Power of Having a Public Voice

In 2020, months after the pandemic closed Chicago schools, Catlyn Savado, then thirteen and in middle school, gave a speech at a local city council meeting that went viral. This, and her continued activism and social media presence, have made her a well-known figure in Chicago's student activist scene. By directly calling out the powerful adults in the community, criticizing the city budgets, and calling for the removal of police from Chicago's public schools, she struck a chord with her classmates as well as adults who agree with her positions. For young activists like Catlyn Savado, Twitter can be a place to speak truth to power. Catlyn's high school principal is following her on Twitter. So are over two thousand other people. In Catlyn's case, it's not just the number of followers but *who* those people are that matter. The Chicago Police, Child Protective Services, and Chicago Public Schools all now follow Catlyn on social media.

"Actually, one time I got called down to my guidance counselor's office because someone from a higher office and CPS [Chicago Public Schools] flagged one of my tweets," explained Catlyn. The feedback she got was that the school would prefer that she voice her concerns through the "proper channels" instead of leading or participating in walkouts or calling for change on Twitter. In fact, this is similar to what I heard from all the politically active students I spoke with who use social media. Catlyn and the others point out that no one has ever made major social change by waiting around for the proper channels.

When Catlyn sees racism in the school system, she calls it out in a tweet. It is not surprising that the school administration doesn't want her to criticize the school publicly, especially now that the head of the teacher's union in another city supports her, too.

At what other time in history would a teen in her situation have that kind of access to speaking to adults in power? It's an incredible platform. On the other hand, it gets tricky when she wants to focus on just being a person, just being a teenager. "Online, I'm also, like, not just an organizer, but I show the very, like, teenager sides of me," Catlyn explains. "Sometimes, [I'm] very vulnerable, so to know that people are reading this or that I'm being surveilled when I'm just being a kid, it's really, really hard." Her activism has created expectations—and yet, one of the most telling and poignant posts I found on her timeline was about living through a pandemic. There was a close-up photo of her face, her eyes peeping out past her mask, with this message:

> *i cant believe that these past 2 years have been real. i was 12 years old when the world flipped upside down. Now, Im in high school. I turn 15 in a couple months and I'm supposed to do something. Be something. I'm still stuck in my 12-year-old body. None of this feels real.*

Other young activists go "off script," too. Cameron Kasky, who became a famous activist in the March for Our Lives movement, along with a group of his high school peers from Parkland, Florida, mostly focuses on gun control on his public platform; but he also used Twitter to come out as bisexual and has shared perspectives on other issues as well.[16] Given that he has over 380,000 Twitter followers, such announcements have significant impact. Today's young activists are not always following a publicist's instruction to "stay on message." They have grown up with social media and aren't afraid to use it.

For young people who want to change the world, social media and its ability to quickly disseminate words, videos, and images offer a powerful set of tools. Whether that means getting the police out of their schools; working against gun violence; or fighting climate change, racist school discipline, or sexist dress codes, social media has offered activists an important platform and space to connect. The pressures on young activists can be intense.

What Parents Can Do:
How to Help Kids Grow Up in Public

Growing up in public drains many kids' emotional energy. It can be stressful and exhausting. We need to make kids feel seen, understood, and validated, because when they go to social media for this, they come up empty-handed. There is never enough: not enough likes, followers, or novelty. No matter what, someone else will always have more. But there are many things that parents and educators can do to help kids navigate this busy landscape.

Tweens and teens are used to sharing only milestone moments or highlight reels of their lives to make them seem perfect. Teach your kids not to get caught up in the trap of seeing their lives from the outside this way. "Communication is crucial," Jacqueline Nesi, a Brown University–based researcher explains. "Let them know that not everything they are seeing on social media is going to be totally realistic. Ask questions about why they might feel like filtering their photos before they post them. These conversations can be really powerful." She also mentions that when we see our kids posting something concerning on social media (like a revealing photo), our instinct is to take their access to social media away; for example, "Because I saw these pictures of you in a bikini, you can't socialize online today." If you do that, Nesi cautions, your child will never come and talk to you about these things in the future: "Social media is such an essential part of their social lives that taking away access to it can't be the main strategy for parents to rely on," Nesi says.

While we should encourage kids not to intentionally make one another feel left out, we must also teach our kids that we don't have to include everyone all the time and that it's okay to not always be included. Normalizing this idea can go a long way in helping our kids prepare for times when they will be left out. It's also important to teach them how to cope with this exclusion when it happens to them. Ask them, "What will you do when [not if] you see your friends go out without you?"

At some point, your child's confidence may waver as a result of using social media apps. Tweens and teens are extra-attuned to peer feedback, so even feeling like people took "too long" to like a photo can be a blow. Help adolescents prevent or process negative feedback as soon as it is given to them and counterbalance their time on social media with activities that restore them. Teach your kids how to pay attention to their emotional temperatures when looking through social media. A group of seventh and eighth graders suggested activities that kids can do when they are feeling left out after seeing images of other kids hanging out without them. For example, they can hang out with pets, watch their favorite show, or even spend time with their parents. The more vulnerable we're feeling, the less time we should spend on apps that push us toward social comparison.

When it comes to body image, experts like Stephanie Zerwas suggest not showing your kids so many photos of themselves. As kids enter puberty, photos where their bodies feature prominently can heighten sensitivities and insecurities. Instead, consider sharing more face photos or pictures where their bodies aren't a focal point. I often talk to kids who have eating disorders. They study their photos frequently. They get stuck revisiting over and over images of themselves and examining how their body has changed over time. Some reminisce about their earliest prepubertal photos constantly and almost always look at the body as an object rather than an instrument that's able to move them through the world.

Conclusion

Ultimately, we want kids to grapple with their "public" audience in an intentional, empowered way when they are ready. We don't want to prevent them from writing their own narrative, and we don't want them to place too much importance on likes, follower counts, and numbers. While we want our kids to be prudent, we don't want them to be so afraid of cancel culture that they can't say anything. We want our kids to be people in their complex messiness, not curated "personal brands." We can help them find their way.

Growing up in public is a lot. A lot of pressure. A lot of distraction. A lot of surveillance. Sometimes, it is a lot of power and influence. Kids are aware that these platforms are giving people space to change the world. That's a positive that adults can build on as they mentor kids growing up in public.

chapter 3

Sharenting:

Balancing Parents' Needs with Kids' Privacy

Parents want to share their experiences on social media, and it's never been easier to show off our adorable kids, from pregnancy, birth, toddlerhood, first day of school, and all the way up to dropping them off at college. We share poignant moments of family time, exciting vacations, and even the occasional "keeping it real" post about the challenges of parenting. Posting about our kids can be hard to resist. But these tech habits can get us into trouble.

At my workshops in elementary and middle schools, I tell kids, "Step into the circle if a peer has shared a photo of you that you wish they hadn't," and some kids step in. But when I ask them to step in if they have experienced a *parent* posting an embarrassing photo, almost *all* the kids step into the circle.

Some kids love being posted about and have been part of the conversation for years. But for many tweens and teens, finding out your parents have been posting about you for years can be an upsetting shock. Malaya, a high school junior, shared, "I didn't really go on Facebook when I was little. So I didn't really know what my mom did or didn't post. A few years ago, I saw my mom's Facebook for the first time. I was *not* happy, because of course moms always have to post the most unflattering pictures. Right away, I was like, 'Oh my god—I have to stop her from posting all this stuff!'"

I've heard many teens and young adults describe the moment of discovering their parents' Facebook page. In Malaya's case, she said, "I didn't make her take anything down. But I was very careful—I told her what she could and couldn't post from now on."

Malaya went on to describe how her visual image was one thing, but it was also her social persona that was at stake: "I play violin, and I told her, 'You are not allowed to post anymore. Especially no more orchestra performances, because I don't want *everyone* to know that I play violin.' It's embarrassing in my opinion to play, like, an instrument, because I don't play a sport. I'm not athletic or anything. So . . . I don't like it. People make fun of me for it. For playing the violin."

Malaya's mother is surely not intending to embarrass her daughter. In fact, her love for and pride in her daughter's accomplishments may be motivating her to post—but she also may be posting for herself, for her own need for validation and acceptance. Our motivation for "sharenting" varies. First, we are proud of our kids and want to mark their important milestones. We used to do this by proudly affixing printed photos onto the pages of a cherished family album, or by sending a pack of freshly printed four-by-six-inch photos to adoring grandparents. Today, it is less common to print pictures and, instead, Facebook and Instagram have become the new family album for many.

Parents benefit from the support of other parents, whether offline or online. Sharing is a way for us to reveal common experiences about the battles we fight and the other difficulties of raising kids. It satisfies a deep urge within to share, empathize, commiserate, and come up with solutions—together. We feel like we are not so isolated and alone in our problems. Like others *understand*. And it feels good.

Yet with all the good things that come with our ability to share our experiences, there is a potential cost that lurks in the shadows. By sharing in digital spaces, are we compromising our child's current and future privacy?

As parents, we are the first stewards of our child's online reputation. It starts from the very beginning with a postpartum photo of mom and baby's precious first embrace. There's nothing like it, and we want to capture the moment. Then we text it to our family and close friends, or even post it on social media. We start posting about our children—publicly—before they can talk. We share because they are beautiful and perfect, and we are brimming with pride and optimism, and we want to share our euphoria with all those who care about us. We share because other people are doing it, and we don't want to seem like we don't love our kids. We share because we are writing a new chapter of *our* personal story—this time as a parent.

Since it's part of our story, we don't stop to think that it's not *only* our story to tell. The other person in the story is our child, and we are telling their story, too. **As our children get older, we can ask for their permission to post about them, and for years I've been advocating that.** But even if they are old enough to give permission, do they fully understand the implications? Do they understand the potential impact on today's privacy—and tomorrow's reputation? Do we as parents understand it enough to help guide them?

Perhaps you're reading this, thinking, "It's too late, my kid is in high school." Today's concerns are more centered on what *they* post, and maybe that's why you picked up this book. Looking back, you're pretty sure you haven't done anything to ruin your kid's marriage prospects, or their chances of getting into a good college, or even running for president someday. And even if you have, well, it's too late now, isn't it? But it isn't! You can take down old posts, change your ways, and have a talk with your kid about this stuff.

Here are some strategies to: (1) protect your kid's privacy, (2) help you manage their digital reputation, and (3) retroactively do damage control (by taking down posts and/or rebuilding trust) if you are concerned about things you've posted about your child.

I will also help you understand how your approach to posting about your child might influence their understanding and approach to digital reputation and privacy. It's up to us as parents to be mentors—and to model the behaviors we want to see in our kids.

What We Post Is a Statement of Our Values

Every time we share on social media, we are making a statement beyond the post itself. Each post contains clues about our values. Our actions display what we think is important and what we imagine (or hope) our "audience" thinks is important, too.

There are many reasons for sharing and many ways we share our parenting experiences. Some parents share constantly, while others share only the "milestones." Some share on vacation and don't share the "regular moments." Some share to show the perfect moments, and some share to show how imperfect life can be. One New York City mom and life coach, Victoria, told me that she stopped using her daughter's image in photos posted on her business's social media page. Her daughter confronted her, saying, "Can you just remove any picture of me off of Instagram? Like, now." So her mother went back and took off several pictures. I can empathize with Victoria. What could be better for my social media posts about parenting than an occasional picture with my kid? But . . . he's not interested in being part of my personal or professional social media sharing, so I have to respect that.

Social sharing can be like a diary or a curated photo album. It can feel private, which is why some parents share with only a very limited number of people. For many parents, the "audience" might be their peers—other parents—or limited to grandparents and extended family. But sometimes we forget the audience or the scope of our reach.

It's easy to overlook the sharing settings on social media, or our phone's privacy settings. Our "following" can be invisible, or at least not top of mind. And as the number of people in your following expands, it can be hard to keep in mind the whole audience when you post.

Your children's friends' parents may be the unintended audience for a post of yours—which, in turn, potentially includes *their* network of friends as well. One Catholic school mother of an eighth grader in Larchmont, New York, told me:

> I was president of the PTA and so a lot of [my daughter's] friends' parents were my friends, too, on social media. So . . . I would post something. Like, little things about her, "Oh, it's my daughter's birthday. I love her sooooo much." But then her friends would say things to her about it. And she did NOT like it. Her friends would just be like, "Oh, like, your mom posted this . . ." I guess because they saw it on their mom's phone? Sometimes they would make fun of her. So she didn't like it at all. She didn't like the attention. She was like: "I respectfully decline." So I stopped posting about her.

It's easy for all of us to forget about the breadth of the possible audience for our shares until we receive a surprise in the form of an unsolicited comment or opinion, or a takedown request from a friend, colleague, or our child. While these platforms make it easy for us to keep in touch with relatives, we want to remain in control of the "invite list."

Taking control means being more intentional about how we share. But *what* we share is just as important. Parents who document every event at their daughters' gymnastics meets are also documenting their own financial and time commitments to their children. This kind of parenting is what sociologist Annette Lareau calls "concerted cultivation," which is a level of intense academic and extracurricular support favored by many wealthy and upper-middle-class parents.[1] Social media can be a place to chronicle and celebrate concerted cultivation.

There is a difference between sharing posts about road trips to the grandparents' house versus taking international flights to exotic locations. Pictures from a fun day at the local water park versus a trip to Disneyland Paris. Sometimes there is genuinely no intent to brag, but a post can still be perceived that way.

Examining Consent: Whose Story Is It?

Social media is not the only arena for sharenting. "Mommy blogging" is a genre in its own right, with many parents—moms *and* dads—garnering huge online followings. Some of this writing is unpaid and "just to share," while others are paid for handsomely in the form of sponsorships or endorsements.

One colleague in the writing world shared that she is part of her college alumni Facebook page and that the level of disclosure about people's marital struggles, challenges with their children and finances—all things that might have once been taboo to share—surprises her. She speculated that the support these posters experience in the comments must justify the risk in sharing. When it comes to our kids, though, the risk isn't just to us—it is also to their experience, their friendships, their self-concept, and even our relationships with them.

Parents could and did write about their children in "old media," but even newspaper columns are much more searchable now. Your child's friends are more likely to be able to pull up your article with a simple search! Christie Tate, the author of *Group*, published a revealing article describing some interpersonal conflicts between her daughter and one of her daughter's friends. Her daughter asked her to stop writing about her, yet Tate refused to do so. As any parent knows, our children's stories can be hard to separate from our own. In response, Tate cited her own rights as an artist and a refusal to bow to the "self-sacrificing mother" trope. She describes the encounter with her daughter this way:

> *Could I take the essays and pictures off the Internet, she wanted to know. I told her that was not possible. There was heavy sighing and a slammed door. When I had pictured our first serious conversation about how the Internet is forever, I always thought we'd be talking about content posted by her, not me.*[2]

Tate agreed that she would not continue to post new images of her daughter without her approval. However, Tate refused to take down old photos or previously published articles. "None of them seemed embarrassing to me, though she might not agree," wrote Tate in an essay published in the *Washington Post* titled "My Daughter Asked Me to Stop Writing About Motherhood. Here's Why I Can't Do That."[3] Readers of her essays tended to side with her daughter. They felt that by not removing the photos and essays as her daughter explicitly asked, Tate was violating her daughter's rights and also damaging their relationship.

Writing about your child's friendship issues is more than writing about "motherhood." A parent can write an essay about "parenthood" and focus on decisions about new clothes and sneakers for school, complaints about applying to middle schools, and figuring out when visits to the pediatrician or dentist are needed. We can do so without disclosing a lot about the child other than he's going to middle school, wears sneakers, and sees a healthcare practitioner from time to time.

The difference lies not just in what and how we share, but also in the motivation behind it and the potential consequences. Sharing something as personal as our kid's friendship struggles could impact our relationship with our child or her relationship with friends. After years of talking with kids who feel violated and exposed by their parents, I've come to believe in erring on the side of privacy. If it could be problematic later, don't share. When it makes sense, we can ask for informed consent from the child or teen, and if there's any doubt, don't share it. The very fact that I write about children and technology sometimes feels burdensome to my son. It is possible I am a bit more ponderous with all my research on kids and tech than parents whose job is not immersed in such matters . . . and it's way less cool than the parents in our circle who work in VR or in the gaming industry. My son asked me not to book speaking engagements at his school or in our school district. To me, this was a fair "ask," and it was easy to accommodate.

Another writer I know had to make a serious change when one of her daughters asked her to stop writing about her. This mother's writing about open adoption had been followed and loved by many loyal readers. However, she made the sacrifice. Prioritizing the emotional health of her daughter, she instead started to write a wonderful fiction series that included some open adoption material. Her other research-based nonfiction writing and advocacy work continue, but *without* the stories about her own family.

These stories about our children are *their* stories to tell. Yes, I value stories about kids that are personal, but I do think we need to honor our kids' requests. Whether they are minors still living at home or we are telling old stories about now-grown children—we should treat these stories as sacred and not take for granted that it is okay to share them.

Feeding Our Need to Share: Selfish or Healthy?

Posting against our child's wishes tells them that we don't value their privacy and that their consent isn't important. Rather than simply never posting about our kids, we can consider whose needs are being met with each post. Is it only for your needs? Is it to show how much you care about your kids? Is it to help other parents? When photographing, writing, and posting about your kids, always consider: Can you meet these needs in other ways? At least balance your children's needs in the equation.

Critiques of sharenting have gendered aspects to them: moms are typically judged more for this kind of sharing than dads. Moms also may feel responsible for presenting and sharing the family's "public image."

In our society, so much of family life is hidden, so the revelations of the interior lives of mothers are extremely valuable, as are the experiences of fathers. But the fact that we rarely see fathers criticized for sharing details about their family lives reveals a lot about the gendered division of the mental, emotional, and physical labor inside of families.

Also, consider the domain. How is publicly sharing fundamentally different from a private conversation? If a daughter overhears her mother talk to a friend on the phone about her grades or her weight or a crush or a recent falling-out with a friend . . . is that any different than if the parent shares in a private social media group? It is important to think of posts as if they *could* become widely public, and also to remember that the very people your kid probably cares most about—their peers' parents and your immediate family—might be the audience for that post. It doesn't have to be published to a nationally known online magazine to feel like it's out there for the whole world to see.

If the disclosure is shared with fewer people—sometimes only one—the intention behind it is different, too. You might hope to receive support from a fellow parent—to garner empathetic assurance or to learn a new strategy to overcome a parenting struggle. Raising kids involves balancing our needs with theirs, including the need for parental community and support with a child's need for some privacy. Every parent needs to weigh these issues carefully in the digital age.

Boundaries and Their Unique Contours

You might be surprised when your child confronts you about a photo you shared—or comes to you upset about something that someone else has shared. You might agree or disagree that it crossed a boundary. But the distress on your child's face will make you want to solve it . . . fast.

No parent is spared this lesson. The best example I can think of is when Gwyneth Paltrow's fourteen-year-old daughter, Apple, called her mom out on Instagram for sharing a photo without permission. Even celebrities with professional "handlers" and PR expertise can misstep. This is somewhat reassuring.

We have to consider timing as well. As kids grow from babies into toddlers, then from preschoolers to tweens—things change. While you might feel okay with less restrictive boundaries disclosing about a preschooler, what happens when they start to read your posts and scroll back in time? Or even more tricky—what about the kids who *want* to be shared about at a younger age, but might not understand the full consequences yet?

Teens and young adults may go back and prune old pictures when a romantic relationship ends, but what about their parents? One mother of an eighteen-year-old son was upset when her son "demanded" that she delete family photos of an outing from two years before because his ex-girlfriend was in the photos. The mother felt violated that her son's current girlfriend had been looking at the mother's old posts. She found the new girlfriend's "snooping" to be invasive. The mother complied with her son's request, which he made on behalf of his girlfriend, but resented the intrusion and didn't like taking down images of family events that were important to her.

This incident really shows how much ownership we feel over our social media accounts. Had the photos with the former girlfriend been displayed throughout the house, perhaps the mother would have been more understanding, but the idea of the girlfriend intentionally visiting the mother's page and scrolling back in time felt invasive. Perhaps the new girlfriend is being insecure, but maybe seeing how embedded the ex was in the family was difficult. In any case, given that her son is eighteen and might have many more relationships, this mother could have considered taking photos at family events that were family only. Had the photos with the ex-girlfriend been in an album on a shelf, they would not have caused conflict or even been seen by her son's girlfriend, but they were easily accessible on an album-oriented app like Facebook. While we've perhaps seen folks cut someone out of a printed picture or take other measures to erase someone from the past, the more typical resolution is simply not going back to the physical or digital pictures.

We typically think about teens looking at their ex's photos or scrolling back through the history of a current romantic partner or crush, but the possibility that Mom's or Dad's social media could be the source of conflict or jealousy is fascinating. This story sheds light on the way social media and sharenting can bring up surprising issues.

A Family Plan for Sharing

Having explicit discussions about boundaries—with your spouse/ partner, your children, or even with extended family—can be helpful in clarifying your own "family policy." Talking about boundaries and setting some "ground rules" about what is kosher (or not) to share about the family can help avoid future issues. This is the job of a mentor, and we need to assume the role gladly.

Another strategy is for families to lay out a family "editorial policy," especially when kids are a little older and would like to have a say in the decisions about what is allowable or not. You might serve the role of "editor in chief" or maybe even delegate that to your child if she's ready for the responsibility.

You can have "editorial meetings" or quick check-ins to make decisions about *when* it's appropriate to share as well. Maybe no one can know about Mom's promotion yet, and we need to keep the celebrations in the family for now. Or maybe there's a new baby on the way, but we're not ready to announce it yet. Or your teenager got multiple acceptance letters to college but doesn't want the world to know until she's picked her place.

In these instances, it's important to make sure that your kids understand *why* the family has to (1) wait to share, and (2) be united on the timing of the disclosure. We've all felt it—sometimes the urge to share good news is irresistible. But there is a huge benefit to making this a family decision and having your kids be a part of it. It shows them that this information has value, both in content and timing. Not to mention that it fosters a sense of togetherness and camaraderie.

Outside the Family: What about What Other People Post?

What if you never post anything about your child? Maybe you're not on social media, or you feel confident that you are never the one in violation. Can you rest easy? Sadly, no. Why? Because of *other people*.

Sharing something about your child can come from anywhere. The child's grandparents, aunts or uncles, cousins, or their school friends. Or what about your friends—or your kid's friend's parents? None of these people may be up on your house rules and policies. None of them may have thought about these issues. They just share.

If you're not out in front of this, a violation will sound the alarm, letting you know about a boundary you never realized you needed to state explicitly. One mom who works in marketing and is social media savvy said she didn't realize she needed to explain why something wasn't okay until it happened: "My mother-in-law took pictures from my private Instagram and printed them for her Christmas card without asking. My daughters, fourteen and seventeen at the time, were so upset. I had to explain to my mother-in-law that it was not okay to do that (for so many reasons)."

This kind of misunderstanding shows that even something we share in public (e.g., on Instagram) is meant to be viewed in a certain way. We have an intention about it. But the tools we use to share are used differently by different people, and we might find ourselves having to clarify boundaries that might seem "obvious" to us. The only way to mitigate this is to have clear and explicit conversations about the issue, because what's obvious to you may not be obvious to others.

It's possible that you may get some pushback. "You're making a big deal out of this," someone might protest. They might not see why this is important to you, despite your best efforts to explain. This is where a family policy is a show of strength and unity. "We got together as a family and decided on these ground rules." They may not understand, but it's harder not to comply when you've said that it's not just your wishes, but your kids' wishes, too.

Different Kids, Different Preferences

One family policy may not be enough to cover the complexities of having more than one child. Each child in a family may be in a different stage of maturity, or each may simply have different privacy preferences. Cassandra is a mother of two and lives in a university town on the West Coast. Her experience is a great example:

> My youngest is more than happy to be posted about: photos, quotes—embarrassing, beautiful—doesn't matter. She's all about putting herself out there. My oldest doesn't want any pictures taken of him EVER, and rarely gets mentioned on my social media. He was scrolling through my Instagram the other day and said, "Wow, I see who your favorite kid is." I told him that if he let me take pictures of him (let alone post them), he'd have more presence there. But these were his choices. He sulked off somewhere after that. It's like you can't win. If I don't ask, I get grief for posting embarrassing stuff. If I ask and respect the "No," I get grief for "having a favorite."

I love this story because it is about a parent trying to do the right thing, yet she still can't please everyone. But there is a great conversation to be had about how else to document the more private kid's childhood and achievements. Maybe it isn't on Instagram but another outlet—maybe a printed mini-album every month or every year with pictures to be shared *only* with the family. Perhaps that would restore the balance.

Also, just because the youngest is happy to be posted about does not mean that there shouldn't be boundaries. As she matures, she may feel differently about some of the shares. Sometimes, we may not want to share, even when our kids beg us to. At her daughter's request, Michelle made a video of her daughter and a friend dancing to explicit pop songs with TikTok-inspired dance moves.

Her eight-year-old didn't intend for her dance to be seen in a sexual way; she just felt great about her dancing and wanted it to be shared. Michelle thought about posting it, but realized that if she posted the video without managing privacy settings, she could be inadvertently sharing it with someone who could repurpose it with that intent. Her adult wisdom helped her make a different decision. She told her daughter, "Let's show it to Grandma, and you can show it to your friend when she comes over. But we don't need to post it." Then her daughter forgot all about it. That video might be better in the family, as your child may see it differently as she matures.

To be clear, I am not suggesting there is anything shameful or problematic about her dancing, the music, or letting kids engage with popular culture . . . just that the video an eight-year-old is eager to share might be best shared with a smaller group of people, or not at all even if she *wants* you to share it, based on your adult judgment. Indulging every impulse certainly sends the wrong message and may encourage your child to perform for the camera when they could be living in the moment. And many kids tell me they cringe at videos that they posted or their parents posted when they were younger.

Different Spheres of Privacy

There are many misconceptions about how the younger generation regards privacy. The prevailing opinion is that they "share everything," and don't seem to mind "living in public." After all, today's middle schoolers have never experienced the world before social media and the internet.

Facebook was started in 2004, Twitter in 2006. Both gained wide usage shortly thereafter. Anyone born in those years simply accepts this as a part of today's life. There is no reference point for them about what privacy was like *before* the internet. Telling them our stories about it doesn't help; it just makes it seem like we're out of touch as parents.

But, of course, like many issues regarding parenting, it's more complex than that. Kids *do* care about privacy—their landscape just looks a little different than ours. Let's look at these differences, as well as a rubric to help you strategize for different kinds of privacy.

Small Privacy vs. Big Privacy

For many young people, it is easier to understand privacy within their own network—parents, extended family, friends, and their (hyper) local community. Privacy within these circles feels more crucial to protect, because they are close relationships and thereby can have a big impact on social standing. I call this "Small Privacy."

On the other side of the spectrum is "Big Privacy," which gets more abstract. For instance, health records, test scores, the data that we generate when using web services, facial recognition, algorithmic tracking, or geo-tracking. This type of privacy is harder to conceptualize because (1) it's not always obvious in day-to-day transactions, and (2) often we've granted permission to companies to use this data in ways that we don't fully understand.

Naturally, kids are more sensitive to "Small Privacy" because it's tangible and immediate. A misstep is easy to spot because it affects them directly. A breach ("Why would Dad read my text message?")

or an unwanted disclosure ("Why did my mom post my test scores on Facebook?") can be painful to them because they can easily imagine its impact on their local social sphere.

Issues of Big Privacy can escape kids' notice and their concern. Are they aware that YouTube's algorithm is tracking search terms, clicks, and time watched? And that it's using this information to fill out a preferences "profile" to generate a set of tailored suggestions for the next video? And that it's designed to keep people on the platform at all costs so that YouTube can keep serving ads to them?

Do kids care that Spotify operates in the same fashion, using "interaction data" to glean more and more information that they can sell to advertisers? These platforms seem to be doing us a service by tailoring the content to our preferences, but make no mistake— serving us is secondary to making sure that we as consumers are available to those who have paid for our attention.

We adults can understand this, but it's harder for kids. They see a free platform that's fun and does what we want it to do. But behind the scenes are data-mining machines that exploit our personal information for profit. This is a trade-off that we might make willingly, but being aware of these hidden costs and accompanying risks makes us at least try to use these platforms responsibly.

As we teach kids about Big Privacy, we want them to take more control over their data. It helps to start by looking at Small Privacy with your kids and to give them more power over what their peers see and learn about them.

SMALL PRIVACY

Each of us has our own social circle, and your kid begins to form their own as soon as they are old enough to interact with those outside the home. Playgroups at the playground, day care, and preschool mean that your child is starting to have their own friends and form their own connections.

Year after year, this social circle expands and becomes more distinct from the one you shared when your child was preverbal.

There will be points of overlap, however, no matter how divergent the circles are. These can serve as a great way to start teaching young kids about issues around Big Privacy. It can show them how information can travel beyond the confines of their small, contained network. When we as parents post about our kids, their friends' parents might see the post. Now your kids' friends might be privy to a story that your kid didn't want to disclose.

Such are the issues of sharenting, and we might use this as an opportunity to model good ethical behavior to our kids. You might say, "I'm so proud of you for all the improvement you've made in your math scores this year. Do you mind if I share this with your grandparents?" Most kids would probably be happy with this. But what if you push it a little further by saying, "Do you mind if I share a photo of your last A+ math test on my social media account?" Would your kid feel uncomfortable? Would they push back a little? Now you can talk about why.

SMALL PRIVACY THOUGHTS: Who's going to see the post? Can you anticipate the reaction? What happens if the reaction is really positive? What if there's no reaction, or not much anyway? How would you feel about these outcomes? Is it worth it or should we just stick to sharing it via text message with Grandma? Will someone close feel left out when they see this picture? Why is sharing it this way different than posting to social media?

This gets kids in the habit of thinking outside their immediate circle and understanding the broader implications of what gets shared and how it travels.

BIG PRIVACY

Thinking outside their small circle opens the door to talking about other issues around Big Privacy. Now you can talk about how other people *outside* your intended audience might be seeing the information you share.

> BIG PRIVACY THOUGHTS: What information is "safe" to divulge in setting up a social media profile—and what info is best *not* to supply? Why do they need certain info and what are they going to use it for? When is the risk too great that we might abort the sign-up process?

We have to go little by little with this, because the issues are complex. But overlapping social spheres offer a good entry point. And as always, it's better to offer some control. Posting to the local parenting Facebook group to look for a pediatrician who is uncircumcised-friendly, or a therapist to help with school anxiety, or a group to facilitate your child's social issues could be a major violation of their privacy. Parents do all of these things for the best reasons—they are genuinely trying to find help or support for a particular issue—but it can be hard to predict how this information about them might revisit your household and come back to haunt or taunt your kid.

Taking Control over Their Own Narrative

When kids have a say in what gets shared, it can make a lot of these issues feel like a shared pursuit rather than a battle. As kids grow up, they are "trying on" different interests and identities—sometimes at a rapid rate.

Giving them control means giving them some guidance. We don't want to be deterministic, but we also don't want to impinge too much upon the narrative they are creating. Children's privacy expert and attorney Stacey Steinberg says, "When my kids both go meet family that they don't know very well, I want them to be able to define their narrative. If at that moment they're really into soccer, I want them to talk about soccer and not have that family member approach them and say, 'Hey, I hear you're a great violinist' because of the violin pictures that I posted."[4]

While you may be proud of their musical talent, your kids might be more into sports. Talking about and posting about the former and not the latter may feel like pressure to your tween, and they may resist or even resent it. This is hard for us, because all we're doing is showing how proud we are of them! But our expression of pride can easily backfire.

When your kid moves on to his next pursuit, hobby, or obsession— what happens? Twenty posts from the soccer season may lead to what feels like an insult when the interest wanes: "I thought you were into soccer, what happened?" someone might say. Ideally, your kid wouldn't have to deal with that pressure if he wasn't good enough, got cut from the team, or was never serious about it in the first place. All of these scenarios are perfectly acceptable for any child, but you can see how it can imprint the past onto the present.

In a time of rapid growth and change, Steinberg cautions that we want to give kids that fluidity and not trap them into past identities or associations. We don't want to "take away that child's ability to control the narrative." But I would add that we want to help them understand the narrative they are creating. A passion is a wonderful thing, as is finding those who share your passion. Maybe it's okay to go "all in" creating a public record. But doing so mindfully is always a better practice.

Practices for Big Privacy vs. Small Privacy

One practice families will want to consider is conducting periodic digital audits of things that you and others have shared in the past. While it is true that something shared can sometimes be found after being taken down, it is also true that it is far less likely to be found if it wasn't shared widely in the initial post period and then was quietly removed.

Other practices like using initials or pseudonyms to make our kids less searchable are limited in their effectiveness. They certainly make it less likely that someone will do a Google search of your child's name and find a post you have written about them and their bedwetting, but someone who follows you could still look up your family and figure out your child's identity. It is worth imagining this scenario for anything you share.

Some parents do use pseudonyms, but also withhold stories that are just too personal, or stories that are vetoed by their kids. Tech expert Alexandra Samuel shares openly about her son's autism and the challenges and pleasures of being his parent in her published articles. On Facebook, she writes about him with a pseudonym. Her use of pseudonyms is good for Big Privacy, but in terms of Small Privacy, the parents of peers, and her son himself, a pseudonym is not effective. There are stories she won't share publicly at all, pseudonym or not. When she posts about either one of her two children, she sometimes writes, "Posted with permission." I enjoy Alexandra's writing about parenting and find "Posted with permission" reassuring. Otherwise, I feel uncomfortable reading personal stories about teenagers if I am not sure they are aware and comfortable with their stories being shared.

Steinberg acknowledges that not using children's full names does not always provide much of a protection, given that households are so searchable; a child's name is something that a little research gives you if you look up a parent's household. But, she says, making it more difficult to connect your child's face and his or her name might offer some Big Privacy protection, at least in terms of facial recognition linking those two data points. Small Privacy is different. If you talk about "my kid" in one community, and people know "your kid" or you only have one or two children and the details make it clear which one you are referring to, then withholding their name isn't a meaningful privacy practice within your own community. It may be worth doing for Big Privacy reasons, but it also may be worth reconsidering the post if the Small Privacy concerns are significant.

Concerns over Facebook's less-than-perfect privacy practices have many of us concerned—not just parents. I spoke with a number of parents, including several who are computer security experts who don't share their children's faces on social media. Interestingly enough, several grandparents with millennial children told me they were under strict instructions not to share on these channels, making me wonder if this is becoming more common. Some of these families did share that they used cloud-based apps that are password protected and more secure, never "defaulting" to public sharing. Other families may feel the same way, so even if you choose to post your own kids' faces, you will probably want to ask permission from other parents and kids before sharing photos of other people's children on your own social media. Also, foster families, I learned, are not allowed to post, to protect the children's safety and privacy (at least in some states), so overall, it is best to be cautious if photographing your children with their friends. Perhaps just share with the caregivers and don't post.

Resist the Urge to Overshare: #DecisionDay and College Acceptance Posts

One mother, Minna, told me that she's usually thoughtful about consent, but one time her excitement and urge to share got the best of her. Her daughter got into one of her first-choice schools, and Minna posted about it without asking her, and her daughter was *not* happy about that. "It was my bad," Minna laughed now, telling me the story. "She asked me to take it down. We had a conversation about it, and I deleted the post. And what it really revealed for me was that she was having so much anxiety about the debt, and about what she would do, and there was a part in the back of her mind that was really still on the fence about what she wanted to do and she didn't want the pressure of everyone knowing she got into this great school because she wasn't sure what she wanted to do."

Ultimately, Minna's daughter felt like it was her news to share—or not. Minna took down the post and apologized and did not post about subsequent college news, following her daughter's lead about only sharing widely when decisions were final.

If you are in a community with lots of college-bound high school students, you may have noticed a few (or a few hundred) shares in your timeline every spring about where seniors were accepted at college and where they plan to attend. This can get tricky—for kids who may not want their parents to post, for young people who won't be attending their "dream school," and for anyone who is feeling anxious about the future.

Susan Borison, editor in chief of *Your Teen* magazine, who has sent five of her own kids to college, said, "You can feel like if you're not out there and able to brag about your kid with everyone else, it's like a massive embarrassment."

Admissions season can be hard for parents who have young adults on a different path. Maybe your son or daughter is considering trade school, an apprenticeship, community college, or heading into the workforce. Maybe they're planning a gap year for an epic year of service, or maybe they are planning to work and save while they figure things out. For everyone who posts, there are families *not* posting that don't have tuition money right now, didn't get into the places they applied, whose child ran into a mental health problem during high school and is focused on recovery, or who just aren't quite ready for college.

Some parents have told me they wish other parents wouldn't post about college choices. Young people have told me their parents' posts make them cringe. Many of the teens I spoke with are very sensitive about bragging and concerned about making friends feel badly. They have been thoughtful about letting friends know one-on-one, especially if they are applying to the same schools. High school students are also very supportive of friends who don't get in. We can learn from their example.

Often, teens have had more social media experience than their parents and use Instagram and other apps in a more nuanced way.

Some applicants also seek solace and commiseration in the genre of college-rejection YouTube.[5] (Yes, that is a thing. TikTok too.)

Here are a few suggestions when it comes to posting about college admissions:

- Consent is everything. Most importantly—as with any social media post, but especially in the face of big-deal news—get permission. If they say no, just don't post.

- Don't share until they've decided where they're going. If your teen hasn't decided, sharing the list of possibilities may create pressure for them, as people may ask them about these different schools. Also, posting each acceptance one by one may be a bit much for your followers.

- Have empathy for yourself and others! Feel free to use features like "snooze" on Facebook (you'll unfollow them for 30 days) or "mute" on Instagram (you'll stop seeing their posts but not unfollow them) if someone's posts are making you feel stressed. And have empathy for that person's teen, who may be cringing (or blissfully ignorant) about parental posting.

- Unplug and take a break. If you or your child is stressed by the "seniors on Instagram" that some high schools create, or the flurry of sweatshirt-wearing, pennant-waving posts, take a break from social media. Go outside! Ride your bike. Find a way to unplug from mid-April to mid-May at least.

- Remember that life is complicated! Some seventeen-year-olds may seem to have their future planned out. Of my adult friends, I have just one or two who had the correct guess about their adult career path at that age. Many of us are in careers that didn't exist when we were seventeen. Your undecided kid who can admit they are not sure what they want to do is being honest with themselves and with you. It will be okay.

- Don't scroll if it is hurting you. If you do scroll, send empathy toward all who are posting and all who are not posting. We all need it.

What Can Parents Do about Sharing Concerns?

Ultimately, our practices at home offer crucial opportunities to mentor our kids. **Instead of beating ourselves up for oversharing mistakes in the past, we should attempt to clean them up where possible, but also to move forward with increasing awareness of the importance of giving our kids the chance to create their own narrative and value their own privacy, while respecting the privacy of others.**

The following are some tips for sharing about kids while respecting their privacy and autonomy:

- Timing is important. Has your child shared with the folks they want to tell? Don't steal their thunder.

- Project into the future. Will this photo be embarrassing when they are running for office? Getting checked out by a possible future spouse? If in doubt, don't post, or take it down.

- In the moment: Wait twenty-four hours before sharing. The

urge to share often goes away while we are making the decision. This might mean your family has less of a profile or that you get fewer likes (I certainly get less likes now that I share less of my child), but it will be worth it.

— Check in. The conversations with your child about these choices are such an important chance to model your values and hear more about theirs and encourage them to self-reflect. If your child is hungry for likes and *wants* you to post all the time, can you create a safe outlet for your kid where you post just for a closed audience (maybe only grandparents and immediate family)?

— Talk to your kid about consent. If they are old enough to understand sharing, ask if there are certain kinds of posts they don't want to share. And then remember to ask every time you post about them, "Is this okay?"

— Consider limiting the number of full-body photos you post publicly to avoid giving kids too much chance to linger or overfocus on these kinds of images as their body changes and grows.

— Consider the audience. We are all hungry for good news. I am not suggesting that you hold out on grandparents who are eagerly awaiting updates, but take a moment to consider: Who really needs to know? If it is just family and close friends, can you simply send a text or jump on FaceTime? Maybe emailing or even snail-mailing some photos directly would work best.

— What to do with the Mea Culpa Feeling: Review the times you have cringed when other parents overshare, seem to be bragging, or are posting personal details likely to embarrass their child. Do you have any posts that remotely resemble those posts? Can you go back and take them down, or switch them to private?

Now that you understand the nature of sharenting and have a handle on the rules of engagement, you'll be in a better position to develop family policies that feel right for you. Throughout the development of your child's reputation, think about what constitutes an acceptable level of sharing of their physical likeness and information about them. Proactively communicating these preferences with friends and family won't completely prevent anything from being posted that you would prefer had not been, but it will go a long way. You won't always be able to enforce what you recommend, but knowing that you are an advocate for your kids' privacy and that you respect their wishes will cultivate a sense of safety and trust. Further, your kids will be more likely to come to you for help if they share something they regret, or a peer shares something without their permission.

chapter 4

Too Much Information:

Are Classroom Apps Undermining Independence and Motivation?

I n the last ten years, digital apps and online portals that track and share our kids' behavior and academic performance in real time have become the norm. Apps like ClassDojo, PupilPath, PowerSchool, and Infinite Campus give parents unprecedented access to their kids' school life. When it comes time to apply to college, "guidance software" may show your teen how they compare with peers on a chart—which can be helpful but can also be deflating and anxiety provoking, especially if it isn't accompanied by nuanced, human guidance. Further, this software might ask for a lot of deeply personal records of the student's behavior, and opting out may not be easy.

Teachers have always communicated with parents about significant behavior issues, and schools mail report cards regularly. High school students had class ranks and some idea how their performance compared with others. But parents did not get day-by-day updates on when a child interrupted a teacher, missed an assignment, showed up late to class, or didn't do well on a quiz. Now we can access our child's school performance from our phone, tablet, or laptop just as easily as we can check the weather.

This technology might seem like a win-win: it makes it easier for schools, parents, and students to communicate about students' progress and behavior. Unfortunately, the technology gives us 24/7 access to surveil our kids, which can undermine their opportunities to develop independence and intrinsic motivation—the motivation to do something for its inherent satisfaction rather than for a reward.

Students not only obsess over their grades as they are constantly updated, but they also worry about how their parents, who have instant access to the same information, will react. Parents can get stressed as they get bombarded with minute-by-minute information about what their children are up to—and whether that information makes a difference in their overall success at school or not.

You might think, "Whew! Dodged some stress there" if you or your kids' schools don't use these online tools. Still, one thing is true:

> The culture of surveillance is shaping our children's sense of identity and independence—and impacting our mental health, our family's connectedness, and our ability to self-define in adulthood. This impact starts as early as kindergarten.

Monitoring Our Elementary Kids' Behavior

It's the first day of kindergarten. Your adorable five-year-old comes home after school, ready to sign up for and create her own avatar on the ClassDojo app. Her teacher, she tells you excitedly, will give her points whenever she follows classroom rules, like raising her hand before speaking. The teacher will also dock some points if she doesn't. A few days into school, she learns which behaviors earn her points toward coveted prizes, like a visit to the treasure box, feeding the class pet, or being a "line leader." Depending on the teacher's updating habits, you may get pinged with updates throughout the day on how well your child is sharing, sitting crisscross applesauce, staying quiet when directed, and following other classroom expectations.

ClassDojo is now used in 95 percent of elementary schools in the US.[1] Part of its appeal is its gamified aesthetics—familiar to any child who has played online games. Students collect positive points when they engage in appropriate behaviors such as "working hard," "staying on task," "following instructions," and "helping others"—and negative points when they engage in inappropriate behaviors such as "not listening," "not staying seated," and "wasting time." (I shudder when I imagine my own workday being held up to similar scrutiny, although this kind of surveillance through AI is creeping into the workplace, too.) Teachers assign points to a group for collective behavior, awarding points to the table that cleans up first. At the end of the day or the week, students typically trade points for a reward, or the child with the most points may be given public recognition or a prize.

Some schools use these apps in coordination with their overall behavior management "system," such as Positive Behavior Interventions and Supports (PBIS). Systems like this tend to rely on the belief that all students can learn appropriate behaviors if they know what is expected of them. The idea is that instead of punishing students when they misbehave, PBIS programs focus on preventing negative behaviors by rewarding positive ones. In PBIS schools, ClassDojo can be used for positive or negative points.

Of course, elementary schools have always had systems for tracking and reporting children's behavior—although until recently these were all analog. Did your teacher ever write the names of kids who were misbehaving on the chalkboard for all to see? If so, she or he was using a very simple classroom management technique: public shaming.

Most teachers and schools today use more formal behavior-management systems. For example, teachers might give students a paper "fix-it ticket" when they engage in "severe" or "significant" misbehavior. Students are supposed to reflect on what they've done and write down a plan for how they plan to "fix it." They bring the ticket back the next day signed by their parents. Of course, the idea of getting in more trouble at home for getting into trouble at school is part of the disincentive or fear factor that is supposed to keep students highly motivated to avoid a "fix-it" ticket. Some teachers still use the controversial behavior chart method where a student might "clip up" or down based on behavior, and the chart is up in front of the whole class in order to shame and control the children who are struggling to stay in line.

Digital behavior-monitoring platforms extend the reach of these systems by sharing minute-by-minute data on students' behavior with parents and caregivers. Teachers can share pictures of students and their work, make classroom announcements, or individually send messages to parents. ClassDojo in particular makes information accessible in multiple languages and outside of school hours, reducing the barriers that many families face when trying to be involved in their children's education. Especially during the remote school phase of the COVID-19 pandemic, many elementary school teachers relied heavily on these apps to communicate with students and parents.

Some teachers credit the app with helping them manage behavior in their classroom more effectively. They believe it motivates good behavior particularly in the lower grades, where kids are still learning basic classroom rules. "The cool avatars truly get my students excited and ready for learning," gushed a teacher in Albuquerque. A special education teacher blogged that she loved the ability to share access to the app with her aides. "Even when I am not with my class, my aides are able to provide the direct [positive and negative] reinforcement," she explained. "And consistency goes a looong way with my kiddos!"

But how does it feel to grow up so closely monitored? And do these apps really *transform* behavior or just bring about short-term compliance?

Can You Motivate Good Behavior with Apps?

Developers of classroom management software like ClassDojo claim that their apps are primarily designed to motivate good behavior. What they actually measure are *outcomes*—how well your child has met the behavioral expectations set by a teacher. The digital app ascribes intention to kids' behavior: it imagines that children are in full control and can simply decide to behave well just to earn points. The problem, of course, is that this is not the case. So much of a child's ability to meet behavioral expectations is both internally wired and also externally influenced by what is going on in that child's life.

Self-regulation—the ability to manage one's emotions and behavior—allows kids to show patience and control their impulses; it allows them to stay seated at their desks, to remain quiet when the teacher talks, to follow directions like raising their hand. In short, it allows them to "behave well." But self-regulation varies not just by age, but by gender, developmental stage, and physical maturity. Boys, for example, are generally less externally regulated in elementary and middle school, and therefore have a harder time meeting behavioral expectations than girls.

Children's life circumstances and temperament have an overwhelming effect on how "well" they behave. For a child who is hungry because he didn't get breakfast, exhibiting self-control, focusing on a task, or being patient with others is simply harder. Students with ADHD or nonverbal learning disabilities may have more difficulty meeting typical behavioral expectations. A child who has sensory issues might find it hard not to run their hands along the back of someone else's chair or hum during tests; children who struggle to express themselves and their boundaries verbally might be more likely to push another child on the playground. Many kids also can't meet a teacher's expectations simply because these are not age or developmentally appropriate.

It is not that these kids don't want to "be good," it's that the expectations are not possible for them to meet, or they need scaffolding and support to get there. ClassDojo and other behavior-monitoring apps simply reinforce what the teacher and parents already know and expect: a child who struggles with self-regulation will collect more negative points on the app, or struggle to earn positive points, compared to a child who is, by nature or circumstance, usually able to meet the teacher's behavioral expectations.

These apps rarely help *change* behavior long-term because they are not necessarily used alongside a curriculum that teaches kids self-regulation. They give parents the false impression that the school is *doing something*, but the points themselves offer nothing to help the child learn to manage their emotions or give them tools to behave better. Teachers, in fact, have little training on self-regulation and how that varies in a culturally, economically, psychologically, and neurologically diverse group of students. Schools' focus on meeting state and federal standards and performing well on standardized tests has left teachers with little time to spend on these critical non-academic skills.

If it doesn't change behaviors, why do so many teachers love ClassDojo? Because the app, like any system of rewards and punishments, is fairly effective at getting kids to comply with rules and expectations—in the short-term. But studies show that incentives in general are less effective at truly changing behavior. Alfie Kohn, a thought leader in education, human behavior, and parenting, explains that "incentives, a version of what psychologists call extrinsic motivators, do not alter the attitudes that underlie our behaviors. They do not create an enduring *commitment* to any value or action. Rather, incentives merely—and temporarily—change what we do."

"All the kids get obsessed with points, points, points!" a teacher said about ClassDojo. As kids get habituated to having their behavior monitored and tracked, they learn quickly to focus primarily on the rewards and incentives to comply with rules, rather than on learning.

Getting students to comply with behavioral expectations in the short-term comes at a high price when you consider the long-term effects of habituating our children to constant external monitoring.

The Toxic Effects of Behavior-Monitoring Apps

In addition to being less effective at truly helping children regulate their behaviors and emotions, behavior-monitoring apps like Class-

Dojo can make children who are already struggling feel even worse about themselves. More troubling still is how the apps shift the relationship between students and teachers, between home and school, and between student and learning. Here are the many ways in which having their behavior surveilled and shared with others affects our kids.

Some Kids Feel Defeated

Losing points in public or being excluded for not earning enough points hurts kids' self-esteem. For some kids, even an hour of inhibiting their impulse to get out of their seats or to talk to their friends is a feat. When the teacher doesn't "capture" their good behavior, but then notices them when they talk out of turn, their day is marked with a ding, leaving them feeling defeated or ashamed.

I couldn't help feeling vicarious stress and sadness reading one teacher's blog about throwing a "pod party" of "several hours of outdoor play" for all her sixth graders who don't have negative points. Study after study has shown kids who struggle with self-regulation at school need *more* recess and play. When I picture the "bad" students watching out the window as the other students play outside, I worry about the triple threat—shame, segregation from peers, and being told by adults that they don't deserve to be part of the group. I have reports from parents that, years later, children still talk about the times they got in trouble on their classroom's monitoring system, be it analog or digital; it's imprinted on their memories.

Erin, a mother of two boys, explains that the points system overwhelms her preteen son. "He starts to lose motivation if he has a bad day, because in his mind he has already ruined the whole week," she told me. "We try to encourage him to use it as motivation, but children tend to focus on the negative when it's pointed out to them. Despite the fact that the app refers to the red points as only 'needs improvement,' we know what it really means and so do they . . . they messed up."

Kids notice everything—and they certainly notice other students getting points that they don't. Even if teachers make accommodations for a child who has a problem self-regulating, this creates dynamics that are not always positive. It might be hard for seven-year-old Sasha to understand why another kid, Julian, gets points for "keeping hands to self," when she keeps her hands to herself 24/7 easily, but doesn't earn points for doing so. In the end, Sasha may resent Julian for earning so many more chances at the treasure box.

Resentment can arise among kids when teachers award points publicly and collectively by giving points to a table that works quietly. If a child caused their table or class to lose points—and a chance to go to the treasure box or get a pizza party—their classmates will not like them very much.

"My son is a very calm and sweet child," a mother of a ten-year-old shared. "When the entire [class] table was rated for something, it affected him, knowing that I would see it." Rosanna, a mother of eight-year-old twins, found the point system didn't help her differentiate between her child's behavior and the overall class's. "Sometimes [my daughter] was in control of herself, but the class or table wasn't, so she lost points," Rosanna told me.

The Apps Stress Out the "Good Kids," Too

Even well-behaved kids can become anxious when they feel so closely monitored—not just by their teachers but by their parents, who can see how they are doing at school via the app. These kids internalize the constant scrutiny, making earning points and behaving quite stressful rather than motivating.

Isabel was a happy six-year-old who came to kindergarten with excitement after a great experience in preschool. She loved school and learning and had the classroom rules down: she had no problem sitting still, raising her hand, or following directions. But within a few weeks of starting kindergarten, she started to dread going and fretted over the points. If too many days went by without getting a reward (while others got them), she would feel that she wasn't doing well, or that the teacher wasn't noticing her good behavior. "It's not fair," she would tell her mom. "I never talk without raising my hand, but she never gives me points for that." Or, "Everyone else talks all the time; I never do, but I talked a little today, and I was the only one that got a point taken away." Her mother was heartbroken to see her curious, enthusiastic daughter get so focused on the points rather than on reading and math and coloring and playing with her friends.

Isabel's mother said that her daughter felt the point system was random: the teacher *might* happen to catch her doing something good or bad, so she always had to be on the lookout to keep her points up. Even teachers who don't give "negative points" can make students feel bad when they don't get positive ones, especially when they are tied to receiving a prize.

Constant Updates Are Hell

For some parents, ClassDojo is a source of great stress. Receiving a few pictures of your child feeding the class pet or participating in a special event at school might be welcome, but getting hit with a running commentary of how your child is struggling on a daily basis is distracting.

When parents see their children getting dinged, they worry their children are having a bad day. The behavioral information parents get is typically out of context: Are all kids getting pinged for not raising their hand, or is it just my kid? Does it mean my child behaves in an age-appropriate way? Updates from school affect family dynamics. Not only do kids feel the sting of getting dinged at school, but they know their parents will know about it, too, so now they have to anticipate their parents' reaction. One mother shared her annoyance: "Why is the teacher harassing my daughter (and me) with these points? And do teachers who have their own children believe that informing parents of their kid's daily mistakes is helpful rather than punitive and shaming?"

School Should Be Your Child's "Domain"

School should be a place where children are in charge of managing themselves in the world, and after a tough day, home should be a respite from a long day of learning and socializing. But this might not happen if kids come home to a parent who has been getting pinged all day with their shortcomings and wants to talk about them. Parents who normally give their kids space and are reluctant to talk too much about the school day might feel obligated to press a bit harder if their kid got lots of negative points that day. This may lead parents to focus on the negative or get into a conflict instead of just being with their kids in an accepting and loving way.

During the remote school phases of the COVID-19 pandemic, parents received a lot of information by overhearing the classroom interactions. Many of these parents shared with me that they found it incredibly stressful. I certainly did. Just hearing the teacher's stress and a hint of frustration took me back to my own school days—and the stress didn't help an already overwhelming situation. Parenting author and podcaster Dr. Robyn Silverman described the experience of overhearing remote school this way: "You are a fly on the wall in a room you were never meant to be in." I found this quote also captured the collapsed boundaries between home and school that results from monitoring apps, even when kids returned to in-person attendance.

Compliance Isn't Always Best

Detractors of ClassDojo worry that the app's focus on compliance undermines kids' ability to think for themselves and self-regulate, and also to learn to question authority when appropriate. The late Joe Bower, an internationally recognized teacher and education blogger, pointed out in his own critique of ClassDojo that "mindless compliance is responsible for far more of the atrocities against humankind than needless disobedience."[2]

While most of my own son's teachers have been wonderful, he once had a substitute teacher who behaved dangerously and said inappropriate things to the students. I was proud to hear that several classmates sneaked out of the class to let a trusted adult in the building know what was going on. Their noncompliance was the right choice! Another parent I interviewed for this book described a teacher harassing her transgender son and "deadnaming" him repeatedly and insisting on using non-preferred pronouns. Her son's classmates stood up to the teacher and used his pronouns and name correctly. Sometimes, resisting authority is the right choice and what we'd want our children to do.

Do Online Grading Systems Empower Anyone?

Once your child graduates to middle school and high school, you are more likely to get asked to sign up for an app to monitor their academic performance—a grading portal or LMS (learning management system) like PowerSchool or Infinite Campus.

Long gone are the days when a kid could hide their report card from their parents. Parents could remain unaware of their child's academic performance until they received an end-of-quarter report card. (I managed to be tardy every day of seventh grade, and my parents were only notified at the end of the year.)

Grades in high school can seem like the be-all and end-all in communities where college admissions are the holy grail. In some places, the pressure for good grades starts before high school. In Chicago, admission to the best public high schools is based on seventh-grade test scores and attendance records. Many students and parents believe middle school grades are the ticket to an acceptable or safe high school, and that high school grades are the only way to a "good" college—and therefore a "good" life. Putting this kind of pressure on our tweens and teens can have negative consequences.

This emphasis on grades has led to grading apps that give students and parents access to students' grades frequently and immediately. These comprehensive student record-keeping systems were preceded by a patchwork of databases like electronic grade books, which began appearing in the 1990s. Now the accessibility of data from multiple devices allowed by cloud computing and the proliferation of smartphones have dramatically increased the impact of these grading portals on parents, kids, and teachers.

Today, grade-tracking apps push notifications of any new assignment or quiz grade, no matter how significant, to devices. In some communities, parents can now track *every* assignment and grade—instead of only semester or quarter grades—on a second-by-second basis. While kids and parents can generally set preferences about how and when they receive notifications (and choose whether to pay attention to them or not), this constitutes a monumental increase in the level of communication about a student's performance compared to years past.

Some teens say they like knowing "at all times" where they stand academically. (Although some also told me they like that the apps let them know if they are "ahead" so they can coast for a bit! Others complain that their teachers don't put in grades for weeks at a time, so they have no idea how they are doing.) Parents who like these apps report feeling a sense of greater control, like they are on top of things when it comes to their teen's education. On the positive side, some of the apps also make this information accessible in multiple languages, so caregivers who are English learners can more easily keep track and support their children's education.

Above all, proponents of these grading apps argue that tracking and reporting grades in real time makes it easier for schools and parents to intervene sooner if a student gets behind. It allows them to track incremental progress and enables parents, teachers, and students to work together to assess an academic performance problem, get the student the help they need, and develop ongoing strategies for success.

But like behavior-monitoring apps, grading apps erode the little sense of privacy or independence that educators and parents claim to want young people to exhibit. When a parent tells me, "My kid is so unmotivated," and then goes to check the app, they may not see the way they are participating in a cycle of undermining their child's in-dependence. In decades past, high school students had to manage their performance largely on their own, seeking out help if they needed it.

I Can't Stop Checking: Grading Apps and Anxiety

Multiple adolescents and parents used the term "addictive" when they described their relationship with these apps. Grades are just a click away on their phones, so checking them can become all-consuming and anxiety-provoking.

The research team at Challenge Success, a Stanford-based nonprofit that is working to make high school less stressful, found that 10 percent of the over 17,000 middle school students it sur-veyed check grading apps more than once a day; another 20 per-cent of this group check daily.

Some high schoolers check them even more frequently. They have been led to believe by well-meaning parents, teachers, and school counselors that one bad quiz grade can lower their average—and derail their college chances. It makes sense that they would be on the lookout for grades . . . and with them, an imagined glimpse of what their future holds.

One ninth-grade girl told me she "couldn't stop" checking her grades. "It's something I want to see, even though it does not help me have a good day." She acknowledged that checking grades at bedtime would wreck her sleep, which of course didn't set her up to learn and focus the next day.

Because these apps provide little to no narrative feedback, grade-tracking apps create far more stress than physically returning a graded or marked-up quiz, where you can see what went wrong. If you're a student, finding out that you bombed your English essay when you are sitting in your calculus class can be pretty stress-inducing and can only distract you. Talking with the teacher or taking a moment to reflect on the assignment might be helpful. But not right now. Right now you are in calculus class and need to stay present.

Robin DeRosa, a parent of a high school student and director of the Open Learning & Teaching Collaborative at Plymouth State University, explained the dangers of such a system to me:

> With my daughter, pretty much every little thing that gets graded or calculated creates an alert on her phone. And then [the phone] dings and it's just so intrusive. But it's also kind of like a conditioning system, a little bit Pavlovian. Just like with notifications on Facebook, you can't sort of help but be drawn [to them]. But whereas normally you'd be receiving, say, a bad grade from a teacher in class that could be contextualized and [you have] a relationship [with the teacher] to support you through the feedback, these portals have no feedback attached to them at all . . . It's just grades. It's literally a disembodied number and it [appears] anytime teachers are doing the grading, random times. With all the updates, [my daughter] feels a lot of anxiety, and that anxiety makes it hard for her to want to unplug.

Parents, students, and teachers have shared their frustrations with how these apps limit meaningful, individualized teacher feedback. One popular system doesn't have space for teachers to add comments on assignments and test grades—the field just doesn't exist. Instead, teachers must choose comments from a drop-down menu.

One dad in a college town in Wisconsin shared, "[My daughter Sunni] will get a lot of [generic comments] like 'worked hard' or 'highly engaged,' but they're not really unique or individual." When Sunni gets a generic "worked hard" comment from five teachers, it stops feeling meaningful. It's quite dispiriting. Sunni is not alone: many kids have told me that the experience of being evaluated in this way leaves them feeling unseen.

The Gamification of Learning

The heightened pressure on students, with the instant availability of their grades in real time on their smartphones, has lent the education experience a "gaming" feel. School becomes less about what happens in the classroom and more about the grades and grade point average students are able to maintain. Amy, a parent of two high school girls, told me one daughter checks her grades obsessively. "It completely makes school about grades, not learning." Not exactly the lesson she wants her daughter to learn at school.

Teachers are also concerned about their students' focus on grades. "Lots of high schoolers check their GPAs every day on an app—that's not healthy," wrote one high school teacher in California in response to a survey I sent out. This focus on grades over qualitative feedback is shifting teachers' relationship to students from a mentoring one to a transactional relationship. Seeing teachers as "evaluators" more than educators can make it hard for students to trust them, tell a teacher if they are struggling, or even focus on learning instead of getting a grade.

"My students are highly motivated to get good grades, and they get upset when they see their grades drop. Then they come asking for extra work to raise their grade," Marie Holmes, a teacher at a New

York City charter high school, shared. "But there's no connection to real learning. It's like a game they're trying to win . . . Students ask me all the time, 'If I do assignment X, how many points will my grade go up by?' I tell them I am not a calculator. [I] don't just deal with the points-game every time there's a report card, either. It's every time [I] enter an assignment."

When I interviewed a group of ninth-grade boys at a rigorous East Coast boarding school, I was surprised by their frustration about not having the same constant access to their grades via a grading app as they had had in middle school. Their boarding school only posts grades at midterms and at the end of the year. Despite coming from vastly different public and private middle schools in California, Virginia, New Jersey, and Hong Kong, these young men had all been trained to constantly monitor their scores—if they didn't know their class average, how would they know if they were on track for their futures?

This boarding school is known for being tough, as well as for molding intellectually curious, college-ready students. Classes take place six days a week, and students have regular teacher conferences for in-depth feedback on assignments and performance.

All the boys who had had a grading app in middle school said they missed it and that it was "annoying" that their new school didn't use it. "It's like they don't want us to know how we're doing." One student, who had gone to a large public middle school, acknowledged that having had the app before made it easier to titrate his efforts: "I'd usually, like, check on my grade and see, like, what to get on the next test in order to either raise it, like get to a 90 threshold or get to 95, so it is really annoying not to have it. I don't like not knowing how well you need to do on your next test in order to, like, not drop your grade." So much for engaging with the subject matter or loving learning. Arguably, grades in general are the problem, but more than one student even used the word "addicting" to describe her constant checking.

The ninth graders at the boarding school insisted that, without digital access to their grades in real time, they "have no idea how we're doing." I countered. "But you are there—in class. Don't you just feel how it is going? If you are super engaged, participating, trying hard?" They admitted there was probably some way to tell. But they seemed to feel grades were outside of themselves—handed down, not responsive to effort or engagement—and therefore they felt frustrated that they couldn't check their grades. All four of them insisted that, having had the app in middle school, it was hard to unhook from a digital average that felt like the absolute truth of where they stood.

Not only are these apps taking away students' ability to gauge their own performance, they might be trapping students in self-limiting narratives. Many of these apps allow teachers to view a student's current and past academic history—not just the overall grades the students earned in previous classes, but every grade, assignment, and attendance record. One teacher's impression of a student might color the next teacher's expectations, making it harder for students to be seen for who they are: evolving individuals who grow and change and mature. This is especially true for kids who might have gone through a phase when they underperformed, so they get stuck with a history of being a "bad" or "troubled" kid. Students should have the chance to "start fresh" with every teacher, without their grade history following them around for years.

I heard from so many students who feel overwhelmed by the need to constantly perform. These grading apps remind them they are constantly being evaluated and judged, and that one bad grade might have outsized consequences—for how they are seen by teachers present and future, by their parents, and by colleges. One teen said, "The obsession with grades throughout high school is driving me nuts. I am only looking at colleges where the focus is on learning and experimenting and trying things out."

Unfortunately, opting out of these apps is logistically difficult, as many teachers use these apps not only to report grades, but to assign work. The apps have been cleverly designed to give them a captive audience.

Grading Apps Erode Kids' Independence and Intrinsic Motivation

Grading apps can undermine kids' independence and opportunities to develop their "executive functions"—the mental skills necessary to manage daily life.

By middle school and high school, most students should be communicating with their teachers directly. But parents who are encouraged by their schools to download these grading apps feel like they are an invitation to reach out to teachers about grades. This has led to an increase in parent-teacher contact that is not necessarily productive. "If I give a quiz in the first period," Kathy, a middle school Spanish teacher, laments, "by the third period parents will be emailing me asking I why haven't posted their child's grade yet." When parents are constantly advocating for their kids' grades or communicating on their behalf, they prevent their kids from forming independent relationships with their teachers: asking for feedback, clarification, or help when they don't understand something or didn't do as well as they'd hoped on an assignment. Kids might also miss out on having the experience of forgetting to do an assignment, getting a failing grade, and learning from it. These are the kinds of life lessons that help kids develop their ability to plan ahead.

"I really felt like this technology takes away a kid's opportunity to make choices for themselves," says Angie Aker, mother of two young adults. Indeed, Aker has been a crucial member of the team at Upworthy, MoveOn, and other influential organizations as an adult, and yet she skipped some classes in high school. She says:

> While some parents may see those choices as a mistake, and they want to prevent their kids from making any mistakes, I see those choices as a part of growing up . . . When you make a mistake, or fail at something, you see what those consequences are and learn from it, and you make your own choices differently. But you do it yourself on your own terms. I felt like, you know, tracking my kids' attendance and grades takes that away from them. I skipped classes sometimes and did fine; I knew what I had to do to be successful.

If parents are constantly monitoring how well their kids are doing in class, kids end up "outsourcing" their worries to parents. Lisa Damour, author of *Untangled*, explains that teenagers have a tendency to "emotionally dump" on their parents—to outsource their worries—and leave their parents to "take out the emotional trash."

If kids are constantly being told by their parents when they need to work a bit harder to earn the grade they want, and the parent is always nagging at them, reminding them to complete assignments, and asking them how they did on them, then kids may not develop their own sense of whether they are doing good work and what they need to do to keep it up. It's like monitoring your car's fuel tank: if your spouse always fills the tank, you may not be in the habit of checking the fuel gauge. One day, though, your spouse might not have had a chance to fill the tank, but you'll drive off, not noticing you are running out of gas until it's too late. When parents heavily monitor their kids' performance, students struggle to develop the intrinsic motivation they need to do well in school. This is what happened to Francesca, a high school student from Naperville, Illinois.

When Francesca started middle school, her mom, Kali, signed up for the school grading portal. Francesca knew that her mother checked her grades all the time. Eventually, she told me, "[I developed] this mindset that I was getting the grades to make my mom happy because I never wanted to see her upset." When I spoke with Francesca, she was in high school and had convinced her mom to stop checking her grades, and she was also checking the portal less frequently. "Now . . . I know that I'm getting the grades for myself . . . I still work hard. I mean, I probably put in even more effort now, since I really want to get into a good college. I know my mom wants the same thing, but I need to focus on my goals for myself and not obsess about disappointing my mom or trying to make her happy, because that actually made me *not* want to work hard."

It was clear that monitoring Francesca's middle school academic performance had threatened to undermine Francesca's motivation to do well at school—the exact opposite of what Kali had intended when she signed up to track her daughter's grades.

Portals Can Turn Parents into a Nagging Machine

Grading apps can undermine relationships in your family, even if your kids are academic rock stars. Timing is a big issue, as parents get access to the grades at the same time (or sometimes even sooner) than their teen. High school students say that dealing with grades *and* anticipating and managing their parents' response is a nightmare.

That was the case with Tamara, a student at a suburban high school who was juggling an ambitious course load. She shared that once she got to the ninth grade, the grading portal was a huge stressor for her. "I would check it a lot because my mom would always check it . . . Sometimes she would know the grade I got before I did," she said. "I'd worry, 'Am I going to get in trouble?' Or, 'Is she going to be proud of me?' If I saw that I didn't get a great grade on a test, I knew it wouldn't be a great situation once I got home."

Sometimes kids might get a grade without feedback and find themselves answering questions from an anxious parent even before they've had a chance to find out what answers they got wrong, or what else might have affected their performance. "It's one thing to come home and tell your parents, 'Oh, I had a tough day and this test didn't go well.' It's another thing for them to know before you do!" a student said to me.

Anjana told me that she got a bad quiz grade and had already worked out with her teacher a plan to drop the grade and do an alternative assessment, but then had to deal with the grade all over again with her father that night, even though she'd solved the problem herself. She sighed, "It's exhausting."

Some high school teachers report that parents might see a grade posted and text their kids during the school day to ask about a low grade or a grade point average that has gone down. The stress and distraction this causes is epic. Research tells us that once we are in fight-or-flight mode, we can't take in new information accurately, so both the updates from the grading app and the texts from concerned parents can derail the student's learning for the rest of the day—the opposite of what these apps are supposed to do.

Adolescents need their parents to be trusted allies, but the immediate accessibility of grades made possible by these apps has turned parents into enforcers instead. David, a father of a teenager diagnosed with ADHD, was near tears as he shared how he and his wife began obsessively tracking their son's grades online. "We went through a period of checking it constantly so we could monitor what he got done and turned in," he told me. Because there was often a delay between when assignments were turned in and when teachers input their son's grades, the portal wasn't always perfectly up-to-date, so they would confront their son. "Sometimes he'd swear he'd turned something in that wasn't showing up yet," he explained.

Like David, many families have reported that grading apps have affected the trust between parents and children. If your kid says they turned in an assignment, but the grading portal says otherwise, what do you believe? "My mom always gets emails about missing grades or zero grades, or even like low grades from Algebra II tests," a ninth grader explained. "But most of the time they're either optional things or things that weren't assigned to me. Or open-ended questions and a single space or misplaced parenthesis can make it wrong. So, it's annoying to have my mom come into my room and be like, 'Brandon, why do you have a 50 on your Algebra II quiz?' And I'm like, 'No, Mom, it's actually a 90, or it's actually a 100, but she hasn't graded the second half."

Angie Aker shared that when she first downloaded a grading app, she almost immediately got a notification that her son's test came in and that he had aced the assignment—she thought it was great. But that feeling went away quickly: "I felt really creepy thinking that when he walked in the door at the end of the day, I was going to be like, 'Oh, hey, I see you got a 100 on your test.' I was thinking how that would make me feel if I knew somebody was watching my every move," she told me. "I got to thinking about how we build relationships with our kids. I just think putting them under surveillance in that way removes their choice . . . their ability to connect, to come home and feel like they're telling you something about their life."

Parents may not worry about a B- itself, but rather what the B- means for their kid, and by extension what it means about them. Of course, their kid's grade might not mean they are struggling—they might have just had a bad day. But these tracking apps pressure parents to act in some way: Stay on top of their kids more? Nag them more frequently? Check their work for them?

Like their kids, parents can choose to not check the app all the time. And I've heard from numerous parents that they don't track their kids' grades in high school with PowerSchool because they consider it their teen's responsibility. But of the parents who do, few of them would monitor their kids' school performance so closely or so frequently if these grading apps didn't make it incredibly easy to do, and if schools didn't make checking them sound like something good parents *should* do. Before these apps became available, it simply would have been too onerous or intrusive to contact teachers for this information daily—and pretty tough to extract it from their teenagers. Perhaps that was all for the better.

Who Has (and Profits From) All This Data?

When journalist Manoush Zomorodi, host of the podcast *Note to Self* (no longer in production), was invited to download ClassDojo by her son's second-grade teacher, she asked about the app's privacy policy and who would have access to the data it generated.[3]

ClassDojo, which collects behavior data, raises privacy concerns. The company claims that its mission is to improve relationships and build a product people "actually want." The app is free and does not advertise other products to children. They do offer premium upgrades, including a recently rolled-out "upgrade" allowing parents to pay to use ClassDojo to monitor and give points to their kids at home. Explaining why teachers are free to adopt ClassDojo without permission from their principal or school district, ClassDojo creator Sam Chaudhary claims his app empowers teachers to pick tools that work well specifically for their students and classrooms and removes the middleman of district supervisors who've never set foot in their classroom.[4]

One principal in a large school district in Colorado, Julie Read, told me she does not allow teachers to use the app. She said if a teacher wants to use the app, she finds other ways to support their classroom-management skills. She found that teachers wanted to use it to "tattletale" to parents out of frustration with behaviors they didn't have the skills to navigate. Read pointed out that using the app can "perpetuate more problems than it solves," and we need to be more equity-minded in our solutions.

If the idea of your child's behavior being digitally recorded in this way concerns you, it is fair to ask some questions. In 2014, partly because of pressure from parents and journalistic exposure, ClassDojo updated its privacy policy to guarantee deleting students' data after one year. Chaudhary insists, "We are not a data company." But James Steyer, CEO of Common Sense Media, responded, "Until very recently, there weren't state or federal laws in place to regulate this; it's been a Wild, Wild West marketplace. Many of the people who make these apps forget about the privacy issues involved."

PowerSchool, owned by the private equity firm Vista Equity Partners, takes financial information about a child's family and can use that in predictive analytics about how they might do in school.

The investigative journalists at *The Markup* found that this equity firm has acquired numerous companies that collect children's data, "which they use to fuel a suite of predictive analytics products that push the boundaries of technology's role in education and, in some cases, raise discrimination concerns."[5]

The EHallPass app is used to give students permission to go to the bathroom. Students pushed back on having their bathroom trips documented, and some petitioned their schools to stop using the app. Parents are also pushing back. "I will not allow this app to be utilized in my kids' schools, period," privacy attorney Brad Shear stated to the *Washington Post*.[6] "This is bathroom big brother." While ClassDojo and its adorable avatars may seem less invasive than documenting when students are visiting the bathroom "too much" or for "too long," I think it is important to see all of this surveillance as a continuum that gets young people, parents, and educators used to overreliance on surveillance.

What Parents Can Do: Building Students' Independence

As parents, we should proactively neutralize the unintended consequences of these apps. We should help our children develop self-regulation, which is critical for their future success.

With tweens and teens, we can mentor them on executive function but know that we are playing the long game. Teach them to plan ahead, use a calendar, create helpful checklists, use productivity techniques to make getting stuff done easier, enlist the help of a study buddy, and more. Ultimately, they need to figure out how they learn best and then carry that knowledge forward. Lots and lots of mistakes and failure are common along the way. If they need help at school, then we can advocate with counselors, teachers, and the administration for support, including getting help with study skills, executive function, and more.

Rather than obsessing and tracking the minutiae of our children's academic performance, we should be focusing on helping them develop intrinsic motivation. We can help them identify what they are naturally and genuinely interested in and what problems they want to solve in the world. We should help them learn to advocate for themselves—and to accept their grades, move on, and do better next time.

We should be teaching our kids to be accountable for their work—to celebrate their wins and experience the natural consequences when they make a mistake, misbehave, slack off, or miss class. We need to step back and see how they deal with a situation before we step in to help them solve it.

We also need to figure out what to do about these behavior monitoring apps and grading apps, as they will not be going away anytime soon.

If your kids' school uses them, there are five strategies you can use today to minimize their negative effects:

Be intentional when interacting with grade-tracking apps. Consider opting out of checking grading apps. If that's not feasible, then at least don't download the app on your phone—use it on a device that you don't check as frequently. And disable notifications whenever that is an option. Challenge Success surveyed 4,200 high school parents and found that some schools had successfully reduced family conflict around grading portals by turning off the portal at a certain time in the evening and/or during the school day and/or on weekends. In one school district, they shot down parent access during the school day, as parents were texting their teenagers during class. The superintendent in Rye, New York, a suburb near New York City, sent the following note to their community.[7]

Dear Parents or Guardians:

Communication about student progress is an important aspect of our family-school partnership. Over the past few years, the District's PowerSchool Parent Portal website/app has provided instant access to students' grades to parents/guardians and middle and high school students, 24 hours a day, seven days a week, except when the portal is closed for report card generation.

Unfortunately, we have increasingly seen that constant access to the portal has become a distraction to students because they are frequently checking their grades or GPAs, discussing them with classmates, and communicating with their parents/guardians about grades and assignments during the school day. Students also report that the portal creates a stressful environment during school hours.

In alignment with our work with Challenge Success, and in an effort to reduce student stress and to eliminate in-school distractions, beginning September 2019, students/parents will only be able to access student schedules in the Parent Portal from 8:00 a.m. to 3:00 p.m. during weekdays. The other information in the Parent Portal will be unavailable during those hours. All information on the Parent Portal will remain open all day on weekends, and during the hours before and after school.

If you have any questions or concerns, please contact either one of us.

Sincerely,
Patricia Taylor, Principal, Rye High School Principal
Dr. Ann Edwards, Rye Middle School

You can encourage your district to take measures like this, and you can also adopt this practice for yourself regardless of what the district decides.

Encourage your child not to put the app on their own phone. Checking a few times a semester or even once a week could be fine, but look for other methods to gauge how they are doing. Do they like the class? Are they doing the work? Overreliance on external feedback leaves you vulnerable to losing yourself. Obviously we all need to respond to external feedback at some point, but all of the most innovative people have had to ignore some criticism and trust that they were on the path to something!

If your child is in middle school or high school, encourage them to build strong relationships with their teachers. It's important that students see their teachers as allies and supporters—not as a party in a transaction for grades. Encourage kids to have more respectful and engaged relationships with teachers. Encourage them to check in with their teachers and ask them for feedback, to talk to them when they need extra help, and to express sincere interest. Your child needs to understand that if they only reach out to their teachers after receiving a grade they don't like, their relationship will be about that. Encourage them to learn from their teachers, not just get grades from them.

If your child is in elementary school, express any concerns you may have about how behavior-monitoring apps are being used. If your child's school uses an app like ClassDojo, ask how it is used and how points are given—per kid, per table or group, per class? And how public are the points? If you suspect your child is likely to have negative or anxiety-provoking experiences as a result, advocate for the app to be used in less punitive ways. And above all, speak up. As Lesley Koplow from Bank Street College of Education says:

> If you are troubled by it, you should know that there may be many, many parents in the school community who have that feeling. But they don't necessarily communicate with each other about it . . . Do anything you can do to have a voice for what your children experience from that kind of approach. Because anything that increases stress and pressure on children, when there already [are] a lot of crises going on around them . . . is antithetical to learning.

Reassure your child that points and grades have no bearing on your regard for them. Just as kids need to see teachers as allies and supporters, they need to see their parents in the same light. You could say to your child, "I know that your teacher is doing this, but I'm not going to look at it; I'm just going to ignore it. So don't worry about additional consequences at home for being rowdy after lunch." Let them know that while school might be a stressful situation . . . home is a safe space.

Using these strategies will help your child feel independent at school and safe at home. Free your mind to focus on your own work and life during the school day, which will make you a better parent when your child is around. Your children will learn to advocate for themselves, plan their own work, and cultivate their own sense of "how they are doing." As Manoush Zomorodi's son, Kai, then a second grader, told her on *Note To Self* when she asked him if she should be checking ClassDojo, the daily data about how he behaves in class should be "between me, my teacher, and my table." Well said, Kai.

chapter 5

Setting Boundaries:

Balancing Discretion and Disclosure in a Tell-All World

Imagine being a young adult and having your most personal information—things like medical and mental health diagnoses—shared with the world. That's exactly what Simone Biles, one of the world's greatest gymnasts, has to contend with on a daily basis. When Biles—a favorite to win gold medals at the Tokyo Olympics—pulled out from several events, media and fans were shocked. In a statement, Biles explained that she was withdrawing to focus on her mental health. "My safety was at risk as well as a team medal . . . Physical health is mental health."[1]

The reaction from the world was swift. Many public figures, celebrities, and media hailed her move as a brave and powerful message about the pressures we put on young athletes and the importance of protecting mental health. Biles's fans (of which I count myself) were massively supportive on social media. And yet, there were also plenty of haters, people accusing her of being a quitter, weak, and selfish for pulling out. Some people blamed her for the US women's gymnastics team's silver medal rather than the gold.

This kind of scrutiny is not new to Biles. In the past, she has had to answer questions about her childhood in the foster care system, about sexual abuse by USA Gymnastics doctor Larry Nassar, and about her ADHD diagnosis. We might feel for her, but also breathe a sigh of relief when we imagine that this only happens to celebrities. Who would want their childhood, medical, and professional experiences subjected to such intense probing and public commentary? And yet, as our culture shifts away from privacy and toward increasingly connected and public lives, our kids are experiencing some of what Biles goes through every day.

Over the years, we've increasingly encouraged and even celebrated disclosure. Disclosing personal information, especially if it is a vulnerable thing to share, is often praised as authentic. But we have a complicated relationship with "openness." We cherish authenticity and intimacy. When public figures, vloggers, or influencers share their innermost struggles and challenges online—when musician Kanye West opens up about his bipolar diagnosis and calls it his superpower, or Instagram influencer Bunny Michael writes about being strip-searched after shoplifting as a teen, or YouTube star Brittani Boren Leach loses and publicly mourns her baby—we reward their vulnerability with attention and "likes."[2, 3, 4]

Kids, and especially teenagers, have grown up in this culture that celebrates openness. Social media has made sharing details about their lives—and others' responses to them—instantaneous. Young people routinely post about conflicts with their parents or family, or have semi-covert rants about someone in the community such as a classmate or teacher they have strong feelings about.

Kids don't always get the same outpouring of support that celebrities do. When celebrities disclose personal difficulties, their fans often rally around them—like Biles's fans did when she pulled out of the events in Tokyo. One of my friends posted on her social media, "I thought of Simone Biles as a role model for my daughter. Now I see that she is a role model for me." Compare that to the responses a high school athlete who pulls out of a game for mental health struggles might receive, which would likely be more judgmental and harsh rather than supportive. Unfairly, a more popular kid in a community might receive more support for all kinds of disclosures, while a kid with a smaller "fan base," even at the local level, might not be treated as kindly. Then again, within their own friend group, they might receive significant support. Whom you disclose to and how you do it and what is shared are all important factors that can determine whether you receive a positive, negative, or mixed response.

Even for adults, sharing our difficult experiences or intimate issues publicly on social media or some other forum is a balancing act as we attempt to strike the right tone, hovering between self-awareness and self-deprecation. Anyone who has been on social media for any length of time has seen posts from friends disclosing very painful details of their divorce or some bad workplace relationships or some interaction with their child's teacher. We also see friends in their network not quite knowing how to respond.

Figuring out what to share and what to keep private is a nuanced task. Many parents are concerned that kids will miss the nuances of how and when to share and get a less than warm reception when they do share. In 2020, Lurie Children's Hospital surveyed two thousand parents and found that "52 percent of parents in the survey felt at least sometimes 'uncomfortable' with the way their teen portrayed themself or interacted with others on social media . . . They frequently focused on 'lack of privacy' and 'tendency to overshare.'"[5] In my own research, I've found parents worry that their kids will be shunned by their peers or that their attempt to be open and transparent will negatively impact their kids' future opportunities, friendships, romantic relationships, chances of getting into college, or even careers. Parents also worry that adults they know might see their kid's posts and judge *them* . . . What kind of parents are they anyway if their kids have such *bad boundaries*?

But rather than encouraging kids to keep more of themselves private or to censor what they want to say about themselves online, or trying to catch them in the act of "oversharing," we need to do a better job of mentoring kids on how to be *intentional* about how much they share both online and offline. The first step is to understand *why* our kids share so much about themselves, what they get out of it, and how it puts them at risk. We can only help our kids balance being authentic and open with a healthy need for privacy if we understand the context for their sharing. Ultimately, we need to balance our concerns with safety and long-term consequences with our understanding that culture is evolving away from stigmatizing certain topics that were taboo to mention when we were kids.

Why (Some) Kids Share So Much about Themselves

Educators and parents constantly ask me about kids' tendencies to share on social media. They especially want to know: *Why? Why do they reveal SO MUCH about their personal lives?* What are they seeking?

Today's young people have many motivations when they set out to share deeply personal information. To understand and support our kids, it helps to know their reasons.

To Find "Their People"

Most kids share publicly who their friends are, what interests they have, what books or shows they like, or what political beliefs they hold because it helps them define who they are and find and connect with like-minded people. Most parents are comfortable with their kids disclosing this information for this purpose, although there is still the potential for fallout. For example, kids who disclose their political views may get pushback or judgment from peers, or they may experience rejection in certain communities.

Many young people (and many adults) appreciate the sense of community and group support that can come from participating in online affinity spaces, like a Discord server for fans of a specific genre of anime, or a server for people with a specific diagnosis like ADHD. Finding a group of people like them can be enormously helpful, especially for kids who feel marginalized or vulnerable. For example, a hard-core anime fan who joins a group that likes the same obscure anime she is into can feel safer in that space. She may then be more likely to share her private thoughts and feelings with that group—that she is stressed about her parents' divorce, her family's ability to pay for college, or her sibling's addiction.

These are tough issues to talk about face-to-face, and the social norms at most middle and high schools can discourage openness and vulnerability. Instead, the culture at many high schools celebrates being cool, collected, and "chill"—not being so emotional or caring so much about things. For vulnerable kids, the upsides of sharing their true feelings and thoughts in an online affinity space where they are among people with a shared interest or identity may outweigh the risks of disclosing sensitive personal information.

Finding affinity online can feel incredibly supportive. Sidney, a fourteen-year-old girl who is homeschooled, told me that the friends who participate in the Girl Talk server that she moderates in the Discord app feel like family. She learned about Discord from a comment on a TikTok video that she saw early in the COVID-19 pandemic in 2020. She downloaded the app and joined some communities because she wanted to find people to talk to. "It felt like I had known them for forever, and it had only been like a week or two," she told me. When I asked Sidney about what participants in her "Girl Talk" group chat about, she explained that although they talk a lot about boys, it is not a place to gossip. "We don't just talk about boys that we like," she told me. "We also talk about when boys do something that's really annoying." There is real problem-solving and support in her group. As the moderator, she has a lot of responsibility, like putting members on probation, or even kicking out or banning people who don't follow certain rules of interaction. For Sidney, as well as for other young people who moderate different kinds of online affinity groups, keeping the discussion civil and, more important, *supportive,* is a big priority.

Peer support is incredibly attractive to young people at certain stages of development. Of course, the concern is that young people often turn to peers over adults in crisis situations where an adult would be a safer choice.

To Explore Sexuality and Gender Identities

For many kids these days, sharing their gender or sexual identity online doesn't always involve a big announcement. While some kids might add a subtle sign like a hashtag (typically only known by other people who share that identity) or an affinity symbol like the LGBTQ+ pride flag, or include their pronouns on their Twitter bio, others might add more straightforward signs like #QueerAF or #pansexual. The signs and codes that young people use to identify themselves in terms of gender and sexual identities shift quickly. What's "obvious" to some people may not be "obvious" to others.

My former student Alex, now twenty-seven and a lawyer, told me that as a middle schooler in 2007, he never announced on his MySpace page that he was gay. He felt, though, that the page conveyed he was "obviously gay" anyway: all his friends were girls. In the community where Alex grew up, simply having a social network of twenty or so girls and almost no boys was enough to mark him as "not straight." While he doesn't remember ever coming out on social media, he recalls that when he was out socially—but not to extended family—he hoped his MySpace page wouldn't become public. Now MySpace is ancient history. As I write this, a tween or teen exploring their sexual identity online is likely to find peers in spaces on Discord, YouTube, TikTok, or Instagram, just to name a few. For example, there are many servers that identify as spaces for queer and trans participants on Discord. Within these varied servers particpants can engage in all kinds of conversations. The gender identities of the peers your child relates to will be less obvious in a space like Discord or TikTok (and less binary because it isn't 2007 anymore!).

Some kids explore queer and transgender identities online while not openly discussing those issues with their family. For others, telling family or friends becomes part of a shared experience. For example, young people have shared moving videos of coming out to parents or friends, or opening up about their mental health status. The style of these coming-out videos reflects a fast-moving cultural change. A 2015 viral YouTube video by the Rhodes brothers—twins who came out to their father, who had a very emotional reaction on camera—became the model for an entire genre of "coming out online" videos. The same year, YouTube star Ingrid Nilsen made a video coming out directly to her audience. It has been viewed 18 million times, and many have commented that the video inspired them to come out or that it made them feel affirmed.

While coming out as queer, gay, bisexual, or pansexual is potentially still a fraught, scary, or at least emotional journey for many young people, we're now seeing a new trend of much more understated TikTok coming-out videos. In 2020 and 2021, for example, lip-synchers started "coming out" by pointing to themselves over the lyrics to a song that goes "this girl's straight and this girl's not."[6] These short videos often included a teen pointing to their mother, or sister, or friend while the lyrics chime in "this girl's straight," and then pointing to themself when the song goes "this girl's not." These funny, supportive videos are sometimes staged and sometimes not. Regardless of whether these videos are made with a knowing collaborator, or feature someone who is surprised by the announcement (or feigns surprise—it can be hard to tell), they are far less dramatic: suspense and tears are replaced by joyful acknowledgment. In one of the videos, the clearly in-the-know mom's eyes roll upward and the word "Duh" appears over her head, confirming that she already knew.

Young people who jump on these video trends or add an LGBTQ+ pride flag to their social media profile are coming *in* to the community as much as they are coming *out* to the world. Kids who find an accepting, embracing community—on- and offline—are likely to be safer, even though being out still exposes young people and adults to homophobia and transphobia. Violence, bullying, and homophobic and transphobic folks are still out there. School can still be a dangerous place for many queer and transgender teens, as they don't have much control of whether they attend a supportive, inclusive school or a school where homophobia and transphobia are the dominant experience, but teens have more control of where and with whom they "hang out" on the internet.

Some parents are concerned that coming out online is a big step for a young person and that they can't retract their post once people have seen it. It's true that people's understanding of their identities can evolve—but there are ways young people have navigated that evolution, too. Celebrity dancer Lennon Torres, who became a child celebrity on *Dance Moms* as a kid, addressed her multiple-coming-out experience as a young adult in a TikTok video. In the video, she "comes out" of an actual closet three times: first, she "comes out" as gay, which is received with a loud applause; then she comes out as nonbinary, which merits only medium-volume applause; finally, she comes out as transgender, which gets a faint applause. Torres found a way to not only update viewers on her identity evolution, but also to make a point about the differing levels of support and social acceptance each of these identities typically receives.

To "Come Out" about Their Neurodiversity or Mental Health Status, or Trauma

Coming out as queer can be celebratory. "Coming out" as bipolar, autistic, or as a survivor of sexual assault (all very different experiences in and of themselves), is very different. Each of these can be perilous in their own ways, but some kids and young adults have found that it has been worth the risks.

In my interviews with young people, I've learned that "coming out" as neurodiverse with a diagnosis of autism or ADHD can be like coming out as gay, bi, or pan in certain ways: it involves joining a community. Sometimes these identities converge and overlap, and finding a community that meets them where they are is truly attractive and comforting. Here, for example, is the description for one Discord server for LGBTQ+ *and* neurodivergent people:

> *Hello! Thanks for taking interest in my server. this server is for people ages 16–24 who are LGBT and neurodivergent! it's a safe space here! we have trans bot to test names and pronouns! we have over 150 emotes! (nonverbal, opossum, cats, etc!) we have specific chats dedicated to autism, ADHD, bpd, did/osdd and then a nd chat on top of it! we have voice channels as well and are working on getting a movie night :) we also have fixation and special interest chats, age and pet regression chats, personal diaries, and a community of nice people <3*
>
> *this space is for only LGBT neurodivergent people! we accept any and all neurodivergencies, even if you're self-diagnosed! you are welcome here <3[7]*

The community in spaces such as this Discord server *can* be positive and really lovely, but kids often don't recognize or don't register that they are sharing a space with adults (note the sixteen-to-twenty-four-year-old age range in the server above). Kids often don't think too much about whom they are getting advice from in these chats, or the inherent danger of putting out their diagnoses under their name, especially since there is still a lot of discrimination against people with neurodiverse diagnoses. They might not appreciate that posting about a diagnosis on social media or even sharing it on a group text is very different in terms of privacy than sharing it with a trusted friend or two in person.

Jacqueline Nesi, a psychologist who studies the role of social media in adolescents' development and who works with an in-patient population of teens experiencing mental health crises, finds that teens and tweens have some awareness of the possible downsides of posting about their diagnoses—but it is hard to resist an immediate form of social support. "It can be really powerful to meet people online who have the same concerns that you do, to get the social support that you're maybe not getting at all in your in-person experiences, to be able to find people who have had the same experience as you," she explains. "It can make a young person who is struggling feel like they're not alone."

To Destigmatize an Experience or Identity

Some kids disclose sensitive personal information because they want to destigmatize disabilities and mental health issues. Some of the parents in my survey mentioned this kind of sharing in relation to neurological diversity. "I don't think a disability is embarrassing—if they want to share about it, more power to them." Another wrote, "My son is autistic and very open about it. He was written off by two school systems. I'm proud of how he uses what he's learned, how he's built success, in helping others from time to time." Another parent spoke to the importance of a considered approach. "I think there are sincere, meaningful ways to share online. I would advise not to do it in a flip or unthoughtful way. Think about whether to and how to, but if after thoughtful consideration, the child wanted to, I think I'd be okay with that."

To Engage in Activism, Seek Justice

Some kids feel inspired or even compelled to disclose challenging experiences like surviving sexual assault or being discriminated against to come together with others who have had similar experiences, support each other and, most important, affect change.

At Denver East High School in Colorado in 2020, two male students were named to prominent leadership roles on campus. Almost immediately, several female students posted allegations of sexual assault that named these students as the aggressors. The female students who shared their experiences of being assaulted experienced a mix of support from other girls and some boys, and also criticism and disbelief from friends of the accused. In response to the accusations on social media, the school principal even shared a video statement to students warning them not to post or share accusations: "During the time of an investigation, it's important for us to think fairly and not make accusations, or post or repost information that we're not sure of," he said.[8]

Despite the directive not to post, the girls' disclosures led student leaders to investigate Title IX reporting at their school. They found it impossible to navigate—there were administrative roadblocks, and the reporting website had broken links. Eventually they were able to bring attention to the issue via student walkouts. Further, despite being told not to post, the students were able to use social media to both pressure the school district to change policies and to connect with student activists in Boulder who were working on related struggles. As Lilia Scudamore, a 2020 graduate of the Denver high school, described to me in an interview, her group's ability to contact and learn from the Boulder activists was facilitated by social media. "I found their names in the article about their protest and DMed a student leader. And so she got back to me really quickly and was very supportive. And [Sophia and Bea—two of the Boulder activists] mentored our group on process, what strategies they felt were most effective. They also just looked at our policy with us because Title 9 is super complicated."

In another example of young people disclosing experiences of being targeted, mistreated, victimized, or harmed in order to bring about change, students at various schools created #BLACK@ accounts on social media (e.g., #Black@Dalton) to allow others to share about racist behavior they've experienced from peers and teachers at their schools.[9] These disclosures called attention to ongoing patterns of hostility and aggressions toward Black students. "[The BLACK@ account] highlighted all the racist incidents that have happened at my school—racist, sexist, homophobic, xenophobic [incidents]. It brought a lot of things to light," a student told me. "Even though everything remains nameless in terms of the victims accusing the perpetrators . . . a lot of people figured out what happened or who the post is about." As this student points out, even though these forums are meant to give cover to those who share their experiences, kids can typically figure out who is posting and who is being accused. Those who share their deeply personal experiences are taking a risk.

It's not surprising that teenagers want to use anonymous online forums or their social media instead of going through the "proper channels" to bring light to injustices made against them. More often than not, they are making accusations against those who have perpetuated the injustice or who have a vested interested in keeping it quiet. Sharing about experiencing racism and microaggressions to contribute to a larger social reckoning is a powerful way for teenagers to take moments that hurt them and leverage them toward a more just society. Nicole Furlonge, at Columbia Teachers College, led research into the BLACK@ accounts and was especially focused on those at independent schools. In an interview, she shared with me that the schools that were able to hear the feedback used the opportunity to make positive change. These schools saw the accounts as "an emerging opportunity and moment to get at some deep-seated issues that they hadn't gotten to before, hadn't recognized before" and saw the posts as "data points that were important for schools to think about how to engage."

As parents, we might be worried when our kids push to be on the front lines of fighting stigma, or if they disclose difficult personal experiences—even with the admirable intention to bring about change. We might worry that the world will judge them harshly or shun them for what they shared about themselves, or that our kids will make themselves vulnerable to retaliation or even legal action. As much as we can, we should support our young people's efforts to make society a less oppressive, less violent place. Lilia Scudamore first learned about the Boulder students' efforts from her father, who picked it up on "old media," the newspaper. She reached out directly to the leaders on "new media." This kind of intergenerational support may be obvious, but both groups have skills and inclinations that we can teach each other.

Sometimes Kids Do Post "To Get Attention"

Parents who think kids are just sharing "for attention" aren't totally wrong, either. On one hand, *notoriety* isn't currency for kids. In fact, their peers can be harsh when kids share things deemed "too personal." Dr. Nesi told me that, for teens, the worst insult is to say someone is "posting for attention." Kids have a reflective suspicion and resentment of being seen as too hungry and needy for attention, or "thirsty." On the other hand, kids *do* want attention. Everyone who posts on social media is doing it for attention. Why else would we post? When kids see other people (including us!) sharing unabashedly about their private lives—and receiving likes and attention—they often want to model them. Kids are tempted to share their own personal information to receive the same kind of support or sympathy.

For some kids, the attention that can accompany disclosing intimate details can be a lot. In fact, it can be so enthralling that it may pull some kids to over-disclose or even lie. The surprising phenomena of self-cyberbullying or digital self-harm—when kids set up fake social media accounts to post negative or mean things about themselves—shows that for a small number of kids, the intense attention they can get for certain kinds of personal posts can be hard to resist.[10] A kid who is digitally self-harming needs support.

As we've seen, there are many reasons why kids are inclined to share sensitive information about themselves. But their audience and the context in which they are sharing give us big clues as to their motivations and needs. While one teen might post about his diagnoses in an online mental health community, another teen might post about his mental health on his social media page that family, friends, and classmates can read. Both kids want to be seen. But the different contexts offer a nuanced view into how they see their own struggles and how you might help them "be seen" in a safe way. Understanding where they are coming from—why they share sensitive information and with whom—is key to helping them balance being true to themselves and protecting their privacy. Later in this chapter, I'll offer specific advice on how to do that.

The Dangers of Oversharing

Sharing vulnerable content, even when it is accurate and for health reasons, can invite the worst of the web: trolls, bullying, harassment, and shaming. Unlike adult public figures, kids are often unprepared for potential backlash; they don't have the thick skin or the maturity to handle the consequences of sharing deeply personal material. Also, the stakes for kids are different—they have so many years in front of them that it's harder to predict what doors might open or close because of what they share. Problems can also escalate when kids try to find community in online spaces that may not be as healthy or supportive as they seem. Here are some of the risks kids take on when they share sensitive information.

Unpredictable Responses

When kids disclose deeply personal or sensitive information, it's difficult to anticipate what kind of response they are going to get or what the consequences of that disclosure could be. The upside of sharing in a culture where clicks are money and currency—and more controversy and more sharing means more clicks—is clearer for adults and especially for public figures. Our kids may not have the financial or social support that public figures have to buffet them from the reaction and stigma of what they shared.

In 2020, I had a chance to talk to a group of sixth graders who were in remote school about the fun and less-fun parts of growing up in public. They had a lot to say about the response "regular" kids get when they share deeply personal information on social media—and how that compares to the response celebrities receive in similar situations. All were big fans of seventeen-year-old Charli D'Amelio, calling her "the most popular TikTok star in the world." When I spoke to the girls, D'Amelio had recently been exposed in a leaked video— allegedly vaping. Many people criticized her for setting a bad example and questioned whether a then sixteen-year-old should be vaping at all. But other fans like Nola, one of the sixth graders I spoke with, rose to defend her, suggesting D'Amelio was using an anxiety pen to treat her severe anxiety.[11]

Nola is sympathetic to D'Amelio's challenges with anxiety, as she lives with it herself. She shared this openly with me in the Zoom call with her three friends participating. "Anxiety took a really big toll on my life the past couple months. But people take it as a joke or people think it's not real. They'll [say], 'You're lying' or 'You don't have this.' But it's a very real thing. I have struggled with it since I was very, very little. And I only realized it about a couple years ago . . . that it was anxiety . . . so when people judge me about it over social media, that is one of the worst feelings I've ever felt . . . I guess you could say social media and the internet in general can be really harsh."

Of course, D'Amelio also received some hate online for the leaked video where she was allegedly vaping, but ultimately survived the scandal relatively unscathed. She is now the star of a Hulu reality TV show featuring her whole family. Would a regular kid caught seemingly vaping be believed by the adults and kids in their community if they said it was an anxiety pen? Unlikely, given, as Nola explained, that so many of her peers don't respond kindly when she shares about her own anxiety. (Importantly, her close friends, like the other girls on the Zoom call, are supportive.)

Unfortunately—and unfairly—kids who have the most social support are the most likely to get support for sharing more stigmatized aspects of their identities or deeply personal information. The popular girl who comes out as a sexual assault survivor or reveals she has anxiety may get real social support, while a kid who is already marginalized socially may be denied that support and judged more negatively.

For some kids, the attention that often comes from sharing about struggles can become unhealthy. One father who is a social worker shared that he had to restrict his fifteen-year-old daughter's social media and mobile access after a few problematic posts. "Some kids find ways to fill a need for themselves" he told me. "Cutting is a way of filling a need. Binge eating and purging is a way of filling a need. These aren't healthy behaviors, but they serve a purpose." He concluded that his daughter Ayla's habit of "telling it all" on social media might fill a need, but isn't safe.

"I have observed that [posting about a personal crisis] actually is a sure way to feel worse. Every time kids overly disclose, especially about bad things happening to them, it's designed to fail. The first time they put out the content, they get a lot of response from people. They get all these dopamine hits when people [write], 'Oh my god, you know you're valuable,' 'Don't kill yourself,' 'We love you; we'd miss you,'" he explains. "When they get all the dopamine hits from that strong response, it conditions them to want to do it again. But as we've seen with social media, at a certain point, compassion fatigue kicks in. Instead of saying over and over, 'We love you; you're valuable,' they start to just ignore it. Then you have a kid who's already psychologically vulnerable, who's using that social media to try to feel better, and who ultimately gets the message 'Oh, no one cares if I kill myself because I went from fifty people telling me I'm valuable [when I post] to now getting crickets and silence the seventieth time I go to that well.'"

Reinforcing Negative Feelings

If you are an adolescent trying to grow up and figure yourself out, the fallout from sharing intimate details can have long-term consequences to your sense of self and health. This is especially true when kids share their mental health struggles in forums dedicated to specific challenges like eating disorders, bipolar diagnosis, or a range of other experiences.

Dr. Nesi is particularly concerned about the ways kids congregate around these topics in digital spaces. "If you're already in a really acute state of not feeling your best, [these sites] can make [you] feel like, 'This is sort of the only thing that's out there,'" she explains. "You aren't feeling great, you go online, and you see tons of other people who also aren't feeling great. It can reinforce this concept that the world is not a great place."

Dr. Stephanie Zerwas, who studies eating disorders, is also concerned that affinity groups focused on eating disorders or other mental health challenges can be negatively reinforcing, too, depending on the climate of the site and how oriented it is toward recovery.

On Tumblr, Reddit, and Discord, there is a lot of meta-discussion about the mental health risks that come from seeking affinity spaces in digital communities where there is so little accountability and so much suffering. One poster on Tumblr, "Turtle-dove woods," who self-identifies as a member of various neurodiverse and mental health online communities, believes these heavily used "vent channels" can make people feel worse by affirming the worst parts of their experience. Turtle-dove woods posted:

> Vent channels are easy-to-access compilations of everyone's suffering. This is especially harmful if you're someone who seeks out negative content during times where you're not feeling all too great (i.e., browsing trauma tags) as a means to make yourself feel worse or otherwise fuel the worsening of your mental health . . . You may begin to believe that something you went through isn't "bad enough" or even real if you're not

constantly suffering from symptoms of it (or suffering in gen-
eral). [People] feed into each other's mental illnesses and justify
their own impulsivity by reassuring others of the same things.

Unfortunately, the more a child or adolescent has struggled or has needed supports like an inpatient or intensive outpatient program, the more vulnerable they might be in an online space. To some extent, that's because peer support is incredibly attractive to young people at certain stages of development. I've seen many teenagers turn to peers over adults in situations where an adult would be a much safer choice.

While we might shudder at the thought of a teenager seeking help from a peer instead of an adult, we should also be concerned about the trauma our kids might face if they find themselves supporting a peer in crisis. For example, if a teenager with suicidal thoughts or behaviors posts online about suicide or suicide-related topics, it can have complicated effects in their community of peers. These posts can be triggering to others who are struggling with similar issues, or traumatic for kids who might not know how to help.

Sidney, the fourteen-year-old moderator of the Discord server "Girl Talk," told me that kids talk about everything on the site. "They talk about . . . [everything from] having a really bad day . . . to having to talk [someone] out of committing suicide." As moderator, Sidney has found herself in situations where she's worried about someone on her Discord server. "Sometimes it is scary . . . We've had a few people who have said really serious things and just disappeared. And in a lot of those situations, all moderators meet and talk about how the situation went down. That person . . . eventually comes back after maybe a week or a few days because they just have to sort things out."

My conversation with Sidney raised important questions. **When** someone shares thoughts or plans to self-harm in an app, what is the app's responsibility? Is there a way to report this kind of content? Unfortunately, we often hear about these things too late because the social apps used by children and adults are not set up to reliably intervene when a user posts a comment like this.

The fact that kids are so hungry for spaces to share about their struggles should give educators and policymakers, as well as parents, our marching orders: we need to create safe spaces in schools and communities where kids can get the support they are so clearly seeking from professionals who love and respect teens and have the training to help them.

What Can Parents Do?
Teach Your Kid the Art of Intentional Sharing

As I mentioned earlier, it's critical to understand *why* our kids share sensitive personal information—in what context and to whom. Are they looking to connect with others like them? Are they sharing personal information to bring awareness to a topic? Are they doing it to get sympathy? Once we understand their motivations and what they are risking by sharing, we can respond with compassion. We can show them how to be intentional in their sharing—that is, how to make empowered choices about what to share and with whom. Using discretion, however, doesn't mean that kids should censor themselves. Instead, they should exercise judgment. That is, of course, a tall order for a child or teenager. And unfair that we are asking this much of them at such a young age. **It really ought to be adults' re-**

sponsibility to create a world where kids are not being harshly judged for what they share.

That is unlikely to happen, however, so while it's asking a lot of our kids, we should be doing our best to mentor them on how they can be thoughtful about how, when, and where they disclose information about themselves. And we should work to create a supportive environment so that when kids do share information about themselves, the world can respond in a more thoughtful way. Here are several ways you can mentor your children on how to share sensitive information about themselves.

Mentor Kids on "Intentional Sharing"

You should actively mentor your kids on how to be intentional when they share sensitive information about themselves. What does it mean to be intentional? It means to be thoughtful about how, when, and where to disclose information about themselves to ensure they get what they want.

- **Discourage kids from sharing intense and personal stories for "likes."** But beware of chastising them for sharing information "just for attention." When it comes to social media, we are *all* posting for attention. Reframe the conversation and explain that the more personal the story, the more they want to keep it within a circle of people they trust. But remember, intentionality is not about reining in free expression; it's about exercising judgment, and understanding and considering that there might be consequences to disclosing sensitive information that one can't anticipate.

- **Empower kids to make thoughtful decisions about how they express themselves.** If they are comfortable wearing it on a T-shirt, then disclosing it on social media could feel fine. For example, some kids with ADHD who are ready to disclose their diagnosis buy T-shirts that read "ADHD Is My Superpower." Kids who are ready to come out as nonbinary might wear T-shirts that read "They/Them Are My Pronouns." If your teen is saying, "What is so bad about being proud of who you are and proclaiming it on your T-shirt?" then sharing on social media might make sense for them. **We can try to encourage kids to pause before making any big disclosures. Before they share a piece of sensitive personal information, teach them to ask themselves: "Would I wear it on a T-shirt?"**

- **Bullying is not the fault of the target.** The reality that families keep sharing with me is that a person may be bullied for their identity (including their race, religion, sexual orientation, neuro-identity, or other reasons) whether they choose to disclose. Disclosure is never to be thought of as *inviting* bullying, and bullying is not the fault of the target.

- **Encourage your kids to consider who is in their circle of trust.** How well do they know the person with whom they are sharing sensitive information? Is this someone who is comfortable hearing about personal things? Have they shown themselves to be a good keeper of confidences? Remind young people that it can be safer to share sensitive information in person or on a call, rather than digitally, where it is so easy for something to be re-shared. But recognize that texting and writing things down also feels more private for kids—that's why hotlines allow texting now. You can do it in your home with your parents and siblings in the next room. Voice calls or meeting in person might be more private, but only if you have your own space.

- **Coach kids to trust their sense of what feels right and wrong to establish their boundaries.** Encourage your child to be mindful of their reactions to other people's posts and to listen and learn from these reactions. (Just beware: when it comes to sharing, your adolescent's sense of "too much" might be very different from yours.) One mother, Marci, was shocked when her daughter showed her an Instagram post from a sixteen-year-old classmate: "It's going to happen tonight, I won't be a virgin anymore next time I post." Indeed, the following post announced, "The deed is done." The disclosure was "out there" enough that Marci's daughter broke the "kid code" and showed it to her mom. When kids notice their own reaction to someone else's post—*Ugh, this went too far*—that helps them set boundaries about what they are willing to post.

- **Teach kids to anticipate both positive and negative reactions.** Encourage your child to be aware of the environment in which they are sharing their personal stories. Remind them that every situation and community is different. In some communities, for example, diagnoses like anxiety or supports like taking medication or seeing a therapist are common enough that kids discuss it with their peers. But there are many places where seeing a therapist is stigmatized and where kids may want to be more private about it. Help them become critical "readers" of situations and anticipate how others will react to their sharing:

What reaction did others get to similar disclosures? Is my comment likely to provoke others? Will it create sympathy for me? Is that my intention? How could someone interpret my disclosure in a way that I don't intend? How could they weaponize my disclosure against me? Prepare your kids for the ups and downs that might result after they share sensitive personal information and help them understand their experience might be different from that of public figures.

Mentor Kids on Appropriate Outlets for Self-Expression

If your child begins to experiment with sharing very personal details of their lives, it's critical to have a discussion about what the best or safest places for self-expression are. Dr. Ken Ginsburg, author of *Building Resilience in Children and Teens* and head of the Center for Parent and Teen Communication, explains to his patients that he does not believe a mental health diagnosis is something to be ashamed of. He thinks that when you talk with your kids about de-stigmatization, it is important to emphasize that you are *not* suggesting they keep their diagnosis a "secret." But it's important they understand that communicating with a friend in person is very different than putting something out on social media.

"There should be a piece of ourselves that we should allow to be open to the world, because we can gain support, because we can reveal a bit of ourselves, which will draw people in," he told me. "**But we also each have a sacred story that really should be saved for people who have proven themselves worthy** . . . In a one-on-one conversation, it is far easier to have a positive experience and be empowered in the conversation . . . We want supportive people to give us input into our lives—that involves control and choice. With social media, you can lose that control."

If your child wants to share sensitive information about themselves online, have a conversation with them: Why is it important for them to share in a public space like social media? What are the potential benefits and disadvantages of doing so?

Resist Monitoring Your Kids' Texts and Posts Unless They Are Really Struggling

Lots of teens' communications are simply private. That does not mean they are harmful or need adult intervention. Maybe your child is dating someone and the couple has texted each other intimate feelings. Perhaps some of their friends are talking about personal issues with their parents. A fifteen-year-old might reasonably want to keep many things private from their parents that are not dangerous: friendship issues, crushes, or feelings about drama between other friends. Being a sounding board is a better way of building trust than spying.

We can be clear with our kids that we are there for them if they are in a situation they don't know how to handle, or one that could mean big trouble for them or a friend. But remember to be clear that you understand that they have a right to intimate conversations with friends and romantic partners and that you don't want to intrude.

If your child has a propensity to self-harm in a public way or might post things that will cause great reputational or social harm, you will want to do more monitoring than is typically needed. If this is the case, do it openly, not covertly. You might even need to restrict access to their devices. Cutting kids off from this important lifeline to their peers is hard, but if they are sharing in ways that are harmful to their mental health and long-term reputation, then you might need to do it. Dr. Jonathan Singer, social worker and suicide-prevention expert, says that a parent who looks at their child's communication should consider doing it when they are scanning for something specific, like a threat of self-harm, a threat to others, or similar disclosure. Crisis social worker Lisa Sniderman, MSW, who works in an emergency room, told me that in cases where parents are having trouble getting an adolescent admitted, especially involuntarily because their child is denying suicidal ideation, a text or post that shows their suicidal thoughts might be convincing to a hospital team.

For kids not in crisis, we need to be very cautious about diving into their communications out of curiosity. Teens may represent themselves and their family life to their friends in ways that cause us pain and that might not be great for our relationship—so there has to be a really good reason to go looking.

"Kids will always get their hands on new technology, so taking it away might be a helpful response for only a short period of time," one parent cautions. "Like, okay, let's take a break from you using anything while we do more therapy and work on impulse control, and we shore up your self-confidence. But then it's only realistic that they are going to be back in the world of social media. 'Cause that's the world we live in. Our experience has been that we have to monitor constantly because even with therapy and mentoring and support, our child still struggles."

In an interview, Dr. Singer told me that digital reentry should be considered and careful, for example, for kids who have had a period of inpatient support. If he were working on a treatment plan, he would recommend wading in slowly and not adding all social apps and contacts back right away. He also suggests making a plan with a young person to manage the flood of updates that comes with receiving their phone again after being in an inpatient program.

If you find out that your child is disclosing vulnerable information online, and they are not currently receiving therapeutic support, that is a clear sign that they would benefit from it. Depending on their age and your relationship with their therapist, you can also share with the therapist what you know about sites or channels they may be using.

Give Your Kids Tools to Navigate Peers' Disclosures

Help your child understand the reasons why peers might share very sensitive personal information. Are they asking for help? Are they in crisis? Are they a danger to themselves or another? More important, help your kids discern when they absolutely must tell an adult about something a peer has shared. If a friend consistently shares information that concerns your child (e.g., posts about self-harm or substance abuse), advise them to let you know or to go to another adult like a school counselor. If your child discussed their concern with their friend, perhaps they can offer to go with them to a school counselor. If the friend's sharing is not concerning—but their posts or texts are "too much" for your child—encourage them to hide their friend's social media feed, but still retain the friendship.

The World Is Changing— and Our Kids Are Changing It

It might be difficult to understand why our kids feel so compelled to share such private, personal information publicly—especially when we were so often taught to keep it close to our vest. As parents, we are unsettled by the idea that our kids' intimate information is out publicly, that they have made themselves vulnerable to attack or judgment, and that their disclosure might close doors for them in the future. In those moments, we must remember that, ultimately, the connection our kids experience when they share their stories with others like them—whether it is an affinity group for fans of a certain TV show, or people with ADHD, or people who are queer—can be extremely valuable. It is part of their social life and learning.

By sharing so freely their most personal stories, kids are changing the culture. They are educating others to think beyond gender binaries, they are celebrating their neurodiversity and speaking about experiences that have been historically silenced. They are creating positive communities and connecting with others in ways we might never have. What we experience as discomfort, they experience as empowering. And that could lead to a more inclusive place. That's worth supporting.

chapter 6

Sexting:

When Explicit Images of Kids Circulate

Jianna and Ethan were enjoying the excitement of a first romantic relationship in eighth grade. They sat together at lunch, sent each other texts throughout the day, chatted on apps late into the evening, made Spotify playlists, and annoyed their friends by talking constantly about one another. Although they hadn't been sexually active beyond kissing, they decided to exchange "sexy" photos. While Ethan texted Jianna a photo that wasn't that revealing and didn't show his face, Jianna sent Ethan a topless image that was more identifiable. They promised to keep the photos private. Initially, Ethan intended to honor their plan, but his best friend coaxed him into forwarding the image of Jianna to their friend group. With some reservation, he eventually gave in.

After a few months, Ethan and Jianna ended their relationship and moved on. But unbeknownst to Jianna, her picture kept circulating, passing from classmate to classmate throughout their middle school. Soon, kids started coughing and whispering "slut" when

Jianna walked by. One afternoon, she opened her school email to find a video with her image with sound effects from a porn video playing with it. She slammed her laptop shut, called her parents saying she was sick and needed to be picked up, and refused to return to school.

Few things kids can do with their phones stoke parents' fears as much as sexting—sending and receiving sexually explicit messages, images, or videos via text, email, airdrop, or social media. There are countless reasons why we hope our children won't sext. We worry about whom they might be sending intimate photos to. We are terrified by the thought of explicit images of our child circulating in public, especially since once they are out there, it's hard to get them back. We imagine the worst: their photo or video uploaded to a porn site. We dread the potential school disciplinary and even legal consequences that might follow. Sharing or intentionally creating sexy photos or videos, or even writing racy text messages, may not align with our values. If we learn that our kids are sexting, it forces us to see their emerging sexuality in ways that are uncomfortable for many parents (and profoundly cringey for the kid, too, if they know that you know).

I get why parents worry about this. We've all heard stories of photos, videos, or words meant to be shared privately that ended up making the rounds across the entire school, often followed by negative consequences and a mountain of regret. But whether we like it or not, kids today are probably going to encounter sexually explicit photos shared digitally—or as they call them, "nudes," or simply "selfies" or "pics"—some time in middle school or high school. Even if they never create or send an explicit photo, they may be asked for them, have one sent to them, or at the very least hear about sexting in their school or community.

A study published in *JAMA Pediatrics* found that almost 15

percent of kids ages twelve to seventeen have sent an explicit message, while 27 percent have received one. The study focused on data from 2008 and 2016 from 110,380 participants—some as young as eleven years old—and revealed that sexting has increased rapidly in those eight years. **Newer research from a Project Zero study at Harvard confirms what I've heard from both teens and parents—that the number has increased . . . and that the pandemic was an accelerant.**

These numbers are not surprising, as kids are accustomed to engaging socially and openly through digital means. They are also growing up in an explicit culture where highway billboards feature models in underwear, and social media is filled with influencers posting in suggestive poses, not to mention the lyrics and videos to many popular songs. Sending "nudes" or "pics" or just sexy photos—especially to someone kids believe can be trusted—doesn't feel like as big a leap to them as it might to us. That's why teens can seem skeptical when we try to scare them with the idea that taking a photo naked or wearing only underwear will lead to their social downfall. Younger tweens especially might doubt that they would ever want to do such a thing (*Gross!*). But as they mature, they also may find that some of their friends have shared nudes or suggestive images and *not* experienced disaster.

The uncomfortable truth is that, when consensual and private, sexting can be nothing more than another form of healthy teenage sexual exploration—one that often has no social consequences. If we use fear tactics to shame our kids or scare them into not sexting, we only make it harder for them to seek out adult help if they get into a tricky situation.

Sexting 101

Even the most sex-positive parents know that when you combine adolescent sexuality and impulsivity with lightning-fast technology and social media platforms, things are bound to go wrong sometimes. If you remember back to your teenage years, it's easy to imagine how having a smartphone then might have changed how you flirted and dated.

When I was coming of age in the nineties, I had friends who worked in the photo department of a drugstore in a college student neighborhood of Boston. They shared many stories of "porny" pictures they developed for customers. Back then, if in an impulsive, rash moment, a teenager or young adult decided to share a sexy picture with someone they liked, they would have had to take numerous steps: shoot the photo, wait until the roll of film was used up and ready to be developed, take the film to a photo center, and then pick up the photos from my smirking friends behind the counter a few days later. Only then could they even *consider*, after many days or even weeks since the idea first came into their head, handing the sexy photo to another person. This lengthy process gave plenty of opportunities to reconsider their choice to share the photo or even to come back and pick up the developed pictures. Indeed, these photos often didn't get picked up, and I can confirm that some of them eventually went home with the drugstore employees . . .

Fast-forward to now. Our kids can take a photo or video and share it with hundreds or even thousands of people in less than a minute. Mobile technology has made acting on the same intense impulses that adolescents have always had that much easier (and riskier in terms of wider exposure). For some kids, sexting is a version of spin the bottle. For others it can be a mark of trust and intimacy. For others it can be a way to objectify and feel powerful. "To some degree, sexting has been normalized among teens," a school counselor shared with me. A teen told Dr. Katie Hurley, LCSW and author of *No More Mean Girls*, that sexting "is just part of our relationship . . . That's just what we do."

Even though kids start sending explicit photos and texts as early as elementary school (I've been called by a few schools with incidents in the fifth grade), and it may be common in middle school or junior high, sexting doesn't become normalized among most kids until high school, when explicit photos become less stigmatized and more accepted, especially among kids over sixteen years old. Sexting in high school is commonplace enough that it has even been central to the plotlines of a few TV shows. In one, *Genera+ion*, one of the characters figures out that her twin brother is fooling around with her boyfriend after recognizing a "dick pic" that she spies on her brother's phone. In college, students tell me that sexting can be a very normal part of dating and hookup culture. Not universal, by any means, but not stigmatized, either. The research confirms that older teens are more likely to sext.

Sending Nudes: How It Happens

Several teenagers I spoke with described a culture in which sexting is a casual flirting tactic. One high school junior, Mag, told me that, in her case, it has most often started with a stranger or a kid from school asking her to connect on Snapchat. The boys will often start by sending a photo of themselves shirtless, or of something that's suggestive, but not flat-out "disgusting." "Then, out of the blue," Mag explained, "[they] just send you a dick pic . . . Girls *love* that," she said sarcastically with a laugh. "Or they will just straight up [text], 'Here's my dick, how are you doing today?' Which is weird and gross." Most of the time, she ignores them. "If you're not interested in them, then you block them immediately and you tell all your friends, 'Oh my god, [so-and-so] just sent me a dick pic. That's disgusting. Let's never talk to him again.'" But if Mag was interested in them, she might ask the person why he sent the picture and start a conversation.

Girls like Mag have often told me that, while they are asked for nude pictures, for the most part, they don't send explicit images of themselves. The boys I have spoken to acknowledge that sexting happens; some even admit that their friends have shared nudes "among the guys." But most of them deny personally creating and sending explicit photos. "Once you get older, you kind of get more self-respect and more foresight to not send [explicit photos]," Troy, a senior in a suburban high school, explained to me, "because chances are it's not going to go well."

Although it may seem to teenagers (and their parents) that "everyone" is taking topless photos, underwear photos, and dick pics and sending them to classmates and strangers, research shows otherwise. Like the boys I spoke with, kids are more likely to see an explicit photo that someone sent to them than they are to send an image of themselves. Of the kids whom I spoke with, a few admitted to having passed along explicit photos that were circulating among their peer groups.

The teenagers who are more likely to "send pics" are those who believe sexting is common and typical among their peers. One study showed that teenagers were ten times more likely to sext if they thought the kids that they perceived as popular had sent explicit pictures themselves. Of course, in middle school or high school, it is easy to think everyone—especially the "popular kids"—is dating more, having more sex, and sexting more. According to a fascinating study, "non-popular adolescents frequently overestimate their popular peers' sexual behavior," including sexting.[1] This inaccurate picture of how often and how many explicit messages and photos popular kids share can lead the "non-popular" kids to feel less inhibited from trying to do it themselves.

Why Do Kids Send Nudes When They Know What Can Go Wrong?

Emily Weinstein and Carrie James, authors of *Behind Their Screens: What Teens Are Facing (and Adults Are Missing)*, conducted a comprehensive study of over 3,500 young people and found nine reasons why kids sext, even though they know the risks.

Some of these won't be surprising:

1. It feels pleasurable, exciting, and fun.
2. They hope to impress someone they like, or they are seeking praise, validation, or attention from a crush.
3. They are talking to a romantic interest or crush but not yet official or exclusive and want to signal a desire to move things forward or keep that person interested.
4. They are in an exclusive relationship and want to deepen intimacy or show trust.
5. They can't figure out how to say no. Sending a photo feels easier than dodging the request.
6. The asker is someone they consider a friend, and they worry that saying no will jeopardize the friendship.
7. The asker is persistent and wears them down.
8. They fear consequences if they refuse from an asker who might be mean, aggressive, and spread false rumors.

9. They are being actively coerced, threatened, or blackmailed by the asker. For example, perhaps they have already sent some sexy pictures in the past and the asker is threatening to share those pictures if they don't send new images.

I'll add two more reasons that I heard a lot from teens and from counselors and public health folks who work with teens.

1. To experiment with sexual personae and language that they are too nervous to experiment with in "real life" with a partner.
2. To be validated in their attractiveness (and not just from a romantic interest, but in general). Some kids may do this with social media posts (clothed), but some might share racier photos with the same conscious or unconscious intent. Only very few get through high school or college feeling confident in their attractiveness (or truly don't care). Many teens want at least occasional validation that *someone* (other than their parents, who don't count) thinks that they are cute.

The relatable plot of *Never Have I Ever* features a teen girl who identifies as a nerd and wants to know that attractive, socially powerful boys will *want* to be sexual with her. When the opportunity arises, and she's actually dating her seemingly unattainable crush, it turns out she's not ready for sex (that's okay, Devi! Wait till you are ready), but knowing she is desired feels crucial.

While parents can worry about the *lack* of control you have over an image that is so easily replicated and shared, it is also worth thinking about the perceived control you have over an image versus a live sexual encounter. Maybe you have body insecurities or don't feel ready to get naked in the room with a partner. Maybe you are a survivor of sexual assault or simply have an awareness of that possibility—but an image where you control the angle and the lighting and exactly how much to reveal can feel empowering.

One counselor noted that for transgender and nonbinary teens, the opportunity to experiment with identity and perception via texting (versus in person) can be hard to resist. In that case, she wasn't talking about sexting per se, but just the way "talking" to a crush via texting felt less vulnerable than spending time together in person.

Even before the pandemic sent kids home for months (or years), "dating" was something that happened predominantly via tech for many teens. The whole notion of "talking to someone" could be mostly texting. If your middle schooler says they have a boyfriend or girlfriend, they might be "going out," getting boba tea, or holding hands at the ball game. Or they might be . . . texting. A lot.

I hope these reasons and context can give adults much more empathy for kids and understanding of why they might send pics, even though we wish they wouldn't.

We must actively mentor our kids on consent, flirting, relationships, and negotiating boundaries. We must help them make safe and ethical choices that honor themselves and others. We must teach them to resist being part of a culture of shaming and objectifying others. We must encourage them to act with compassion—and caution—when explicit images or messages end up circulating in their school or friend group. Crucially, we must empower them to get help if someone violates their boundaries. Anyone who's had their privacy violated needs support—not judgment.

What about the Queer Kids?

For queer kids, sexting can play out a bit differently than for heterosexually identified tweens and teens. In at least one UK study, boys ages fourteen to eighteen years old who identified on the LGBTQ+ spectrum were somewhat more likely than heterosexually identified peers to take and send explicit images of themselves to someone they didn't know well.[2] Several boys described sending explicit photos as part of the flirting ritual. First, they direct message when they see someone on social media that they find attractive, then they might exchange explicitly sexual or nude photos, which might then be followed by meeting up, "hooking up," and possibly getting into a relationship.

Unlike some of the heterosexual girls I talked with who told me receiving dick pics is "gross," many (but not all) queer boys in the UK study reported feeling positive about receiving photos from other boys (including explicit anatomical pics, as well as less explicit images, shirtless pictures, etc.). In fact, they told researchers that sexting often gave them validation of their sexual attractiveness, as they don't often get the same body validation that many of their heterosexual peers experience, which is perhaps why they enjoy getting that from unknown people online. "Straight boys have more confidence about how they look because they have a lot of people to tell them," a fourteen-year-old research participant explained. "Whereas if you don't have people to go to you must find out other ways."

Sharing nudes is already fraught with risk for teens. For kids who don't identify with their assigned gender at birth, nudes can be especially problematic. But sex educator Rachel Lotus thinks that sexting, especially explicit "verbal/text-based" exchanges that do not include images, can give nonbinary or trans kids freedom to experiment. "I have talked to nonbinary middle schoolers who have, in some ways, benefited from the safety of that kind of flirt," she explains. "It seems almost like a way of testing it out before doing anything physical. It's also trying on different identities and just feeling around . . . 'Does this feel like a good fit? Am I . . . what I think I am?'"

To a certain degree, many kids who don't identify as queer sext to either get appearance validation or to try on a sexual identity, too. Feeling cute or hot is a desire for many teens, and many straight kids would argue that high school doesn't validate their attractiveness, either. It is an infamously insecure time for many if not most people. For some queer kids—who may feel they are missing out on in-person opportunities to be "checked out," flirted with, and seen as attractive— sharing pics might be especially appealing. These teens may feel like there are few other contexts in which they can have these experiences—an important part of growing up and exploring the romantic and sexual world.

Different Contexts for Sexting

Although we may be alarmed if we find out our kids are sexting at all, there are many contexts and situations in which teenagers may sext—some less problematic than others. Most of the time, kids will engage in "non-pressured" sexting; that is, they send and share explicit photos or texts because they freely choose to.[3] Often, non-pressured sexting results in minimal or zero negative consequences. The teens in the numerous studies cited earlier in this chapter shared stories where sexting was fun, exciting, and pleasurable, and crucially did *not* lead to regret or harm when it happened between people who didn't pressure their partner, and when the images were not circulated beyond their intended recipient.

Non-Pressured Sexting vs. Pressured Sexting

The Harvard study found that in addition to consensual sharing in romantic relationships, friends might share nudes or pics, and that can also be non-pressured. In this context, kids share images outside of a relationship, typically to a group of friends or peers. Potentially for affirmation of their attractiveness, or just as currency in the friend group. While this urge to share outside of dating relationships might surprise adults, I've found that, based on talking to many high school kids and in recalling my own high school friendships, those lines can be blurry!

Bottom line: kids who feel autonomous, like they have free choice, don't seem to experience sexting as harmful, according to numerous research studies. And that's important.

On the other hand, "pressured" sexting is when kids are coerced into sending nude or sexually explicit videos. Repeatedly cajoling someone else to send pics, threatening exposure of previous pics if more aren't sent, or using social power in a relationship to obtain images are all examples of "pressured sexting." The consequences are far more significant here, and the research shows that young victims can experience stress, worry, shame, and depression. That's the type of sexting you *especially* want to help kids avoid or recover from—and certainly to *never* perpetrate.

When Pics Go Around without Consent

If teens send sexually explicit photos or messages to someone they trust, believing those messages will be kept private, but then the photos are shared without their consent, this can leave someone vulnerable. Tamoko sent her boyfriend intimate pictures while they were dating, which he kept private. But after they broke up and moved on, his new girlfriend found the photos on his phone and shared them. Tamoko hated going to school not knowing who had seen the photos and almost failed two classes that she had with friends of her ex's new girlfriend. (Note: As parents, it is important to hear stories like this. If your kid suddenly stops going to a class or has a sudden academic change, there may be a social reason, not an academic/cognitive explanation.)

The expectation for reciprocated intimacy can also lead to hurt. Kaya sent a lot of explicit photos to Sander, a boy she liked. He hadn't initially asked for them, but she sent them in a bid for his attention. It seemed to work. He liked them and asked for more, making her feel special, and suggested to her that they were going to get together romantically. So she kept sending photos. Once Kaya realized that Sander was getting nudes from multiple girls—and that they were *not* headed toward being a couple—she panicked. She felt she "got played." Her mental health was affected as she became consumed by shame and regret. Thankfully, with her parents' and friends' support and a good therapist, she was able to move forward from this experience. Importantly, in this case, Sander didn't share the photos. But knowing he has them makes Kaya continue to feel vulnerable and powerless.

Pressured Sexting

Unfortunately, some tweens and teens are often pressured or coerced into sending nude pics or, worse, are not even aware that explicit images of them have been taken, and then those photos and videos are shared with others.

Girls are more frequently pressured into sending explicit photos so their peers will not think of them as "uncool" or a "prude," or so they won't lose the attention of the person asking for the pics. Sometimes, they are cajoled into sending explicit images. In the worst situation, young people may be coerced into sharing more images or having sex—in exchange for not distributing a photo. This is a sex crime. Photos may even be used to keep someone in a relationship, under the threat of releasing explicit images or messages if they break up, or just "as currency."

In September 2019, for example, Channing Smith, a sixteen-year-old boy from Tennessee, died by suicide after private explicit messages he'd exchanged with another boy were uploaded by a classmate and shared widely without his consent, with the intent to out him.[4] Within hours of this forced exposure, the sixteen-year-old was dead. No amount of juicy gossip, nor level of hurt in a breakup, nor desire for status should lead to actions that left this young man feeling so painfully exposed and betrayed. But as Channing's story demonstrates, the risks of exposure for closeted teens are especially intense. We know that despite overall growing acceptance, in many communities, LGBTQ+ kids are subject to harassment and violence in much higher numbers than cis, heterosexual peers.[5] Even in progressive communities, middle schools and high schools are not universally inclusive places.

For cis, hetero boys, sexting can still be emotionally risky—at one middle school I worked with, a boy's nude photo, intended just for one girl, circulated without his permission, and he felt terribly embarrassed. This scenario happens much more frequently to girls, and the resulting attention and "slut-shaming" is intensified by the double standard, but it can still be embarrassing for boys to have a private image shared widely.

The Double Standard

In a boy/girl heterosexual context, the social risks and consequences of sexting reveal that a double standard is alive and well, even in our "enlightened" times. If you are watching a movie in which a person is being objectified or slut-shamed, point it out to your kid and start a conversation about it. The movie *Easy A*, where Emma Stone's character is slut-shamed but she turns it around, is a great one to watch with your teen.

In some high schools, boys share photos of girls with one another

If you hear your kid—boy or girl—calling a peer a "slut," "whore," "ho," "easy," "thot," etc., intervene immediately. Teach your kid the importance of treating everyone respectfully and sticking up for one another's humanity. If you have boys, talk to them about not caving into pressure to solicit images from girls, to share images with other guys if they do receive them, or to talk about girls and women in a way that is objectifying. If you have girls, talk to them about the importance of not shaming other girls if explicit pictures of them are circulating. It's critical that we teach kids not to weaponize misogyny or homophobia against others.

as "trophies" and as a way to gain status. Getting a nude of a girl who is widely perceived to be attractive earns a boy higher status. One tenth grader at a suburban high school told me his baseball team had gotten in trouble the year before when seniors circulated nude images of girls. Several of these photos were of students at their school; a few were in relationships with members of the team. To be clear, there are many boys who disdain this behavior and would never trade photos of girls. The tenth graders I spoke to pronounced such behavior "gross." One boy said, "I couldn't imagine betraying someone's trust that way."

Nonetheless, when it comes to sexting that goes public, girls usually pay a much higher social price when things go wrong—whether she sent an explicit image or text freely, or under coercion. Aware of these social risks, some girls watermark nudes so if the photos are leaked, they will know who shared. Others might send a plausible nude that is not really them so if it gets out, they have deniability.[6] Finally, some girls warn one another about boys in their communities who have been known to leak or circulate nudes.

One sexuality and health educator described how after two ninth graders broke up, the boy shared with his friends pictures that the girl had sent him. His friends, not content to merely share the pictures and humiliate the girl, were charging money for them. "His reputation only improved after he shared those [photos] with other people, whereas her reputation suffered. She was slut-shamed." The girl even lost some girlfriends in the process, likely because her friends internalized the double standard and wanted to distance themselves from the object of the gossip. "I think it's just the same old story. I wish that things were different at this point in history!" the educator told me. "But the truth is that boys tend to gain social capital [in these situations], and girls tend to lose it."

That mindset of slut-shaming sometimes extends to school administrators. I've seen schools discipline the initial sharer of an image, who was the victim of wrongdoing, not the perpetrator. Another educator told me about an eighth-grade boy who convinced a girl in his class to masturbate while they were talking on FaceTime. She had no idea that he had secretly recorded her until the video made the rounds among their classmates. Even though he had victimized her, the girl was suspended from school, while the boy was not suspended. In fact, the school called her parents to express concern about her "problematic" behavior. Even other girls in her class blamed her and were cruel to her. Not able to handle the humiliation, the girl ended up changing schools. It was clear that in her community, her actions were considered shameful—not the boy's deceit or abuse of trust. The double standard that "boys will be boys" allowed his behavior to be excused, while hers was not, even though she was the victim.

In addition to the risk of exposure, girls are also much more *frequently* harassed with *unwanted sexts*. Many girls I spoke to had received at least a few sexually explicit direct messages and photos of male genitalia. While some shrugged it off and others felt harassed and disgusted, these unsolicited texts and photos undoubtedly contribute to a climate of objectification and sexism. In some contexts, it can also feel threatening.

Several mothers of boys interviewed for this book also shared with me that their sons had received photos from girls unbidden and felt extremely uncomfortable. Due to the "double standard," the boys may have felt like they were *supposed* to celebrate these images, but in reality, it made them feel pressured or violated. Parents and educators should be aware that receiving unbidden nudes can be stressful for kids of all genders.

Legal Issues

While the emotional risks of sexting are borne primarily by girls, the legal risks associated with sexting—pressured or non-pressured—affect everyone, from the sender to the sharer. If there is legal trouble with boy/girl sexting, some parents and attorneys shared that boys are more likely to get into trouble, even if they have an image they didn't solicit.

While creating, sending, and receiving sexually explicit pictures are increasing among teenagers, the laws have not kept up with the technology or the varied possibilities. It is a blunt instrument given the complexities of the different ways kids are making and sharing these images. Two sixteen-year-olds in love exchanging nude pictures are a world apart from a sex trafficker forcing underage people to make pornography. And yet, laws around the country don't quite differentiate between the two. Teens have occasionally been censured, fined, and even forced to register as sex offenders for consensually sending pictures of themselves. And although receiving a sexually explicit image that you did not ask to see is hard to prevent, in many states, if a teen or tween receives one and keeps it on their device or computer, they can be legally liable for having that image.

Some states have made efforts to make child pornography laws more nuanced so that, say, a consensual photo exchanged between two sixteen-year-olds can't lead either of them to be criminally charged.[7] In Connecticut, for example, the ages of those who send and receive sexually explicit photos and messages are now considered relevant.[8] Texas allows an exception for "sexting" if a minor sends explicit images to another minor who is no more than two years older or younger and the two are dating.[9] But the laws around sexting are still a mess. Since legal jeopardy varies tremendously by state, it's important for parents and young people to understand how the laws work where they live. **It would behoove all who care about kids, especially teenagers, to fight for laws that protect them from exploitation, rather than punish, stigmatize, and humiliate them for sharing intimate photos consensually.**

The good news is that most kids who take explicit photos of themselves or who have received or shared them don't face legal consequences, especially from consensual image sharing. That's why Dr. Elizabeth Englander, a psychologist and expert in cyberbullying and aggression reduction, says we should be wary of focusing on the threat of prosecution when trying to dissuade kids from sexting.[10] "Care must be taken when citing the risk of criminal prosecution," she wrote, "as such prosecution seems to be increasingly unlikely, and could actually frighten victims of coerced sexting away from reporting to adults."

What Parents Can Do: Teach Kids to Safely Navigate Sexting

There is nothing wrong with teenagers liking each other, wanting someone to like them, being excited about their bodies and how they are changing, or wanting to be appreciated by someone they like or are attracted to. But we live in a world where sending explicit pictures and texts is not a safe way for tweens and teens to explore sexuality and romance. We live in a world that makes this approach emotionally and reputationally dangerous. In this case, the risks and downsides might outweigh the fun.

The tricky part, however, is that the train has left the station. Sexting has become commonplace enough that preventing or stopping your child from doing it to keep them safe might backfire. "[As with] anything related to sex, it doesn't really work to just tell kids not to do it," Rachel Lotus, a sex educator, told me. "They won't likely be deterred by scare tactics and shaming." Lotus also reminded me that all online activity leaves our kids vulnerable to some extent. "Even a fight between friends can get screenshot and sent around," she explained. "So I'm not sure how you make it fully safe." In other words, sexting is one risk among the many others that kids take when living their lives digitally.

The key is to help our kids become better at navigating the risks associated with sexting. While this might seem like we are giving them "license to sext," it is actually no different than offering them basic sex education. Just as sex education does not make kids more sexually active, educating them about sexting will not make them more likely to sext. Kids with more knowledge are more likely to wait until they are ready, or to not do it at all. **Talking about sexting and helping kids make better choices taps into values that most of us already want to instill in our children. We want to raise children who are thoughtful about how their actions affect them and others, who know how to treat and express interest in another person in a respectful way, who honor other people's boundaries and their own, and who understand the consequences that might follow if they don't.**

Here are some ways to foster these qualities and skills at home.

Don't Put a "Scarlet Letter" on Them

Depending on your household rules, religion, or culture, you might be invested in having your child not engage in any kind of sexual activity. The thing is, kids are sexual. They masturbate, have sexual feelings, get aroused, have crushes, and fall in love. They also want to feel validated, attractive, and crush-worthy. Even if you don't think sexting is the appropriate way for them to explore their sexuality and bodies, don't shame them for these feelings and desires. The adults in their environment already send them all sorts of confusing and often negative messages about their bodies through provocative advertisements and even sexist school dress codes. Talk to your kid about sexting in ways that prioritize their emotional and physical safety (more on this later) and resists shaming, stigmatizing language. And if you find out that they are already sexting, don't react to the situation with your own complicated feelings about their emerging sexuality. While it might be uncomfortable to think about the way your child's body is changing and about their emerging sexual and romantic identities, it is important to stay supportive and focus your messaging around sexting on consent and safety, rather than disgust, shame, or stigmatization. While we might say, "You're only twelve!" and feel like our kids should still be "innocent," that ignores the reality that puberty comes earlier to this generation, and marriage comes later, if at all. The research shows more kids today are delaying intercourse until later ages. Teen pregnancy is way down. In some important ways, consensual sexting is "safe sex," yet it still sends most parents into a panic.

When kids perceive they are going to be shamed for an action, they "hide." This is dangerous. If you are not talking with them about sexting in a calm and respectful way, should something happen that makes them vulnerable to harassment or worse, you might not know about it and won't be able to help. Given the sensitivity and complexity of dealing with explicit images that circulate, there is almost never a case when "hiding" is a good idea. In my experience, tweens and teens are not fully equipped to handle such issues without help from a responsible adult or mentor. It is crucial that your kid knows that you respect them even if they make a decision they regret. And if problems related to sexting arise, you must tread carefully to avoid sending your kid into a shame spiral that may actually compound any public shaming they might be experiencing. You want to maintain trust and openness—it's your best opportunity to help.

Teach Them about Consent

Most of the risk associated with sexting comes from kids not having a clear sense of what consent is. To a middle schooler, pressing "forward" on an image that they've received or that is already posted online and sharing it with others might feel like a benign action, or "fair game." After all, they didn't take that picture and they weren't the ones who originally circulated it. They might not even know the person in the picture, so what's the harm? **Teach your child the importance of never sharing an explicit message or photograph of another person—especially without that person's consent. Explain to them that regardless of how they came across the explicit image or message, passing it on to someone else is unethical, perpetuates that person's violation, and is very likely illegal in their state (especially if the image is of a minor).**

But how do I talk to my teen about *that*?

You can bring it up casually in a car, giving a theoretical example of a "friend" whose child got into trouble.

You can also use the news of a celebrity "scandal" to talk about it. If you are clear that you are sympathetic (for example to Jennifer Lawrence, who had her nudes hacked) and that you feel concerned for *her*, and not judgmental, you are setting your teen up to know that you will be sympathetic and helpful if their own picture was circulating. You can also be very clear that if your kids are in a jam, they can come to you. Attorney Carrie Goldberg is an expert on supporting victims of revenge porn and other digital exploitation. Goldberg says that kids will often hide situations where they are being exploited or threatened with disclosure, so parents need to be proactive to let kids know that they will help without judgement.

It's also critical that you talk to your kids about the different types of consent. Discuss the difference between willingly exchanging explicit images with another person and coercing or pressuring someone to send them. Explain to them that if someone consents to sending an explicit image, they are not consenting to having it shared with others—and they likely would not have agreed to send it in the first place if they knew that this was the intention. Make sure your kids understand that they should also not send an explicit photo to someone unless the person on the receiving end has consented to receiving it.

Goldberg suggests teaching and practicing empathy—it goes a long way in helping teens and tweens understand the harm and hurt that sharing intimate images and messages nonconsensually can cause. "We have to teach young people to imagine how [it would] feel and not reach for the burst of exciting attention or power over someone that would make even considering sharing or threatening to share private photos something they would [contemplate]," she told me. "Ultimately it is empathy, rather than fear of getting into trouble or getting caught, that should drive anyone considering sharing someone else's private texts or photos to avoid committing such a damaging [act]."

Goldberg feels that parents should try to prepare kids for possible sexting situations they might find themselves in so that the element of surprise and the possible rush of sexual, excited feelings won't lead them to make rash decisions in the moment. This conversation will be uncomfortable—it will involve scenarios that many parents would like to pretend don't exist. She recommends asking your kids questions such as: "What are you going to do if somebody really cute that you don't know follows you on Instagram and starts DMing you, then sends you nudes and wants some images of you?"

In her workshops with students, Rachel Lotus, Brooklyn-based educator and founder of The Talk NYC, which focuses on a broad range of topics such as body image, consent, sexting, and gender identity, likes to help teens and tweens think a few steps ahead. She suggests telling your child: "You might be in a relationship with this person this week. And you might feel like it's true love and it will last forever. You might be using sexting as a form of flirting and foreplay. But [what happens if or when] that relationship comes to an end? What will happen to all those [pictures, videos, words] that you've exchanged? So, fast-forward weeks or months or years to that eventuality, and think about how you will feel about all of those things you have shared [being] in that person's hands."

Empower your kid to seek help right away if they are being pressured or coerced into sending explicit images. In addition to teaching them to alert you or an adult they are comfortable with, show them how to keep screenshots of messages sent by the perpetrator, which might help a social media platform take down their accounts and photos— and law enforcement to go after them. Goldberg explains that, often times, those who coerce photos from our kids threaten them with embarrassment (e.g., "Send nudes or I will share the text where you said you would do this terrible thing"). "Kids need to know that telling is power and that you will believe them and take their side," she adds.

Educate Them about Safe Sexting

Most adults don't want kids to sext at all. But given that some young people will do it anyway, there are potentially less dangerous ways to do it. It's important to have a conversation with your child about how to "safe sext." In a paper published in the *Journal of Adolescent Health*, my friends and colleagues Justin W. Patchin and Sameer Hinduja shared strategies for safer sexting to pass along to your adolescent. I'm adapting them with my own caveats here—but I am impressed that they took this step, because it can feel risky for adults to even acknowledge youth sexting, let alone seem to accommodate it:

- Always assume an intimate photo or explicit message might get distributed or seen beyond the person you are sending it to.

- Make any intimate photo unidentifiable. Never show your face, and make sure it does not show any background, tattoo, jewelry, scars, etc., that can help others identify you (or where you live). Consider taking pictures that are more suggestive, rather than explicit; that is, photos that strategically cover your private areas.

- Only send intimate photos to people in your circle of trust. Never send to a stranger or someone you don't know in real life, as they could be falsely representing themselves and their intentions.

- Use technology wisely: send intimate photos through apps that delete them automatically after a certain amount of time. I'd add this caveat, though: **Don't let your guard down. These apps can give you a false sense of security. Many apps can be screenshot, allowing people to save explicit material and share it later.** Avoid posting intimate photos on social media apps that have sophisticated algorithms and facial recognition technology that can tag you instantly. Remove any tags, location stamps, and metadata from your photos so your username and other identifiable information are no longer attached to the photo.

- Delete any explicit images or messages you've received or created from your devices. Keeping them might carry criminal implications, and hackers and friends with ill intentions might find them.

Talk to Them about Appropriate Flirting

In addition to helping kids engage in safe sexting, we need to do more to help them learn how to flirt or express interest in someone in *positive* ways. Obviously, no one wants flirting lessons from their parents, but if you are watching TV or a movie together and see good flirting versus bad or manipulative dating "tactics," use them as opportunities to discuss. Some of the movies I grew up with haven't aged well on the consent front, so while we might enjoy watching *Say Anything* or *Sixteen Candles* with our kids, don't be surprised if they point this out to you! *Friday Night Lights* was a big discussion starter in my house.

Boys need to understand that an unsolicited dick pic is not the way to endear themselves to most girls or to impress them. Not only could you get into trouble for harassment, you are unlikely to win her heart. The girls I interviewed for this book were universally grossed out by them. Even if the dick pic came from a boy they found otherwise attractive, the photo tended to diminish their interest in them. In the context of a relationship and when sent consensually, some kinds of sexy pictures can be acceptable. But kids need to understand that dick pics or requests for nudes "out of nowhere" are usually not welcomed or an effective kind of flirting that leads to positive interactions. But they can absolutely lead kids to trouble.

Give Them a Reality Check

If you have a kid who does seem to care a lot about what the "popular kids" are doing (e.g., following kids who don't follow them back on social media, or observing the ins and outs of the relationships of kids with a lot of social status), then it might be helpful to remind them that these kids are no more likely to engage in sexting as a way of flirting or starting relationships than anyone else. You could even share the study I cited earlier or other research on kids and sexting to educate them and counter the assumption that "everybody is doing it."

If You Catch Your Kid Sexting

What should you do if you find out that your child has been exchanging consensual sexts or photos with someone? (Hopefully you weren't just snooping on their phone, but maybe something popped up while the phone was lying around.) Or perhaps you know your kid is in a relationship, and your intuition tells you that pics have been shared.

Or maybe they even tell you. These photos or texts, fortunately, have stayed private, but you are still feeling a little worried.

Adolescent specialist Dr. Katie Hurley reminds us that, for parents, staying calm is crucial. "You could say, 'Okay, you sent those photos. How are you feeling about it? Want to walk me through it? How does this app work?'" She reminds us that love and crushes can be very powerful, so parents need to talk about emotions with their kids, not just about the explicit exchanges. Parents need to remember how huge and consuming these big feelings are. "Because we're so bad at talking about emotions, kids are just kind of trying to figure it out on their own," she says. Also, for most kids, it can be very traumatic to talk with parents about their shame or, worse, to live with the fact that a parent may have seen an image, video, or words that were meant to be private. It is important to find ways to express that your child is not a horrible person, a freak, a pervert, or a slut.

Finally, especially if your child is older, maybe you don't need to say anything. If this is your college-age son or daughter or an older high schooler, you may want to simply pretend you didn't see their phone and try to wipe what you saw from your brain. You could bring it up as a theoretical later: "I know some couples send racy pictures these days, do you think your friends are doing that?" and see what they say.

Bottom line: adult reactions and fears around sexting can definitely exacerbate the consequences of "experimental" sexting that would otherwise be harmless. This drives kids to hide in situations where they may have been pressured or coerced. **We never want our kids to be so afraid of getting in trouble or of being humiliated that they keep secrets—that make them even more vulnerable to exploitation.**

What to Do if a Photo Gets Out There

Finding out that your teen or tween has shared an image and that it has gotten circulated is a stressful situation in which your kid does need your help. In that moment, you might be tempted to chastise your child—*How could you be so careless? What were you thinking?* Often, in situations like this, parents let out their frustration and worry by showing anger.

But this is not the moment to punish your child, or to discipline them (e.g., take their phone away). Realize that you are walking into a deeply traumatic experience for your child. How you react upon finding out is pivotal in how this trauma gets dealt with. Are you going to amplify your child's trauma by punishing them and getting angry with them for something that they're already in pain about? Or are you going to create a supportive environment to show them that you are there for them, that you're their ally?

Tweens and teens who are in the middle of being humiliated online have a high frequency of depression and suicidal ideation because they don't know how to escape the pain. The humiliation feels inescapable. They need your support and, in many cases, therapy. Often, kids won't tell parents everything, so talking to a counselor (or even a lawyer, if things are very serious) might be helpful. And basic fact-gathering is also necessary: what was sent, who sent it to whom, when, and how. You want to be as calm and supportive as possible so that your child will actually tell you as much information about what's going on as they can.

For most kids, talking with their parents about a private moment that has become public—or living with the fact that a parent may have seen an image, video, or text meant to be private—can be traumatic. Phyllis L. Fagell, a middle school counselor and author of

Middle School Matters, recommends first validating your child's feelings. "Put yourself in the mind of that kid who is feeling vulnerable and insecure," she suggests. For example, you might tell your child, "I can imagine why you don't want to go to school. I probably wouldn't want to go to school, either, if I was humiliated and felt like my friends were judging me, or people were lying about me." Often, kids feel like no one hears them or believes their truth. By paraphrasing their experience, you not only demonstrate that you recognize what's happening to them, but you also show that you understand the incident's emotional impact. You're saying, "It's okay to feel this way. You're in an emotionally safe space."

Report Explicit Photo Shares

If a graphic image of a minor appears on social media or on pornographic websites, then it is important to try as hard as possible to get the image taken down. If you choose to take matters into your own hands, a stern letter from a lawyer to the teen who is posting photos, and to their parents, might be enough to get them to take it down. Sadly, you'll find little to no help from the authorities, or even your school. Laws about child pornography make reporting sexting complicated; in many states, taking an image of your own body as a minor—and sharing that image—could put minors at risk of being charged with "self-production of child pornography." And if you report sexting to the police or even your kid's school, the explicit photos, videos, or texts can become even more public before the situation is resolved. It is important that you and your child think through the various scenarios you are likely to encounter. Ask your child to consider what these might look like, and if they are ready to deal with them.

However, if your child is being stalked or threatened, then alerting the school and law enforcement may be appropriate and necessary. Depending on the circumstances, administrators may or may not find punitive action necessary. Cases like these can feel like they are never-ending and that the incident is still all everyone is talking about. But the buzz of gossip will recede eventually. Most people will understand that the child here is the victim, not the perpetrator of harm—and that alone can garner sympathy.

Conclusion

Ultimately, instead of simply fearing sexting, we must actively teach and mentor our kids on consent, flirting, relationships, and negotiating boundaries. By emphasizing the importance of tuning into their own feelings and other people's feelings, we are mentoring them to make safer and more ethical choices that honor themselves and others. Crucially, we must empower kids to get help if someone violates their boundaries. We need to lead by example in resisting being part of a culture of shaming and objectifying others. And if explicit images or messages end up circulating in our kids' school or friend group, we must teach our children to act with compassion—and with caution. Finally, if your own child's image is "out there," we need to keep their mental health in focus and be supportive rather than punitive.

Ultimately, we want to live in a world where teens can feel empowered and safe to explore their sexuality without being exploited or shamed and without harming, exploiting, or shaming others. We want to live in a world where kids navigate the complexities of romantic attraction with as much support and good self-esteem and boundaries as possible.

chapter 7

Damage Control:

When Things Go Wrong

Hannah was a first-year student at a large, diverse suburban high school in Illinois. In the early days of the lockdown, Hannah—who identifies as white—reposted a meme that blamed China for the emergence of the COVID-19 virus. It was an ill-fated attempt at humor, and the xenophobic overtones initially eluded her. Since her school had pivoted to remote classes, she wasn't seeing her friends and classmates during the initial weeks of the pandemic, so it took a while for her to realize that her peers were offended. They didn't comment, and a few even unfollowed her, but she didn't think about it much, as she was adjusting to remote school. Several weeks in, Mira, who was in her math class and considered her a "friendly acquaintance," texted Hannah directly in a Google Hangout during class. "Do you even get how racist and stupid that meme was?" Hannah scrolled back to the meme and recognized that the other girl was right. She felt remorseful and stupid—and took it down immediately.

The damage, however, was done.

When Hannah went back to in-person school the next year, the consequences of posting that meme became evident. "She had a reputation as 'the girl that shared *that* on Instagram,'" Mira told me. "A lot of people didn't like her after that." Mira acknowledged that Hannah probably didn't realize the impact the meme would have or how it would affect people. "I think she's tried to learn from that mistake, and gradually people are recognizing that she's grown as a person . . . But she's always going to have that post as a part of her reputation."

We live in a "gotcha" culture. In an instant, we can post our thoughts—well-considered or not—on social media, where our friends and followers can not only read them right away but share them with others at lightning speed. Ubiquitous cameras on our smartphones allow people to catch us in our worst moments—from doing something embarrassing to behaving in clueless ways to saying and doing harmful things—and expose us to the world. We may even be the ones exposing or commenting on other people's failings, from a momentary frustration to something more problematic—it can all be captured on social media. As a society, when we catch people engaging in harmful behavior, we are increasingly deploying the full force of social media to punish them, to make examples of them, and to make sure that we demonstrate our distance from their poor choices by shaming them.

Kids, especially teenagers, act impulsively all the time. The teenage brain is different.[1] Emotions are felt more intensely, rewards are amplified, and risks can seem less present. Both risk and novelty are more compelling during the teen years. The imagined reward of "Everybody's gonna think it's funny" may outweigh the negative consequences that they might not have considered: "This might actually be problematic because it's racist/hateful/misinformed."

Kids May Be "Just Kids," but They Don't Get a Free Pass

Here are a few mistakes that are common among tweens and teens and came up repeatedly in my interviews:

- Carelessly taking a video of themselves making a crude hand gesture or using profanity

- Making a video where they intentionally (or unintentionally) appear very cozy or affectionate with someone else's sweetheart, causing rumors and disruption in their social circles

- Sharing videos of themselves making an unkind joke about a peer or a teacher

- Take selfies where they are drinking underage, vaping, or using other illegal drugs

- Taking a video mocking someone's disability

- Wearing a racist Halloween costume

- Making fun of someone's accent or body type

- Simply "liking" or reposting peers doing any number of problematic, thoughtless things ranging from unintentional and immature to hateful and damaging

It is painful to think about these possibilities, and we all imagine our children *would never*. But . . . they might. Kids are trying to be known. They're trying to "rise above the noise" and gain attention from peers. And sometimes they mess up. Big time. Even if your kid doesn't mess up, *as far as you know*, someone in your community might, and you and your teen or tween will have to make choices about how to respond.

And yes, some of these actions are beyond merely thoughtless. A racial slur and ableist mocking are harmful and perpetuate abuse in ways that can multiply; on the other hand, using bad language or vulgar gestures may not earn your teen respect or brownie points, but it won't have the same harmful impact on your community.

Let me be clear that I am not here to be an apologist for kids taking actions that are ableist, racist, homophobic, misogynist, or xenophobic. Excusing actions because they are "just kids" can be problematic, especially when the acts are perpetuated by high schoolers or college students. After all, we've seen all too many incidences of terrifying violence and terrorism perpetrated by people who are still young themselves. Teens can and do hold one another to standards, and their schools and communities have expectations that they are learning to live in a community and that they will treat others respectfully. As one anonymous student wrote on the @BipocIgnatius Instagram account (defined in its bio as "A safe space for BIPOC students and alumni of @IgnatiusChicago to share their stories of racism"):

> *Y'all are 14–18 years old and that means you need to start learning how to hold yourselves accountable. We (BIPOC students) should not be having to call you out in order for you to start speaking up for what's right . . . I have had to call out multiple white friends for being silent and that's not my f***ing responsibility.*

And yet, despite our disappointment and even disgust with a young person who uses the internet to post something problematic, we need to get curious about why this happens and figure out how to help kids reckon with the results. Every day, teens willingly post these images without considering the consequences. Their peers have their smartphones out all the time, making it that much easier to catch a friend or peer on camera saying or doing something regrettable or maybe even indefensible. Anyone might post a picture or video without their friend's consent. The public outcry and shaming that often follows— potentially out of proportion with the offense—can be devastating and deeply isolating. A thoughtlessly and hastily posted meme on social media can lead to friends unfollowing them, to being canceled by their larger cohort of peers, to receiving school disciplinary actions, and to being judged by the whole town or community, even by people they don't know from places far beyond their hometown.

These consequences are in stark contrast to how *our* mistakes were treated when we were growing up, pre–social media. Back in the old days our transgressions were not broadcasted widely for everyone to comment on them. For instance, my college friend used to write "Heil Heitner" on his letters to me in a very ironic and what he thought funny way. Neither of us thought he was being anti-Semitic. I took this as a joke. Between us. Perhaps misguided. Importantly, we never had a conversation around it where I said, "This isn't okay." However, today, this would be called out in a big way if he were caught in a screenshot writing this to me. What would that have done to his reputation, back then and even up to today? He has a prominent job now, and had he texted or DMed me instead of writing me snail-mail letters, someone else could have seen and shared. Or if we'd had a falling-out, I could have shared the letters.

Today, the onslaught of negative attention that follows a public shaming can be so overwhelming that dealing with the public outrage itself—rather than how a young person behaved in the first place—becomes the focus.

A Range of Problematic Posts and Consequences

Shayna, a teenager attending an urban private Catholic high school, told me that a girl from her school got "a little canceled" after posting pictures of her and her family traveling in Mexico during the COVID-19 pandemic, when people were advised not to travel. "[Going to Mexico] just seemed like not a very *conscious* thing to do when people are dying," Shayna said. "Maybe if you do go, don't post about it."

In another example, Jasper, Diego, and Izzy, neurotypical freshmen at a suburban high school, sometimes sat together at lunch with Howard, a classmate who is on the autism spectrum. Howard sometimes sang to himself and responded to other boys' attention with intensified behaviors. He seemed to feel Jasper, Diego, and Izzy's attention was positive—even if their intentions were not always kind. While they were often friendly toward Howard, they sometimes also mocked him among themselves and recorded his singing on their phones. One day, Jasper and Izzy suggested singing a song with Howard, which Diego recorded. Jasper sent the video to another friend, Oscar, who thought it was funny and posted it on their school's anonymous social media account. A week later, Oscar, Jasper, Diego, and Izzy were individually called into the principal's office. They were each suspended. All four kids involved with making or sharing the video claim that they didn't have any intent to hurt Howard or make him feel bad. Oscar said to his mother, "Literally, I got a video that I thought was funny, and I passed it along. *It wasn't even a thought.*"

When Oscar's mother relayed the story to me, I asked her if there was a way to help her son understand disability, like volunteering as a buddy for Buddy Ball or doing other activities. This is only something I suggest with a remorseful kid or a young person who is ready to learn. If a young person is actively homophobic, for example, I wouldn't send them to volunteer with queer youth outreach; or if they are actively racist and committed to those beliefs, I wouldn't subject a targeted community to that hatred. Instead, I would first work with a therapist trained in helping people to confront and unlearn hate. While it is painful to consider where our children could have learned such attitudes and behaviors, we need to consider our own language and beliefs. Have we ever stood by without intervening when such language is used, perhaps afraid to intervene?

Another story that shows how the long memory of the internet can make the consequences of a harmful choice stick to a person, potentially forever, involves Charlotte de Vries. She was recruited to play field hockey at the University of North Carolina at Chapel Hill. After an Instagram video of her saying a racial slur as a high school junior went public, she lost her spot on the team. De Vries apologized and hopefully learned a lesson about how harmful that word is and how it carries a legacy of violence. The consequences of that single act were significant. Her admission to UNC–Chapel Hill was rescinded, and she was also kicked off of the national field hockey team. Eventually, de Vries was admitted to Syracuse University. Two years later, however, in the midst of a racially tense moment at Syracuse, the video resurfaced and exposed her *again*. In response, she expressed her remorse and was appreciative of her "second chance."

Black student athletes at Syracuse pointed out that Black athletes growing up in the United States don't get second chances. Speaking to a local nonprofit newsroom, Gabrielle Cooper, a prominent former basketball player at Syracuse who graduated before the video resurfaced, told the school's paper she felt "disrespected" by the university's choice to admit de Vries, knowing about her video.[2] "A lot of things deserve a second chance," Cooper told the paper. "People should get another shot on a lot of things. That's not one of them."

Another story. When Jordan Blue was a junior at Baraboo High School in Baraboo, Wisconsin, he was photographed standing uncomfortably among his classmates, more than half of whom who were making a Nazi salute with their arms or making a white nationalist "okay" symbol with their fingers. This picture included most of the town's eleventh-grade boys, dressed up and in a public spot in town, right before the junior prom. Seconds earlier, the photographer, a father of one of the classmates, had told the teenagers to "make the sign"; some responded with the "Heil Hitler" arm gesture, while others merely waved, and still others kept their hands at their sides. The photograph lived quietly on the photographer's website until a small local Twitter account shared it.[3] Another local woman shared it with several journalists on Twitter with an exhortation for the local schools to "do better."

The picture went viral. Right away, the boys and the community were under fire (all but Jordan, whose reaction precipitated an outpouring of support and earned a "Be like #JordanBlue" hashtag). Soon the small town of Baraboo was crowded with national media. The high school's teachers and administrators got endless angry emails and phone calls, and the school even received bomb threats. On Twitter, some adults advocated sharing the photo as widely as possible to forever cement the damage to the kids' reputation. "Remember their faces, don't hire them. Don't let them in your college," tweeted one.

Meanwhile, parents of the boys who were in the picture became protective and encouraged their sons not to speak about the incident. Instead of reckoning with what they had done in the photograph, and the bigger picture problem of the culture of racism and homophobia at the high school, the school administration initially shut down the conversation.[4] While a few of the boys in the picture made individual apologies to Jewish families they knew who felt hurt and threatened by the photograph, there was no systematic conversation or attempt at restorative conversation.[5] In fact, the media blitz and the protective reaction seem to have prevented students who regretted their action from coming forward and facing the truth of how the gesture had affected their neighbors and friends.

In the case of de Vries and the kids in Baraboo, the troubling actions were a documented *performance* by the teens. De Vries went on

Why would kids post something that will get them into trouble? In *Brainstorm*, psychiatrist Daniel J. Siegel explains that brain changes in the early teen years set up "four qualities of our minds during adolescence: novelty seeking, social engagement, increased emotional intensity, and creative exploration. Teens seek rewards in trying new things, like connecting with peers in different ways." As Dr. Siegel points out, these changes to the teenage brain have many upsides, but they do have some downsides as well, and social media can be a place where these consequences are amplified because of widely available sharing and digital permanence. An advantage of the novelty-seeking teen brain is that teens are willing to try new things and take on positive challenges like a new sport, new friendships, or a hard class. On the other hand, "impulsivity can turn an idea into an action without a pause to reflect on consequences."[6] Like sharing a meme in the blink of an eye.

Instagram live with a friend, laughing and repeating the racial slur while expressing shock at themselves. They were also vaping. They seemed conscious of their transgressions, and the very act of posting seemed to have been a bid for . . . notoriety? It is fair to ask: *What were they thinking?* Here, as in Baraboo, the camera provided the occasion to commit the action.

These four scenarios involve a similar dynamic: photographs and videos are used against kids to shame them via social media. Now, public shaming is nothing new. In fact, it's been around forever. While we no longer brand people with a scarlet letter or place them in the pillory in the town square, there is something about shaming that human societies seem to be drawn to. Today, public shaming is, once again, on the rise. Books like Jon Ronson's *So You've Been Publicly Shamed* and Sue Scheff's *Shame Nation* have documented how this resurgence is powered by our digital technologies and social media, which can amplify both our mistakes and the fallout we receive for them.

"Kids know there are consequences to posting the wrong thing, but when it happens, it is brutal. Canceling online is one thing; canceling in real life is super lonely. And there are no boundaries anymore between online and real life for these teenagers. It's all mixed up. There are no clear boundaries, and it's never ending. It's all night long. It's first thing in the morning. There's no break from it except for the hours that you're actually sleeping."[7]

—Dr. Katie Hurley

Whose Schools? Our Schools! How Communities Can Support BIPOC Students

When racist posts appear, everyone expects schools to find and address the offender and to support directly targeted individuals. Building or rebuilding trust with BIPOC students, especially after incidents of racism, is also crucial. Principal and anti-racist school expert Henry Turner learned this from experience. Turner, along with his DEI colleague Kathy Lopes, cowrote *Change the Narrative: How to Foster an Antiracist Culture in Your School*.

Turner took on the principalship at Newton North High School in Massachusetts in the nationally tense election season of fall of 2016, and just a few weeks into the school year, a small group of students made a video of themselves driving around the school driveway with a Confederate flag. The video went viral. Students, parents, and people outside the school community expressed their opinion. Some students of color, frustrated by this on top of incidents in previous years, felt it was time for direct action. Meanwhile, white supremacist groups threatened to show up if there was direct action outside the school. Concerned for students' safety, Turner focused on listening to students, readily agreeing to a 10:00 p.m. Google Meet. Turner and the students were able to agree to an in-school action that included over five hundred students and staff that offered a chance for students to be heard.

The students shared experiences of the racism they would experience daily, from both students and staff, and the lack of connection they felt with the school. At the end of the protest, Turner took the microphone and expressed his support for the movement and his pride that their school had been able to host such an event. The pride of the student leaders was clear, too. They knew they were making a difference in their school.

Later, the school experienced another incident, a series of racist posts on social media. The administrators diligently investigated and identified the creators and supported the victims. They felt they had addressed the problem thoughtfully, possibly even "created a textbook example of how to respond to handle these incidents." But students of color felt ignored and unheard—because although the administrators had dealt with the situation, they hadn't addressed it with the larger community, and the students said, "We don't think you care that this happened."

A visible response is crucial, Turner emphasized. After such an incident, "administrators need to do everything they can to show up for and build trust with their students of color." Parents, community members, and administrators need to not just find and give consequences to offenders but recognize that an incident like this requires a community response to deal with the deeper-seated problems.

I have witnessed this, too. Recently, in my own community in suburban Chicago, there was a racist incident at a local high school, and parents, community members, and teachers, including educators from other high schools, did a solidarity walkout alongside the students at the school. We stood on the sidewalk near piles of snow and listened to students, some of whom had walked out with-out jackets into a Chicago winter. One student, Briyanna Manzanares-Etienne, took the mic and said, "Why does it take the publication of the discrimination we are experiencing every single day for our school to finally acknowledge our pain?"

When there isn't a direct response to address the needs of the community, the gap leaves people hurt and grasping. Sometimes in an effort to do something, to get some response, people amplify the incident—an understandable impulse to seek justice and judgment by a wider public—when it feels like the school or immediate community has done nothing.

Why do these incidents seem to happen so frequently? While teens overall are more likely to support Black Lives Matter than adults, the deep rifts and systemic racism in our society affect teens, too.[8] Also, social media can feel like an attention game—and the bolder statements or more outrageous posts can elicit a reaction. In some cases, a young person may say a racial slur because it feels like an exciting, transgressive game, and they may not comprehend the weight and violence of their words. The phenomenon of online disinhibition, where people might say things they would never say in person because the audience online feels abstract, certainly contributes to the prevalence of these kinds of incidents.[9] Sometimes drugs or alcohol contribute to the disinhibition. Sometimes the post is only intended for a small audience. This doesn't diminish the impact a harmful post can have, but it is important to attempt to understand intent when we respond. It gives us a clue that anti-racist education must go deeper than simply forbidding slurs, but making sure young people have a deep understand-ing of racial terrorism, colonialism, and the violence toward BIPOC individuals and communities that is embedded in American and world history. Anti-racist education ideally starts early—in *How to Raise an Antiracist*, Ibram X. Kendi makes a compelling case that anti-racist education in preschool give kids what author Jason Reynolds calls "antibodies" to our societal sickness of racism.

In Owatonna, Minnesota, a small, predominantly white town, the community experienced an incident where a white kid posted a video of other white kids using a racial slur.[10] First the post led to a physical fight, where a Black student was arrested. After this, two more white students posted racial slurs on social media. Following a fight and arrest at school, Black students, who were a small minority at the local high school, demanded change, saying that they experienced racial slurs and other interpersonal racist violence at school all the time.

Adding to the outrage of students and families of color, when racist incidents happen at schools where BIPOC students are targets, Black students often experience disproportionate discipline in the aftermath. In one school, a Black member of the wrestling team was suspended for four days for sharing his white teammate's racist post with another Black wrestler. School leaders may focus initially on shutting down the sharing and containing the conversation—rather than the content of what was shared and what it revealed about the school climate that their Black students face every day. The Black students were disciplined for sharing the post because the principal said it contributed to the climate of unrest at the school; the school ended up punishing the victims of racism who were concerned about their personal well-being rather than focusing on the problems that led to the racist content in the first place.

However, over time, the students participated in mediated meetings and attended diversity training. Because of the ongoing conversation, several of the white students involved in the initial post seemed to have grown in their understanding of both historical and contemporary racism. It took time. The kids involved were initially reluctant to acknowledge how much their words and actions hurt their Black classmates, but they grew to recognize their own responsibility to stop perpetuating racist views. Parents and school leaders should view incidents like this as a symptom of a bigger problem—an indicator that the whole community has work to do.

Documenting police abuses can be powerful agents for social

change, but it is less clear how widely circulating a video of a kid saying something terrible accomplishes a similar goal. It is important to address the behavior, through consequences for the person who posted, and empathetic and practical support for those targeted, but simply fueling outrage doesn't accomplish what some might hope it does. Further, making "an example" of a teen or tween also paradoxically risks absolving others. It makes one person or small group the "bad guy"—while the whole community gets a free pass from examining their own behaviors.

In Leesburg, Virginia, fifteen-year-old Mimi Groves uttered a racist slur on a video message she made when she got her learner's permit. A classmate shared the message a few years later when Groves got into college. Once the footage was shared publicly with the college, Groves was forced to withdraw. Shaming her may have offered some outlet for the frustration that Black students experienced at the school, which reportedly was "rife with racial insensitivity, including casual uses of slurs," but naming Groves as the sole perpetrator of racism left the racial culture of the larger community at Heritage High School in Leesburg unexamined. This is a school district where the *failures* to teach against racism have been persistent and extreme. Educators in that district made Black students portray people who were enslaved during "lessons" on the Underground Railroad. Given the community's history, letting Mimi Groves become the exemplar for racism when she was essentially forced to withdraw from the University of Tennessee can make the community feel vindicated without doing the necessary work: *See, we had a racist person here, but she got caught and got in trouble. The problem has been addressed.* When one person goes viral, it becomes all about that one person—not about the whole community. It *might* make some feel vindicated, but it doesn't usher in a new era of understanding and acceptance—that would take more work.

Keeping young people out of college can feel satisfying if it seems like they "got away" with something in high school. When the Baraboo photo went viral months after it was taken, thousands of adults commented on social media calling for boys in the photo to be kept out of college. But . . . don't we *want* them to go to college? To meet people who are different from them? And have their beliefs challenged? What is college for, if not to help raise consciousness—to challenge preexisting ideas? College isn't just a prize for doing well in high school or for being a good kid. It is a place that could potentially correct some of their deficiencies and offer lessons that push back against ignorance.

All communities should be doing proactive, anti-racist work and holding up a mirror to the whole community, not just reacting when these things come to light in a social media post. Too many high schools are unsafe environments where students who are targeted for their racial identity are left to fend for themselves. It should surprise no one to see young people wielding their skills on social media as a weapon or a shield when they have been otherwise ignored. In addition to incorporating anti-racist teaching into the curriculum, parents should support schools holding young people (and teachers!) accountable for racist actions in the setting where they occur, and initiating a thoughtfully planned, restorative process that gives everyone a chance to learn, heal, and understand the impact of their actions. It is especially important for students who have been targeted to be heard and to be able to participate in the restorative process in a way that prioritizes their safety.

Part of the "solution" to viral shaming is making sure there are proper channels for reporting. Schools need to focus not on shutting down the conversation as crisis PR, but on moving the conversation forward in a way that addresses the root of the problem. We need more principals to say yes to the 10:00 p.m. Google Meet like Henry Turner did. And we need more anti-racist school leaders in general, which requires a willingness to reflect on white supremacist thinking and its harms at a deep level.

Until schools and communities get better at restorative practices, self-examination, and real consequences for perpetrators of harm, we should expect racist behaviors to be documented and shared on social media as a way of exposing their behavior widely and attempting to bring about accountability and consequences.

I asked Dr. Traci Baxley, author of *Social Justice Parenting*, what parents can do when racist incidents like this happen in their communities. She told me, "We can teach our kids about being upstanders . . . to arm them with the information they need to be able to stand in their truth, right, and to be able to . . . talk back, you know, to things that don't align with their core values. But I also think it's really important that we teach our kids to draw boundaries, because sometimes we can get lost in that, trying to be the martyr in some ways. And so I try to tell my children that, you know, I want them to be the upstander. I want them to be able to hear people's perspective and also give their own. But when it starts to kind of infringe on their mental health, they have a right to set boundaries around that."

Parents can put pressure on school leadership and their wider communities to make school, home, and community safe for those targeted, rather than focusing on maximum exposure to the harm—because, in some ways, that is also multiplying the harm. Shaming via exposure and social opprobrium without intervention may be dangerous. The harms could outweigh the "positive" intent of drawing a line in the sand. There are documented cases of adults dying by and attempting suicide after public "cancellation," so doing this to teenagers is just not safe. As a community member, if the need to express outrage drives you to action, try to find ways to support the targets of the hateful speech or actions instead of focusing on re-sharing the post or focusing on the offender.

Shame vs. Guilt

While guilt can prompt corrective action, social researcher Brené Brown writes that shame can lead to further destructive or hurtful behavior. She describes shame as "an intensely painful feeling or experience of believing that we are flawed and therefore unworthy of love and belonging—something we've experienced, done, or failed to do makes us unworthy of connection."[11] Taya Cohen, an organizational psychologist, says, "That's the key distinction between guilt and shame . . . 'You did a bad thing' vs. 'You are a bad person.'"[12] A person who posts an angry rant on social media "might feel guilty and later apologize," but "a so-called shame response to the same situation would make you feel like a horrible, worthless person," which might not lead to the same level of corrective action, since you are then in the shame spiral. One of the problems with shame, especially if it is heaped on by many people, is that once a person feels worthless, taking action to repair the wrongdoing might feel impossible.

We may not feel sympathetic toward the Baraboo High School boys who were pictured making a Nazi salute. After all, shouldn't they be held accountable for their offensive behavior? Yet, if the adults in Baraboo had not shared the photo out of shame, but had addressed the implications with the kids and urged them to repair relationships with friends and neighbors, and had the adults also examined the wider culture of racism in their town, that could have been transformative. Instead, many became defensive. Hiding and finger-pointing do *not* lead to transformation. Do the kids who made the Nazi salute feel bad about what they did or about being caught and exposed? When kids in a community are exposed for racist acts, does the community of adults that raised and educated those kids share in the responsibility and therefore the obligation to self-examine?

PUBLIC SHAMING IS ESPECIALLY DAMAGING FOR KIDS

While we should never condone kids' offensive actions, adults should be cautious about weaponizing social media against them. We should question what our purpose is for doing so. Sometimes public shaming is a way of "virtue signaling," disavowing the inappropriate or hurtful act. The more thoroughly we shame the kid, the more we're trying to distance ourselves from them. Other times, public shaming is a way to mete out punishment and make permanent a child's worst moment. But if you really want to understand where they got that hate, disdain, or fear, you have to engage with them. Directly.

Instead of teaching their kid to be better when faced with that level of attention, many parents will do what the parents of the Baraboo kids did: encourage them to go underground, rather than deal with their anti-Semitic beliefs (or even their cluelessness about history). It's essential to consider what decisions, experiences, and education led to the filmed moment. **What if it wasn't "just one moment"?** Rather than teaching kids "Don't get caught," we need to be sure we're teaching them not to be hateful, racist, xenophobic, homophobic, etc. We need to teach them not to go with the angry mob, which is on the internet, trying to recruit kids (especially white boys).

Reckoning with one's actions and their impact on others is part of growing up, and it's going to be painful at times. Getting exposed and shamed online for Nazi salutes or racial slurs is not the way we want our kids to learn—even watching it happen to others may not teach the lessons we might hope for. But we *do* want kids to face their own ignorance and learn from their mistakes. We want kids and teens to reckon with privilege and to understand that systemic racism does affect them. Young people of color and others who have been targeted urgently need spaces to call peers and adults into awareness and accountability.

PUBLIC SHAMING CAN BACKFIRE

Truly remorseful kids have a better opportunity to make things right if they are allowed to take restorative actions such as apologizing in person, taking a class, and speaking or writing about what they have learned. While shaming might seem appropriate for perpetrators who double down on their offensive behavior or seem to be faking remorse, total shunning from the community can have tragic consequences.

If we simply shame students without asking hard questions about the origins of their actions, we may isolate kids. Once isolated, they may become more entrenched in antisocial beliefs. Christian Picciolini, a former white supremacist leader who is now an anti-racist educator, argues that marginalization or shunning can make youth even more vulnerable to recruitment to hate groups. "If there's one thing I learned along my own journey, it's that having empathy and offering compassion—often for those we feel least deserve it—*is* the only path toward change. Hold people accountable for their actions, question things, speak truth to power, get mad as hell, prepare to fight back if attacked, but drill down to the underlying motivations that led them there. Having lived on both sides of hate, I see it in ways that are difficult for most to understand. Strangers, people I believed hated me on principle alone, showed me empathy when I least deserved it. It was a triumph of humanization over demonization. Now I use the same tactic—*to see the child, not the monster.* This mantra is the foundation on which I build the trust necessary to help people disengage from extremism."[13]

In the wake of a viral moment when people are directing their understandable anger at someone who has behaved badly, it is hard to gauge a "proportional" response. Parents of the perpetrator may experience an urge to push back against those they perceive as "haters" and ignore the criticism of their child's behavior. The sheer weight of people's attack can immobilize parents, making it difficult to figure out an appropriate next move. "You go into immediate protection mode," says Michael Una, a strategic communications expert who has helped companies put out public relations "fires." Our instincts might tell us, "We're turning off all our phones."

And why wouldn't we? If a kid you care about committed a transgression, but an angry mob is calling for the child to suffer long-term repercussions—ranging from being "canceled," to being expelled from school, to being blacklisted by colleges and employers—it can feel like a transgression *against* the child. When parents read comments like "Make sure they never get a job," they perceive a clear threat and move to defend against it, like any parent would. Even if parents are disturbed by what their child has done, they may still become their crisis PR managers.

"When everyone on the internet is mad at you, the experience threatens your very concept of yourself," Una explains. "You must accept the level of punishment that's being visited upon you by the internet, which no one actually deserves. So in one sense

[families] are doing the right thing by blocking [it] all out, but then they have also lost that opportunity to actually learn from the experience."

The high school in Baraboo received bomb threats, and the town was besieged by the media. Parents there simply wanted their children to have as little public association with the controversial photo as possible. But by discouraging their kids from coming forward, parents instead hurt their young adults' chances of truly reckoning with the impact of their mistake. The way the situation was handled in general robbed them of that opportunity. Instead, parents adopted a defensive posture. Universal blame was thrown around without any level of nuance. There were denials and attempts to bury the story. Baraboo could have had a moment where kids—and their parents— thoughtfully confronted their own racism. Instead, most folks ended up walking away unchanged.

How Parents Can Help Stop the Cycle of Shaming and Help Our Kids Become Better People

The first thing we must do to change the dynamics of public shaming is to model the right behaviors to our kids. There is a long history of using the press to fight moral battles when people in power have ignored us. Shaming a hospital for suing its own patients may be a good use of this power. Heaping vitriol upon a high school kid for their actions is weaponizing social media against someone considerably less powerful.

After her family moved to a wealthy Atlanta suburb, Dina's eighth grader, Karl, joined a group of kids that made Dina nervous. Karl was invited to a pool party, where a girl handed him a bunch of vaping pens, and he posed for a goofy picture that looked like he was smoking them all. "It was a stupid, stupid photo," Dina said. Karl told the girl to delete it immediately, but she didn't. Instead, she posted it on Snapchat, where kids screenshotted and saved it. Later that summer, a parent found the photo and shared it with all the parents in this social group, encouraging them not to include Karl in their kids' social gatherings. Karl was dropped by his friends and ostracized. The social shunning was so painful that he left his new school, started being homeschooled, and sought treatment for anxiety.

Although it's unusual for parents to be responsible for "canceling" another child, this isn't the only story that I have heard of it happening. It is troubling enough when kids do this to one another, but it is particularly painful to hear about a photo being weaponized against a kid *by an adult.*

If you are ever tempted to share or comment on an image or video showing kids at their worst (especially if they are identifiable), ask yourself: What are your motivations for sharing? If you live in the same community as the kids, can you speak to them directly? Can you speak to their parents? If not, can you notify the kids' school's teacher, principal, superintendent, or the local police? Teach your kids to do the same.

Of course, if you see someone doing something harmful—such as behaving in ways that are hurtful, racist, or homophobic—you must respond. The distinction here is that posing with the Juul harms . . . no one. Vaping harms the "vaper," not others. If you do see a post documenting a harmful act, focus on identifying the perpetrators and seeking accountability. Prioritize caring for and making safe members of the targeted communities.

Teach Your Kids What Consent Truly Means

Explain to kids that they can't just assume a video or photograph of another person is okay to share; they must think about how the other person might feel once their image is out there. But context matters, and it's important that the person you are getting consent from understands the whole picture. In the case of Jasper, Diego, and Izzy—the freshmen who made the video of Howard, a classmate on the spectrum—and Oscar—who shared it—Howard may have consented to the boys videotaping him because he was enjoying their attention, but he might not have fully understood the boys' motivations. So what would true consent have looked like in that case? The boys might have had to ask Howard, "Hey, can I take this video of you behaving in this way that lots of other kids think is weird and funny, and post it to this underground account so people who don't even know you can laugh at you singing?" Had they really considered consent in these stark terms for themselves, they might have realized that what they were doing was hurtful.

The following are some considerations about posting photos and videos:

- **Don't post something that's not yours to post.** Don't share something that's not your story to tell, whether it is a video of someone that you took without their permission or something that you know will cause reputational harm.

- **Be careful about anonymous accounts.** It is easy to get into trouble there. Nothing is really anonymous. Reposting something to a school's "confessions" account or "tea" account doesn't take away from your accountability for sharing something hurtful.

- **Humor is complicated.** Someone may be the target of a joke. We can explain to our kids that sometimes a word is "allowed" for some people but not others. For example, in a circle of women friends, they might use the B-word as a humorous greeting. Boys and men should avoid the word.

- **Rethink the urge to record.** Kids often reach for their phones out of discomfort, or when they don't know how to deal with a situation. And they've all been encouraged to record: "If you see something that's weird, you know, take a video, that's how you deal with the situation." A lot of it has to do with *Hey, I want someone else to validate my feelings about this.* I've talked to parents of three different kids who were suspended for taking nonconsensual videos of other kids engaging in sex, so although you may think this is obvious, let kids know that if they walk in on people having sex in a school bathroom, the way to deal with their discomfort is to head back out the door, *not* to get out their phone. In one case, the mother said the only thing her daughter documented was the feet of the busy couple under the stall . . . but it turned out one of the two participants was identifiable through their footwear, and the video caused significant embarrassment and harm. Recording a fight instead of getting help can put people in danger. Recording friends who are drunk or high can have all kinds of consequences. On the other hand, there have been times when recording was essential and brave; for example, when a teenage girl recorded George Floyd's murder. Our phones are powerful recording devices. Motivation and context are crucial here.

- **Rethink the urge to share.** Kids share very quickly. Yes, if your kids see a hateful or threatening or vile image, they should tell their parents and administrators, but they should also resist posting it on social media or even texting it to someone, which can perpetuate harm. *Tell*, don't send.

What Can Parents Do
If Their Child Is the Target of Public Shaming?

When our kids make mistakes that lead to "being canceled" or public shaming, it's important that they feel safe confiding in us. This requires laying the groundwork for open communication. Spying on our kids by reading their text messages (especially covertly) may encourage them to expend energy hiding from us instead. Being open and direct about any monitoring we are doing is crucial in building trust. It's our right as parents to be aware of what our kids are doing, but even more important is making sure they know *we are there for them*, no matter what. Kids should understand that no mistake makes them unworthy of our affection or support.

Our role, therefore, is to support our kids through their ups and downs and find the lessons in those downs—though that's sometimes easier said than done in the face of a public fallout. Public shame can make kids "hide," which is dangerous, because when this happens, we can't help them. That's why when a problem arises, we must tread carefully to avoid sending our kids into a shame spiral that may actually compound the public shaming. We want to maintain trust and openness—it's our best opportunity to help.

When your kid gets caught up in a public maelstrom, do the following:

1. Validate your child's experience.
2. Keep them safe.
3. Take steps to examine their actions.
4. Take steps to repair harm.
5. Take steps to move forward.

CALM THE STORM

"If a child is in a state of high emotion, they're going to feed that [frenzied, gossiping] energy," school counselor and author Phyllis L. Fagell explains. "What you're aiming to do is to tamp down the excitement around the incident and help extinguish it from the conversation, so people aren't continuing to gossip about it." Work with the school's counselor to prepare your child for kids' reactions. While some peers may tease or insult your kid, others might express sympathy or support. Unfortunately, anything that keeps the incident at the forefront of people's minds keeps the rumor mill going. Working together, you, your child, and the counselor can rehearse some generic responses. If someone says, "I heard there was a video of you vaping that got sent around," Fagell suggests a response like, "Yes, that's true, but it's in the past, and I don't want to talk about it anymore." She adds, "They can just come up with that dry story or that dry response and the end of the response could be 'I'm not allowed to say anything.'" Fagell explains that making the response "totally unsatisfying" is a good strategy; it's hard for gossip to spiral indefinitely if it hits a dead end.

Once a child's emotional safety has been addressed, you can begin addressing their physical safety. What may have started online can easily affect their face-to-face social world. Tensions that begin (or intensify) on social media or via text can even erupt into physical confrontation at school or outside of school. There are some situations that are so isolating that a new start might feel helpful. A jury of their peers might be even worse than the abstract threat of "the public" or even getting suspended from school. As a society, we have to figure out how to move forward, and there may be some benefit to starting fresh, possibly by changing schools, if that is a possibility. And while it's important not to overreact, we *do* need to respond. We need to soberly evaluate the situation and identify if there is a legitimate threat or imminent danger.

TAKE STEPS TO MOVE FORWARD

As a parent, you can't reverse time and prevent your child's transgression from happening. Focus on deeper reflection, rather than a quick reputation Band-Aid. "There needs to be space to admit that [they've] done something wrong," Michael Una says. "Then [they] can say, 'I'm accepting all the judgment that comes with that.'"

Reflection also requires helping a young person think through these questions: Why did doing that offensive thing seem appealing? What emotions framed it? Was there another way those emotions could have been expressed? If your child finds themself in a similar situation in the future, what choice would you like to see them make instead? What choice do they hope to see themselves making? And are there steps they can take to prevent this from happening again?

After reflection comes contrition. And embracing the consequences of their actions is the first step toward contrition. Doing so says, "I see what I've done, and I aim to make it better." It's a show of good faith, a statement that they care. When this is done openly, in public, the community can start to heal.

In extreme cases, young people who have caused harm may need to put out a statement online. But the first step is to take it offline and really understand what has happened. "The right consequence serves as a lasting reminder to do the work of continuing change," wrote Hanna Stotland, a former attorney who now works as a consultant specializing in admissions (and readmissions) of high school and college students who have run into significant disciplinary challenges.[14] Stotland also works with high school and college students accused of sexual assault. I admit that I was ambivalent about meeting with Stotland at first because I was concerned that she would be an apologist for sexual assault, a crime that too often goes unpunished on campus. But I learned a lot about how the disciplinary process works (and doesn't work) when I spoke with her.

"My work with [these students] requires them . . . to push back against the temptation to place blame on others; to prove, not just to announce, that they are working to change," she explained to me. "They have to disclose the worst thing they've ever done or the worst thing they've ever been accused of."

Conclusion

Of course, we'd all like to avoid the need for damage control in the first place. Rather than be reactive, we want to be proactive—especially when it comes to racism, homophobia, and other forms of oppression. Being proactive is ideal. It is important to emphasize character, rather than the threat of consequences, to prevent harmful incidents from occurring.

But when they do occur, we need to respond. Parents need to *help* and teach—with a focus on creating a safe environment for the targets of the harm and for the community. Parents of the kids who have created harmful posts need allies who can help them look honestly at the situation and avoid utter denial. Embracing the consequences is the first step of contrition. When this is done openly, in public, the community can start to heal.

At every step, we as parents see our children at their best and at their worst. We can help them move forward from their worst moments. We do that by holding them accountable in age-appropriate ways. We can make it clear to them that *they have our support* in moving forward even if they have done something disappointing. Then we can build out from there, enlisting the community to help our kids grow up as well. In turn, when we do the same for other kids in our neighborhoods and schools, we are building a support system that makes *all* of our kids safer and more responsible.

chapter 8

Who's *Really* Looking at You, Kid?
Are Colleges Actually Stalking Kids' Posts?

How much do colleges really look at what my kid and his friends have posted?

Will something my kid posted prevent them from getting into the college of their (and our) dreams?

Does my child need to explain her disparate interests to package her "personal brand"?

Should my foster son "sell" the adversity he's been through to make himself appealing?

How can my complicated, brilliant, but unevenly performing teen see themselves as a human being when their counselor keeps showing them a representation of themselves as a dot on a scattergram?

These are some of the most common and fervent questions I get from parents whenever I give a talk. They speak to the stress that we parents feel these days about our kids' futures. We've become incredibly invested in their success. (Our overidentification even manifests in our speech: How many times have you heard a parent say "we" are applying to college?) It's no surprise then that some parents say their worst fear is that a stupid (or drunken) post might ruin years of hard work and education.

In my interviews with parents, high school students, and admissions officers, I learned that parents and kids both may overestimate how much digital surveillance is actually happening. Young people are divided about how "fair" it is for colleges to use a digital search about them in the process. Carrie James and Emily Weinstein, researchers at Harvard's Project Zero and authors of the informative book *Behind Their Screens*, found that an almost equal number of teens found it "fair" versus unfair for colleges to check their social data. While slightly more teens found it fair, I was surprised to see that a majority of educators and parents in the poll found it fair.[1] It seems like parents and educators believe that this is happening, and they are okay with it. The good news is, for the most part, it isn't happening. I also think we should rethink how comfortable we are with it.

These are some common worries parents shared about their kids' digital reputations and college admissions:

- If my kid's gaming channel on YouTube features videos of him swearing, will colleges see him as profane? Will they think he games more than he studies?

- Could my daughter's Instagram dance reels and TikTok videos and the many comments on them about how "sexy" she is cost her admission to her top college?

- Should my scholarship-applying athlete salutatorian daughter scrub all her high school partying photos from social media?

- What about my son's complaints on social media about a certain teacher or internship boss?

- Is it okay to have wide-ranging activities that don't "go together"?

- Is it okay to quit an activity that no longer brings you joy or does that make you seem "inconsistent"?

We hope our emerging young adults will see themselves from the inside out—by being true to themselves and their own values. They should claim their own voice, opinions, and interests. Still, we know that the world is looking at them from the outside, and that kids growing up with constant awareness of their public presence and searchability may overemphasize seeing themselves from the outside in.

The Myth of Personal Brand: Focus on Character Instead of "Branding"

When we parents fret about our kids' reputations online, we are not so much worried about whether they are seen as "good people," but how their very public life will affect their future, and by extension how *we* will be perceived as parents. College and job prospects can seem like rewards for a childhood and adolescence well lived—and thus parenting "well done." After reading stories in the media about teens who lose scholarships or have their admission offers rescinded because of something they posted, we wonder, *Could that be my kid next?*

To prevent that from happening, we often scare our teens into having a sedate virtual presence, even a perfectly curated one. We urge them to scrub anything from it that may seem questionable: *You won't get into college if you post a picture of you wearing* that*! You can say goodbye to that internship if they find a post where you're swearing!*

Yet high school is a time when we lose influence over our teens. When they stop listening to us, we are tempted to invoke the threat of ruined college admissions chances to scare them into complying with our requests. But when we threaten kids with the future (e.g., colleges and companies won't want you if you post that!), we are weaponizing the idea of the "public" for our own agenda. There are two consequences:

1. We are not being honest with them about why we don't want them doing these things. If we don't want our kid swearing on social media, there are lots of great reasons we can give them for why it's not a good thing to do. Not getting into college probably isn't the top one—and a few F-bombs on social media posts are unlikely to keep them out of college anyway. In keeping the conversation narrow about swearing, or clothing choices, we risk missing the bigger conversation about character. We are letting ourselves off the hook from having tough talks with our kids about what kinds of behaviors and values they want to be known for in the many communities they participate in.

2. We are sending the message that from an early age kids must cultivate a "perfect" online persona—a personal brand—that they can deploy when they have to "sell themselves" to college admissions officers, potential employers, or even potential dates. Putting pressure on them to always "be on brand" is an unacceptable limitation for any human, especially teenagers who should be free to experiment with their identity, grow, and change.

Instead, we should encourage our kids to work on their personhood—their character, their values—for the sake of making a positive impact in the world, not for the sake of "selling" themselves to colleges and future employers. And this is not just online, but in every aspect of their lives. Then their authentic character will shine through as they grow up in the public eye.

The Problem with "You Won't Get into College If You Post *That*!"

Although parents often think their kids are oblivious to how they are perceived by others on social media—*He didn't even think before he posted that!*—kids today are acutely aware that as they post images, videos, and comments, they are "curating" an online presence or persona. The tension is that, well, they are teenagers, experimenting with who they are. The digital persona they may want to communicate *at that moment in their lives* may not be one you are happy about. Your teenager may want to be known as sexy and "hot." You probably don't. They may want to be known as a grunge skater or as someone who doesn't care about anything. You probably don't want that, either. Parents tell me over and over: they are terrified their teenagers—who share and reveal more on social media than they are comfortable with—will post a picture or comment that will cost them admission to their top college.

The reality is, our kids' futures—especially their college careers—don't depend on their social media profiles. When applying to college, if your child isn't eliminated by some overarching criteria such as not meeting the minimum grade requirements, the admissions committee will consider their file for only five to seven minutes. High school college counselor Jim Jump told me that "in the last ten to twenty years, [colleges] are getting many more applications. They're not hiring more staff to read those applications. Students and parents would be appalled to realize . . . how little time colleges spend reading applications compared to how much time students spend on applications." That short amount of time does not usually include an extensive online background check of candidates, or a deep dive into their social media history.

Colleges Don't "Dig up Dirt" on Social Media

For the most part, colleges expect that most applicants are reasonably good human beings who are still developing. They trust that young people are who they say they are on their college applications. Admissions officers don't go out of their way to dig up dirt on applicants. "The agreement is that your application will be reviewed fairly on whatever you report," explains Sonja Montiel, an independent college counselor who's been guiding high school students through admissions for over twenty years.

Tina Brooks in the Pomona College Admissions office agreed. "We don't check a student's social media as any part of the admissions process. On occasion, staff members may look at a student's social media." That may happen, Brooks explained, if the student includes a link to a URL to show off some relevant work they've done, like a video they starred in for an extracurricular activity. If the website includes links to social media accounts, an admissions officer might follow that link and peruse the applicant's profile.

A 2019 survey conducted by Kaplan revealed that 36 percent of admissions officers acknowledge *sometimes* checking *some aspect* of an applicant's social media, an increase from 2018.[2] However, they self-report that this is not something they do routinely, which means 64 percent of surveyed admissions officers report never checking *any* social media for *any* of the thousands of students they review. In all my conversations with college admissions staff, they emphasized the time limitations that would make an extensive "background check" implausible.

Colleges Rarely Reject Students Because of Their Social Media (But It Does Happen Sometimes)

An applicant at a highly competitive college is far more likely to be rejected because of "fit," grades, or simply because the admissions committee chose a different student with achievements, talents, or background that better rounded out the incoming class in a certain way—rather than because of an online misstep. But when it happens, it is typically because a social media profile raised significant red flags about questionable or potentially problematic behavior.

"We found a student's Twitter account with some really questionable language," said one admissions officer. "It wasn't quite racist, but it showed a cluelessness that you'd expect of a privileged student who hadn't seen much of the world. It really ran counter to the rest of her application." Another admissions officer shared that "a young man who had been involved in a felony did not disclose his past, which is part of our admissions process. His social media page shared his whole story. If he had been forthcoming, we would not have rescinded his acceptance offer, but we had to." Yet another admissions officer said that pictures of a student "brandishing weapons" gave him pause when deciding whether to admit the applicant. These are all examples of admissions officers deciding that a student might bring an undesirable trait (i.e., racism, insensitivity, unethical behavior, violence) to campus.

How likely is it that your child will be rejected for anything they posted on their social media accounts? According to a 2017 survey by Inside Higher Ed, just 7 percent of private schools report having done it at least once. But a whopping 93 percent of them said they have *never* turned away someone over a social media post.

When I asked journalist Jeffrey Selingo, author of *Who Gets In and Why*, if a social media profile can really torpedo an applicant, he agreed it is *incredibly rare*. But in the unlikely event that students are rejected due to something they posted, the college probably learned about these posts from someone who took it upon themselves to report them. "That's how these schools are finding out about something on social media," said Selingo. In other words, admissions officers aren't out there scouring social media to find posts that will disqualify kids, but they may investigate the posts if someone brings them to their attention.

Although the number of students who have been turned away from colleges because of their social media is quite small, many of the parents I meet believe this is a significant threat. The media does love a good takedown story—for example, some students whose offers were rescinded from Harvard in 2017 got a lot of media attention.[3] When we read stories like this, it is hard not to worry, especially since some of these cases have revolved around messages shared in private groups, just to a few friends. There is likely no way the university could have found something like that without it being brought to their attention by a third party.

Overemphasis on College Admissions
Sends the Wrong Message about What Truly Matters

Should we encourage kids to think before they post and not share every passing thought? Well, yes. But we should do it because we want our kids to avoid offending and harming others with their words or actions because it is inherently the right thing to do, not because we're afraid they won't get into college. We don't wait for our kids to hit or say something mean to another kid in the playground and then tell them, "Next time, don't get caught." Most of us start teaching our kids that hurting others—physically or verbally—is bad from the time they are toddlers. Similarly, we shouldn't wait for our kids to offend and hurt others (or themselves) online, either.

We should focus our energies not on catching and "cleaning up" unwanted behavior, but on helping our child to become as good a person online as they are in their in-person relationships. We need to talk to them about empathy. We need to model ethical behavior and expect it of them. We need to teach them how to balance their rights with those of others in a sensitive way. We need to show them how to respect and treat themselves and others well. We need to teach them that being a decent human being is its own quiet reward. No badge, blue ribbon, or Ivy acceptance comes with it—and that is okay.

Positive Steps for Kids to Take Online

Teaching kids to "clean up their social media," or warning them not to do this or that because it might close doors in the future, *seems* like a good idea in theory. After all, presenting ourselves in the best light to colleges, potential employers, and the public at large is something we were encouraged to do ourselves when we were teenagers. That was fine advice—if you grew up at a time when "being in public" was limited to in-person interactions or one-way communications like applications and resumes. But for kids who grow up online, their everyday actions are constantly being captured by academic and behavioral apps and by their classmates, friends, and family. Making sure they are presenting themselves publicly in the "best light" is not so easy. In fact, it is a twenty-four-hour-a-day job.

By the time they are teenagers, many kids develop a sophisticated sense of how to "storycraft" themselves online. Contrary to what we often believe, kids are hyperaware that their digital footprint might be difficult to escape in the real world. Many already tailor their behavior because of the mounting pressures created by social media and the sense that one wrong picture or post could lead to social shunning or ridicule, or yes, a derailed future.

Maya, a member of the student government at a prominent public university, told me that she has been concerned about her digital reputation since middle school. Now in college, she stresses about social media constraining her actions as a student.

"I was at a party off campus, and another girl, a student I had never met, beat me up. She elbowed me up the face and punched me in the mouth and the eye," Maya shared with me. "I didn't hit her back or defend myself because . . . guess who's in that fraternity? The reporter for the school newspaper, who covers student government. And I'm the vice president of the student body." Maya was worried that if she defended herself, she would end up in the student paper, which of course has an online edition.

"What was going through my mind while I was getting beat up was a headline: 'Student Government Officer Punches Girl at Fraternity Party.'" The police had been called. Maya was terrified that the student paper, which regularly sweeps police reports involving students and publishes them, would put a link to the police report of the incident on Twitter. "I didn't want that to become what I was remembered for, or what people would see when they search my name. Especially since I want to go into politics after I graduate."

Maya's story about her worries during this violent encounter is unsettling. Some young people have internalized the fear that their future rides on a perfect digital footprint to the point that protecting their reputation feels more urgent than defending their own bodies. We as a society should consider whether we want police reports and mug shots to run online and in the paper. Who is it serving? Is it really keeping us safer? Should our children grow up fearing searchability and scandal to this degree?

Many students like Maya describe the overwhelming pressure to "be perfect." The anxieties they felt in high school about cultivating a perfect digital footprint to get into college continue to haunt them in college as they worry about getting internships and jobs. The truth is that new college graduates face a very different job market than the one we faced when we came of age. Some companies do review a candidate's social media when considering them for a job. But before you urge your college-age kid to get offline completely, recruiters have also said they are less likely to interview a candidate with no obvious digital footprint.

Syndhia Javier, a recruiter for Lyft, is focused on attracting first-generation college students and people of color to lucrative tech positions. When she visits historically Black colleges, she teaches students the importance of getting their coding and engineering work "out there." According to Javier, an engineering or software development student is far more likely to not be noticed because they aren't on GitHub (a place where developers can share code publicly and work on projects together), than to be dinged because of a photo of them partying on Instagram. "A lot of the recruiters are in their twenties, and college is still pretty recent for us," she explained. "If you say something awful on there, yeah, that's not good, but we're not digging through your drunk photos and judging you . . . We want to be impressed by your smart work, so put that out there." According to Javier, for a young college graduate or a third- or fourth-year college student investigating graduate school and a career, "putting yourself out there" on LinkedIn or STEM-specific sites like GitHub can be important, just as joining professional organizations can be.

So while teenagers and college kids should think before they post and self-audit their social media history periodically, we need to lower the stakes and be clear when "putting yourself out there" really does matter. The digital lives of middle school and high school students should not be a nerve-racking act with punishing consequences for thoughtless posts, not posting much at all, or posting without a consistent "message." People are allowed to have disparate interests or may find themselves entangled in unexpected, unfortunate situations like Maya did.

Tweens and teens are complex and evolving—not a consistent, polished "brand." Do we really want to teach them that they should or shouldn't do something just to impress others? Or do we want to help them grow into the multifaceted adult they want to be, and not the easily digestible brand they think they *need* to be?

Colleges and employers are not looking for perfect. But they are looking for authenticity and character, even if it's not part of their official criteria. Richard Weissbourd, a senior lecturer at the Harvard Graduate School of Education, is also the director of the Making Caring Common Project. He leads Turning the Tide, an organization dedicated to reforming the college admissions process. With his colleagues, Weissbourd has come up with a framework for thinking about character in four ways: "*performance character*, which [includes] things like diligence, grit, and, discipline; *intellectual character*, which is about passion, engagement; *ethical character*, which is about your personal behavior (for example, whether you're kind or fair and your interpersonal interactions); and *civic character*, which is about whether you think about the larger good and a commitment to justice and have some understanding about what fairness and justice are in your communities."[4] In many ways these are the character traits that admissions officers and job recruiters are looking for in candidates already.

Rather than thinking of "character" as something that a seventeen-year-old should develop at the last minute to get into college or land a good job, parents would do well to nurture, model, and encourage these different character traits throughout childhood and adolescence and help teens reflect their different character traits in their applications, resumes, and social media.

How Much Do You Reveal in a College Essay?

We also want to resist the "sell your pain" narrative that has become an insidious part of the "personal brand." As we've already discussed, kids today are comfortable (and used to) sharing a great deal about their lives—and not just online. An issue that has come up over and over again in conversations with both parents and teenagers is the consequences of kids sharing sensitive information about themselves in their college applications. An admissions essay is *far* less public than a social media post. Still, sharing deeply personal information with admissions teams is not without risks.

I spoke with Miles, a recent high school graduate who now attends a competitive liberal arts college. For his common application essay, Miles chose to write about his anxiety and the role it played in him leaving his high school's gymnastics team, where he had been a successful team leader. Miles got into several elite colleges, so his disclosure certainly didn't hurt his admissions, but every admissions officer or college counselor I've talked to advises caution about sharing a diagnosis in essays, unless you make clear that you are functioning pretty well now. Counseling centers at most campuses are overwhelmed, and as unfair as this may be, colleges feel overburdened, so you don't want to sound like you'll struggle too much. Also, it's worth pointing out that Miles's grades and recommendations were very strong; he wasn't a struggling student, and in the essay, he detailed how his struggles with anxiety led to activism and participation in local politics.

Revealing sensitive information may not always work, however. Dr. Stephanie Zerwas advises her patients against detailing their experience with eating disorders in a college essay. "[Colleges] increasingly understand mental health, and they're somewhat more willing to provide treatment resources," she told me. "At the same time, they're overloaded with the number of kids with these issues who are coming through their front doors. So, it can be really dicey to disclose."

Gilit Abraham, a college counselor at a large high school in a mixed-income community, agreed, adding that "with our students who have gone through some counseling and developed some coping skills, it might be okay to integrate their experience surviving a parent's suicide or a violent relationship into their college essay."

After all, these can be defining experiences. But a student with evident mental health issues who is not seeking out assistance is "just going to raise red flags that might hurt their chances of being admitted. If they're just kind of baring their soul, it can be dangerous," said Abraham.

Alice Moody, a writer and college essay coach working on Chicago's affluent North Shore, feels like adversity can add depth and dimension, or make the applicant seem less privileged and sheltered if it is approached thoughtfully. Of course, having an essay coach like Moody to help a young person shape their personal story into something much more than "trauma porn" is a huge privilege in itself—and while ultimately it may help the author gain new understanding and empowering perspective on their own narrative, I struggle with the unfairness of it all.

Young people, especially kids with identities that have been marginalized, have a sense of the ways trauma and challenging life experiences can be commodified as a narrative. Elijah Megginson, a young college student, wrote a powerful editorial for the *New York Times* about resisting the pressure to "gain pity" by recounting experiences of lack or trauma. In the editorial, he writes about his former middle school teacher, who urged him to examine his identity "because while struggles are important, they're not my only contribution." Megginson explains that as he wrote his college application essay, "it kept sounding clichéd. It was my authentic experience, but I felt that trauma overwhelmed my drafts. I didn't want to be a victim anymore. I didn't want to promote that narrative. I wanted college to be a new beginning for me."

Megginson wanted to look forward, not backward. Although he may not have known it, he was following former Dartmouth admissions officer Becky Munsterer Sabky's advice from her book *Valedic-*

torians at the Gate to write about an experience that informs an admissions committee about character and maturity that *isn't* obvious. For example, if your water polo team voted you captain every year and that's on your application, admissions officials will already know that you are a leader. Instead, Sabky suggests you dive into an aspect of that leadership experience that schools wouldn't be able to tell just from seeing your record.

In the end, Megginson chose to write about how he helped his mother's patient, who was in a wheelchair, and about his relationship with his middle school janitor. These stories gave the admissions committees a window into the realities of Megginson's life—without making him feel like he was commodifying his own experiences.

When we support young people in telling their stories, we should be wary of encouraging them to "sell their pain," especially when it doesn't benefit them in the long run or makes them feel bad about themselves. Often this misguided advice to write about painful and challenging experiences in college essays is rooted in a racist and classist imagining that the difficult experiences students have lived through are the most valuable asset they bring to the table. As adults, we can tell stories about hardships and losses we experience, but for a young person to find themselves defined by those experiences is problematic.

Counselors working with students who are members of marginalized groups, first-generation college applicants, students with disabilities, or students who have been through difficult experiences like homelessness or early parenthood would do well to check in with their own biases before counseling a student to make their intimate, personal story the centerpiece of their college application essay. The confidential recommendation letter could be a better place for counselors to let colleges know that these young people have managed to survive and move through adversity, while telling their story in a respectful way.

Seeing Your "Chances" on a Chart: The Naviance Effect

While some well-resourced high schools have an army of counselors shepherding teens through the process of college admissions, many schools have a few counselors serving hundreds of students through this intensive process. A relatively small percentage of parents can afford to hire private counselors, leaving many high school kids "under-advised," which exacerbates existing inequities.

College counseling software aims to close that gap.

For simplicity, I'll focus on one of the most commonly used software packages—Naviance, now owned by PowerSchool. If you're not familiar with Naviance, it is a popular "guidance" software that manages many aspects of the college search and application process. They claim that they processed the submission of 6.2 million college applications in 2021. Forty percent of American high schools use the program, and many of the high schools that don't use Naviance use other guidance software, like Scoir, Cialfo, and MaiaLearning.[5]

While this type of software can help students be realistic about their odds of admissions, it comes with many potential pitfalls. Most sixteen-year-olds are understandably unfamiliar with the vast array of college options out there—four thousand or more institutions of higher learning—so if they search only a few colleges to compare their grades against, they won't see the large variety of schools they could be considering.

Teens might end up with an "outside-in" view of themselves because of college application software, which represents them in a graph or "scattergram." There, your high school performance is shown as a dot, along with all the other college hopefuls at your high school, and if you're at a certain point in the graph, you are more likely to get into the college, but if you're at a lower level, you're less likely to get in. This dot makes it appear as if all you've pursued and achieved is clocking in as a score.

While containing the college search in a specially designed "engine" like Naviance, MaiaLearning, or Scoir may be convenient, and I'm certainly a fan of the Common App and the option to send transcripts and recommendations digitally, there are other tendencies and practices that these software can encourage that are more problematic.

- Peer pressure/crowdsourcing the options: the software can push young people to only apply where other students from their high school are applying.

- Narrows a student's search too much.

- Intensifies social comparison and competition instead of seeing the whole person.

- Compromises students' privacy: students shared with me that sometimes you can tell who someone is based on their dot on the chart (especially if they are admitted to a school that only one student in the class above yours is going to).

- Influences students to consider the universities with well-resourced marketing engines, rather than the best match for their interests and financial resources.

- Triggers a stream of email and content marketing: when your child clicks on a university, the university gets notified, and that student becomes a "lead" who now receives emails, pop-ups, social outreach, and mailers.

Naviance's matching algorithm strongly favors colleges and universities where students from their high school have matriculated on a regular basis. It's easy to get overwhelmed by a long list of options, so it can seem helpful to reduce one's research to a list of twenty schools that others in your child's high school have applied to. But a teen who only considers options where their classmates are regularly applying could miss out on a great college that would really fit their needs. Naviance can play right into a teenager's tendency to follow their peers.

Narrowing the Search (Maybe Too Much)

While the counselors and admissions staff I interviewed agree that software like Naviance can be helpful, they also worry about students using it without nuanced expert guidance, ideally by a person who knows the student and the college process well. When it comes to scattergrams and data, students are ranked based on quantifiable data like GPA and test scores. However, the graph doesn't reveal the student's "best fit" based on more personal characteristics. Apps like Naviance can be useful primarily to get a ballpark estimate of a student's odds of admission.

Darnell Heywood, director of college counseling at Columbus Academy, points out that a little data is a good reality check, especially at high schools where students are groomed to obsess about the "Ivies" and other prestigious colleges. For example, most students with a 3.0 GPA are not going to get into one of the most competitive colleges in the country barring something *very* exceptional. Seeing the "hard facts" can help students move forward with a realistic plan rather than taking the advice personally—*Oh, that college counselor just doesn't like me*. But counselors agree that the apps need a human being to balance their impact. Several students I interviewed saw classmates crying when they first looked at Naviance.

At high-tuition independent schools, the extensive college counseling available can help a disappointed student figure out where to apply even if they learn that their dream school is a "reach." But for students at under-resourced high schools, there is significant concern that students could "under reach" or give up entirely on applying to college if they rely too heavily on the apps and get discouraged from applying. The students who most need personalized college advice are often the ones who get the least.

For every student who needs the reality check, there are also students who will give up on applying to a school where they actually *do* have a chance and are misunderstanding the graph or discounting other factors that might help them. When we over-rely on tools like Naviance (and the ratio of counselors to students at most high schools means many students are forced to over-rely on these tools), we risk misdirecting our students on important decisions.

College counselor Sonja Montiel admonishes, "Who are you, [Naviance], to be that gatekeeper? Who is this one platform . . . telling students that this data set determines what your outcome is going to be?" Montiel says that while the data should be a reality check—it is true that you will not get into highly competitive colleges without a rigorous curriculum, strong grades, and more—it shouldn't be the be-all and end-all. "If your dot is close to the line and you have other attributes colleges should know about—go ahead and apply!" Ultimately, we should also be aware of algorithm steering and make sure to counterbalance the information we get from apps with as much high-quality advice from college counselors as possible.

Social Comparison Makes Naviance Kind of Like Instagram

Let's look at what it *feels like* for teens to see themselves as a dot on a graph in the college counseling software. This dot representation, the "comparison feature," is one of the most gripping, stress-provoking, and sexy parts of using this software or its competitors. The graphs and visuals show students who might be interested in a certain school how they compare with others *from their own school* who were accepted or rejected from that school in the past. It turns out that this has an outsized influence on a student's decision because it feels so personal. At smaller schools in particular, it's quite likely that students actually know the past students and where they got in—or didn't. And there's important data that shows this scattergram can influence students to slightly undermatch, which has potentially damaging effects. Imagine a student who is dissuaded from "reaching" and instead dampens her expectations.[6]

Guidance software like Naviance exposes young people to even more social comparison, in addition to their already crowded social media worlds of followers and likes. One student described how depersonalized Naviance *feels* to her, and how it reduced students to their scores and numbers without any nuance:

> *If you're a really good writer, that's not necessarily a statistic that's going to be on that little graph. It doesn't really encompass everything that's actually important. And also, like interviews, your activities. It's definitely discouraging, but also kind*

of frustrating, because that's not like the best representation of how I could fit into this particular school.

Ultimately, we need to be thoughtful about how our kids will use this kind of software.

We need to be careful not to over-rely on Naviance and its competitors. We need to be careful not to obsess about the scattergram and social comparison. And we need to make sure we're not overlooking schools that few or none of the students at our child's high school have applied to. Consider the software *just one* of several tools, another information resource. But we should keep a close eye on the impact of this software on a process that is already fraught and inequitable.

How Parents Can Help: Encourage an "Inside-Out" Perspective in an "Outside-In" World

As parents who ultimately want to help our children become adults with the self-knowledge to make good choices throughout their lives, we want to get past the idea of "jumping through hoops" to get into college.

- **Remove the threat.** Trying to change your child's behavior on social media by using a meaningless threat about their future prospects will only alienate them. They may see their friends posting similar images, videos, and comments and getting into college just fine. If you do not like or approve of the behavior your child is capturing on their social media, talk to them about the behavior and why you don't think it's appropriate, how it may affect others, or whether that truly reflects their values and who they want to be.

- **Show your kids how to align their actions with being a good person.**[7] Kids are impulsive and live in the now. They might not realize that their behavior online is not reflecting the best of them. If your child posted something you think is insensitive or could inadvertently hurt someone, ask them to consider whether their actions are in line with the kind of person they want to be: "I know you are a good friend, but that kind of attempt at humor might make it hard to see that you are."

- **Coach kids to be self-reflective.** Get your child to think about their character and whether it is reflected in their online posts.

- **Share your mistakes with them openly.** By talking about your missteps honestly—and how you addressed them—you are showing them that no one is perfect. Kids need to know that we all make mistakes and that perfection is neither attainable nor something to pursue. Also share with them how you corrected your mistake and limited the damage it caused—and most important, what you learned from the mistake. Maybe you congratulated someone on social media for news that wasn't yet public. Show your regret for having done something that didn't go as intended or didn't reflect the best of you. Tell your kids how you apologized—not because you got caught, but because you are genuinely sorry and want the other person to know—and how you would do things differently next time you are in a similar situation.

- **Discuss relevant news items with your kids.** The media loves to write about college admissions scandals or an employee who gets fired for something they posted online. These stories offer a good opportunity to talk to your kids about character and doing the right thing. Remind them that the real lesson of these cautionary tales is not that you have to "watch what you post," but that you need to behave online the same way that you behave in person. If you wouldn't say something to someone face-to-face, maybe your motivation or intent for posting or commenting online about it is not coming from a good place.

Conclusion

Ultimately, we want to live in a world where teens are not encouraged to build a "personal brand," but instead can spend these important years trying new things and figuring out who they really are.

chapter 9

The Keys to Thriving as Emerging Adults

For parents who are used to knowing so much about their kids when they're living in their house—the food they eat, when they wake up and go to sleep, what their plans are, how much stress they're under—the transition to life after high school, and the accompanying changes to your rights as a parent, can be especially challenging.

Many parents are nervous about their eighteen-year-old's ability to handle basic life skills; emotional issues; and their own digital records, privacy and, ultimately, their long-term reputation. Many parents don't think they are mature enough.

They are not entirely wrong.

For most young adults, turning eighteen years old might mean the beginning of adulthood, but it's not a magical turning point into "full grown-up." Neuroscience informs us that adolescent brain development continues into our twenties. Researchers use the term "emerging adulthood" to refer to the developmental period that comes after high school, but before some of the traditional markers of "full adulthood" take place.

Once upon a time, marriage, homeownership, and entry into a

long-term profession were some of the key markers of adulthood: young people left their parents' homes when they met someone and put down roots of their own. But today, these are no longer meaningful as indicators of living an adult life.

Now multiple career shifts are the norm, and people are getting married at a later age or forgoing marriage. Moving out of the parental home straight after high school or college is financially impossible for many. As for owning a home, well, that may take even longer depending on the housing market. Emerging adulthood has been extended by economic and social forces that are bigger than my family or yours, and young adults remain in that emerging stage longer than in past generations. They are also thriving in this longer emerging stage—so we don't necessarily need to despair.

We do want to make sure we aren't unwittingly extending this delay or encouraging dependence in ways that are unhealthy or unproductive, though. As we've seen throughout this book, growing up in the public eye, under intense digital surveillance from parents and peers, can mean that our kids get used to our checking in and being there. According to adolescent psychology professor Michaeline Jensen's research, parents and traditional-age college students are still checking in during the college years. And they are doing it a lot. But I will urge you to consider that this is the time to transition to scaffolding and support *from afar*. Even if your child is going to college and still living at home, or living at home and transitioning from high school to work, you can move into a mentoring role and step back more and more from doing things *for* your emerging adult.

We need to support young people to take ownership of and be responsible for their own successes, to advocate for themselves, to use sound judgment, and to be good stewards of their personal information. While the digital world makes their lives easier and more convenient, it puts their most sensitive information at risk in ways that we are just now learning about. Whether it comes to protecting their identity and passwords or managing their healthcare records and making doctor's appointments, we must teach our adolescents the skills they'll need to be digitally independent; manage their health, financial, and educational records and information; and protect their privacy and reputation.

It's also not too late to prepare *ourselves* for a time when we no longer have access to every detail of our children's lives.

For parents who have already started or been through the college admissions process with teenagers, this will give you some clues about your child's independence and your readiness to let things go right or wrong. This may feel like absolutely the worst time to let them fail by missing deadlines, but it is good to know exactly how much initiative they showed in the process.

Perhaps your teen has handled or plans to handle their college application process on their own—or maybe you read their essays or suggested teachers to contact for recommendations. Almost all families must be involved in the financial parts of the application, like deciding what schools are affordable, filling out the FAFSA form, and comparing financial aid offers.

Even if you resisted (or plan to resist) getting too involved with choosing college options, researching them, and applying, you will still likely be an emotional support for your kids as they run into issues of adulting. Many young people are not used to managing their most sensitive records and information, or bureaucratic activities such as filing taxes and keeping records, holding on to social security cards and passports, managing health insurance and doctors' appointments, filing for financial aid, and so on. It's important to onboard our emerging adults into the administration of adulting.

Knowing milestones are coming is good for both parents *and* emerging adults, as they need to be prepared to decide together how much information emerging adults will share, if consent to share information makes sense, and what the long-term plan for independently managing their own academic, healthcare, and other information looks like. Building trust-based relationships and healthy communication with your kid will set them up for success. But starting to talk with them about health issues when they're already in control of the information, and you no longer have access to it, is really difficult.

This chapter offers you some suggestions for crucial conversations to have before a child turns eighteen to prepare both of you for the next stage in your relationship.

Challenges for Parents and Kids at College

So many young people do struggle with adjusting to college, or somewhere along the way. It's important for parents to be able to separate the typical rites of passage of possibly entering the romantic world, or navigating the wide availability of drugs and alcohol and parties, versus knowing when a young person is in crisis and may need more support. Navigating their new life—including making new friends and potentially living in a totally new environment—can be a lot and can throw even a previously easygoing kid who has never needed therapy or medication into a tailspin for a time. And that's not something we can always predict. If you are dealing with more of a crisis, *The Stressed Years of Their Lives* by B. Janet Hibbs and Anthony Rostain takes a deep dive into how to support college students who are going through significant mental health struggles.

Many parents are blindsided: once our teens turn eighteen, they are entitled to total academic privacy—even if we are the ones paying their bills. If kids are used to having their academic work heavily monitored by us, they may have become dependent on it. But that can change. Their grades, their attendance, etc., are protected by privacy laws—specifically by FERPA (Family Educational Rights and Privacy Act), which means the college has no obligation to inform parents of grades and dropped or failed classes. This is humorously depicted in *The Sex Lives of College Girls* when Bela's parents force her to greet her political science professor in a restaurant and he doesn't recognize her because—she's actually dropped the class, unbeknownst to them!

Grade Privacy Laws

FERPA is a federal law that gives students rights over their education records. Students have a right to review their own education records—including student discipline, consent to disclose identifiable information, and more. Students must opt in to providing their parents access to their academic information and records by signing an Education Record Information Release.

This means you won't receive your child's report cards or attendance records, or have access to their professors, unless your child signs the waiver.

Whether it is the allure of new social freedoms or new access to drugs and alcohol or a less structured schedule, sometimes students who have done well in high school will struggle in college. If parental monitoring of grades has been a driving force, removing that as a motivator and organizer can leave some new college students floundering.

Reina, a mother of three young adults, described her middle son's challenging transition to college from high school. He was hoping to go to an elite school and was so disappointed that he didn't get into his dream school that he had trouble adjusting, even though he ended up at a "flagship" university in a neighboring state. He was admitted to the honors college. But . . . that didn't work out.

"Each semester [my son] was taking honors classes and would text me, 'I got a hundred percent on this thing,'" Reina shared with me. "But halfway through the semester, he got tired and bored—and interested in going out with his friends." Reina's son's grades took a turn for the worse. He lied to her, telling her he was getting all As. Initially, he had given permission for his parents to access his grades, a way that some families get around FERPA educational privacy rules, but as soon as he started doing poorly, he rescinded their access. "I did not realize that he had shut me out. I could still pay his bill, and I could see his past records, but I couldn't see his grades anymore. And he lost his scholarship," Reina told me, shaking her head.

Especially when it comes to academics, many kids, like Reina's son, are motivated in high school to do well, to a large degree, because they know their parents are keeping close track of their grades. They are *extrinsically* motivated, as we explored in chapter 5. But, in college, not used to being accountable to themselves, they often lack the ability to motivate themselves (intrinsic motivation), and their performance suffers.

When parents fail to build trust-based relationships and healthy communication with their kids, talking with them about these issues when parents no longer control the flow of information is really difficult. And kids don't know how to turn to their parents for productive and healthy advice when they most need it. Further, if we monitor our kids too closely during high school, we're not developing a trust-based relationship, where our kids can come to us for advice and support if they are struggling.

A dean at one highly competitive university confirmed to me that there are situations where parents come to town for graduation, but their student is not going to graduate and has not told their parents.

For Reina's son, not getting into the highly prestigious private schools he'd applied to was a blow to his self-image . . . but also a reality check.

When her son came home on break, Reina told him that he was in danger of losing his membership in the honors college and his scholar-ship. When he went back, he again reassured his mother that things were going well and he was working hard, but he had a 2.9 GPA. She told him that he'd need to live at home for a year and attend community college, as the tuition without the merit scholarship was too much for their family. She told her son, "You blew it . . . It was a big deal for us to have that scholarship." But her son really didn't want to move home, and Reina and her husband worked with him to come to a decision—he'd move back to the state where he was in school, work part-time, and go to school part-time so he could get state residency and gain access to in-state tuition. He'd also be getting some real-world work experience and taking fewer classes; both seemed like a good plan.

Ultimately, slowing down and working part-time gave Reina's son more time to grow into independence. It was a big transition for Reina and her husband to let their son be responsible for all of his own fi-nances.

"I've helped him financially a few times," she told me, "but he works full-time. He's working at Jimmy John's and at a parking garage—jobs that will allow him to claim residency."

Reina pointed out that he'd have to file the paperwork with the university himself, documenting his work and lease and getting a driver's license in-state. "We're not doing it for him," she told me. "We'll pay tuition, but only at the lower in-state rate, since he blew the scholarship." And he'll need to do all the "bureaucratic hoop-jumping" to get residency himself.

Reina hopes when he can move back to campus housing, he might consider being an RA so he's with more people. But she has also seen him "pull himself together," and although she might have wanted to protect him from the blow to his self-image, she acknowledged that it was probably better that it happened now than further down the line. The moment of realizing that even though he is smart and accomplished, he doesn't get a special pass to keep his scholarship if he keeps getting Cs . . . He'll survive. And he might do *better* in the workplace and in life because of this experience of failure.

Medical Privacy Laws

We can also be blindsided by medical privacy. We've heard about the nightmare scenario—a faraway college student has an urgent medical need, like a bike accident on campus, or ends up in the ER with a high fever or from consuming too much alcohol. **The hospital won't talk to you if your child is eighteen or older, unless they have signed a waiver.**

HIPAA (Health Insurance Portability and Accountability Act) is important to know about. HIPAA has already been a presence in your child's life, giving your child time alone with their doctor after their thirteenth birthday. These laws in the US are designed to protect our

The Privacy Rule protects all "individually identifiable health information" held or transmitted by a covered entity or its business associate, in any form or media, whether electronic, paper, or oral. The Privacy Rule calls this information "protected health information (PHI)."

"Individually identifiable health information" is information, including demographic data, that relates to:

- The individual's past, present, or future physical or mental health or condition.
- The provision of healthcare to the individual.
- The past, present, or future payment for the provision of healthcare to the individual.

This means your child's doctor or medical practitioner can't share their records, details, or health incidents with you or anyone else unless they agree and sign to give permission.

---

personal health information. If your child is in an accident or admitted to the hospital for a physical illness or mental health need, you will not be able to speak to their doctor if they are over eighteen, unless they have waived certain rights; the default is that doctors will not speak with you.

Preparing Kids to Navigate Health Information

Eighteen is not the ideal time to start preparing young people to manage their healthcare. It is best to teach them from a young age how to be their own advocates and how to navigate their rights to privacy. Deborah Gilboa, a family doctor in Pennsylvania, is a big advocate for growing children's autonomy starting at around age twelve. When I spoke to Dr. Gilboa, she pointed out that for a healthy tween or teen who only visits the doctor annually, that's just six times to practice before they become adults. If your child has a chronic health issue and sees doctors more frequently, then it's even more important for them to start learning to self-advocate, to understand the medications they are on, and to talk with their health providers.

She recommends helping kids "practice" these skills at every annual visit starting at age eleven or twelve. She suggests encouraging them to spend time with their pediatrician without you in the room so that they can practice talking with them about how they feel and what they're worried about, and ask any questions about their bodies, or alcohol and drugs, without you there.

Many of the young people I talked to were surprised when they turned thirteen (different ages in different states) and the doctor offered to see them alone or even "kicked their parents out of the room." These interviews helped me to prepare my own son for that moment so we both knew it was coming.

If you are looking for a pediatrician or specialist for a tween or teen, look for a practitioner who supports emerging independence. A good practitioner will let adolescents know what their privacy rights are, but will also often encourage teens to be open with their parents when it makes sense or is safe to do so.

Dr. Gilboa described introducing her patients to the idea that she can be their advocate and support on a confidential basis as a crucial turning point in their relationship. She explains that "in our state, once you get to be your age, there are certain things that you can talk to me about. And I'm not allowed to tell your parents unless you give me permission. I make that really clear to them. So I can do a well visit exam and code that once a year for certain issues. And we can have lots of anticipatory guidance conversations, and we can talk about birth control. We can talk about STDs. We can talk about marijuana. We can talk about mental health issues."

Dr. Gilboa described situations where she would let the patient know that a parent might be able to glean certain information about what the doctor and patient discussed in the visit. She might say to an adolescent, "But if you have a diagnosis that I have to do something about, your parents might see that on their insurance statement because I have to put in a diagnostic code. Do you think that's a concern?"

For example, this happens if Gilboa sees an adolescent patient who needs birth control. "Because that's a particular diagnostic code, I actually have to have a conversation with the patient, letting them know that depending on how closely their parents read their mail, they could find out. Now, I'm also trying really hard to convince these kids to include their parents in the conversation because it's safer and it's healthier if they do. So I'll often say, 'We can invite your parent back into the room and we could have some of those conversations. So they know what's going on with you.'" But if the patient really feels unsafe or unwilling to do that, then she advises them that "the only way to be positive for sure that it won't show up on your parents' insurance bill is for me to send you to Planned Parenthood or one of the other free clinics."

Gilboa also shares that suicidality and homicidality are not protected by HIPAA.

These are some of the skills young people need to have in order to manage healthcare:

- Making appointments

- Writing down questions before a doctor visit to make the best use of the visit

- Managing medications

- Carrying their health insurance card and their photo ID

- Phone skills: They need to be able to call the doctor if they're having symptoms and need to do a phone consult. Learning to call for a prescription refill and even negotiate with insurance is important. Often, young people who have grown up texting are less familiar with voicemails, how to escalate a concern up the chain of command, etc.

Why do tweens and teens need to learn phone skills? You don't want the first voice call they ever receive to be offering them a job or a scholarship and they are just clueless, not knowing what to say or how to respond appropriately. Make sure that they know how to pick up the phone when it rings and to turn it off if they need to have it on silent. I've met parents who panic when their children don't respond to their voicemail at college because they never set up voicemail or never knew to even check voicemail.

Preparing Young People with Chronic or Ongoing Health Needs to Independently Manage Their Own Care

If you are supporting a young adult who has needed mental health care in high school and you are sending them to college, it is important that everyone is on the same page about the supports and protections that you are going to put in place to make sure your child is safe—while keeping their autonomy and privacy in mind, of course.

Kids under eighteen years old with chronic conditions from migraines to type 1 diabetes to asthma often have no choice but to comply with treatment plans, so long as they are under the close supervision of their parents. Parents have a special responsibility to be sure that once kids are on their own, they have gained the skills to advocate for their health, talk to healthcare providers, summarize their health history, etc.

The more complex a young person's healthcare needs are, the more critical it is that they and their parents plan thoughtfully for this transition. Meredith Balogh was diagnosed with type 1 diabetes when she was twelve years old.[1] Her mother taught her how to manage her blood sugar and her medical records. The first few times Meredith got on the phone with medical offices or health insurers, she was a scared high school student. Eventually, she became a "medical ninja," who helps other people negotiate their medical care and bills. Meredith said, "At fourteen, my mom had me get on the phone with insurance." While Meredith initially felt her mother was throwing her into the deep end, she is grateful now that her mom taught her how to obtain medical records and self-advocate in a system that can disempower even the savviest adult patients.

"Kelsey," a student at Stanford University quoted on the T1 Everyday Magic website, describes how her parents fostered her independence, which increased her confidence in caring for herself with a chronic condition.[2] "The best thing my parents did for me last summer was gradually transferring responsibilities to me that had been theirs for the past 10 years. They started by having me order my own prescriptions over the phone . . . then I started picking up my prescriptions, calling companies to change my shipping address, and anticipating when I would need to refill prescriptions. It really helped that I had a couple of months to learn all of this, but it also made me appreciate all the work my parents have done to make sure I never run out of insulin or that my pump supplies always arrive on time."

Challenges for Kids Who Had IEPs and 504s

Families face extra steps in the transition to college if their students have learning differences. These parents have been heavily involved in their child's academic life. For years, parents tirelessly advocated for them and routinely communicated with their case managers, counselors, teachers, and school administrators about their child's performance. Losing that access suddenly can make parents feel helpless.

Ruth, whose son and daughter both had IEPs (individual education plans) throughout grade school and high school, describes how unsettling it's been to not be able to monitor her son's academic progress. "He didn't want us parents to know what his grades were, so we had no idea," Ruth told me. "When we'd ask how [he was] doing, he completely ignored the question.

"They [the college] literally do not communicate with you. And that . . . comes as a huge shock for parents who have been navigating the special education system," Ruth explains with frustration. "You've been like a tiger, and you've been in those IEP meetings, and you've been communicating with the counselor and their case manager and everything . . . They turn eighteen and you fall off a cliff, nobody will talk to you."

Preparing Our Kids for College or Life after High School

Ultimately our kids' digital reputation, the ways they represent themselves online, and the ways they navigate the world of algorithmic privacy and reputation are going to be on them. And before they leave our nest, we need to both negotiate with ourselves and with them the separation of both their academic records, which are going to be protected by FERPA when they're eighteen, and their health records.

And even if we do have them sign a waiver to give us access to those things, we really need to moderate our relationship to that information. So maybe we are going to ask them to show us their grades, but we're not going to check in about week-to-week homework anymore.

It's not uncommon for college students to voluntarily share their grades and involve their parents in their academics, as they've been accustomed to having their academic work monitored by us. At least while they are doing well. Other kids don't want us to see their grades at all. If you want to look at your college student's grades, discuss your expectations with your child, and decide together whether they should sign these forms over or not. Establish whether it is fair to make getting good grades at school or not skipping classes a condition of paying tuition.

Whether we like it or not, in the US, the expectation from colleges, federal loans, and the whole "system" is that parents pay for college. Information about academic progress or disciplinary actions is not automatically shared with parents or guardians. Many schools have websites or handbooks that state a version of this: "It is the student's responsibility to communicate such matters to family members and others, as needed." If parents and students do decide that parents should have this access, the student can sign a FERPA waiver. A FERPA waiver for parents can be partial—there may be forms online at universities, where students can grant some but not all access to parents.

FERPA exists for good reasons. For example, parental oversight may be forcing your child not to explore interests because they know you are monitoring them and may put pressure on them to avoid subjects for varying reasons, like practicality, politics, and religion. When I taught queer cinema at Lake Forest College, I had a student who hesitated to sign up for the class because they feared outing themselves to their parents in their transcripts. In this case, I allowed the student to take the course as an independent study to maintain privacy.

While ideally parents wouldn't use their economic power to try to dictate their young adult's life, I've seen too many students afraid to come out to their parents as LGBTQ+ for fear of losing economic support to naïvely believe that parents don't wield their power this way. A society where a university education is free or heavily subsidized would reduce this financial leverage in a way that would be healthy for family relationships.

For Reina's family, a bike accident was a wake-up call. Since she couldn't be in two places at the same time, her son had to learn to fend for himself. He had an accident at work while he was delivering sandwiches, and broke his arm. Reina said, "He had to go through the whole process of going to the emergency room and showing his insurance card and going to the follow-up appointment and getting the X-ray and then dealing with his employer for workman's comp since it was a workplace injury." According to Reina, this gave her son a "taste of what it is to be an adult. And I really tried not to coddle him through the whole process because I didn't have access to his medical records."

And he did it.

What Parents Can Do:
Planning for Independence

Young people need to be accustomed to fending for themselves in crucial ways. Some readiness skills to work on include the following:

- **Making decisions independently:** Up until now, your child has been relying on you but now needs to shift. Start this shift in high school, if not earlier, when you can be the one possible source to "bounce things off of." Later, your young adult can build the trust to come to you to ask, "Can I drop this class?"

- **Knowing important information:** Many students still text parents for their social security numbers. Your college students will need this number and need to keep it private, so texting you for it is less ideal. **Before they leave home, think about helping them set up a folder for important documents and numbers. If they keep it on the computer, it can be password protected and even encrypted.**

- **Managing their own finances:** Many undergrads have parents deeply involved in their financial lives (beyond paying tuition). Parents are holding passwords for banking, for example. They are helping students set up accounts. They are also Venmo-ing money back and forth, which, unless you are careful with settings, is public information.

- **Communication skills:** Does your teen know how to answer an email or send one seeking information in a polite way? Could they reach out to a department head to ask for a meeting? Do they know how and under what circumstances to email a teacher or professor? Can they leave an appropriate voicemail? Have they set up the voicemail on their phone?

- **Body care:** Does your teen take care of their own body, with regular showers, tooth brushing, keeping track of their own medications if they take them, wearing sunscreen before spending time in the sun, etc.? No one is perfect (I've gotten sunburns as an adult), but overall if they rely on you to remind them, then they should work on this before leaving home.

- **Problem-solving:** Do they know how to ask for help or to make use of help that is available? Do they know how to research the help they need, like where to start if they need tutoring and office hours?

- **Conflict resolution:** Can they disagree with someone and respectfully hear the other person's views, and find a solution or simply agree to disagree? Could they experience a slight or minor offense and shrug it off? Can they help others see the molehill and not a mountain? Can they be faced with an upsetting situation with people who are not already good friends—perhaps a roommate they didn't choose—and find a way to negotiate it while avoiding permanent bruising to the relationship?

- **Making friends:** Do they know how to ask for someone's phone number or how to pursue a connection with someone they want to get to know?

The good news is that digital communication, which for 40 percent of college students is a *daily* activity with parents, *can* be supportive and positive.[3] Overall, several studies have found that when a young person has some control of the frequency and doesn't feel hounded, the contact with their parents can be supportive and helpful.

Conclusion

Ultimately, as parents, we want a world where our young people are really *seen* and understood, not just watched and surveilled. As parents and educators, we can make this happen with both individual changes in our own families and collectively working with others to push back against weaponizing social media, overly surveilling kids at school, and creating public narratives about our children that they will have to overcome.

By supporting our kids' privacy now, and helping them learn to set their own boundaries, we are supporting them in the process of becoming authentically themselves as adults. By focusing on character and not simply external consequences, and by holding them accountable for mistakes and not simply covering them up, we are preparing our children to be the ethical conscience of our society at a time when we need that leadership and moral compass more than ever.

acknowledgments

This book started via conversations with parents and educators at schools and workplaces, especially in the last five years since *Screenwise* came out. Big thanks to the many young people, educators, and parents who have shared their stories or who have asked questions that lead me to fascinating discoveries.

I was lucky to meet my literary agent, Jill Grinberg, after *Screenwise* came out, and I hoped we might get to work together. In our early meetings, when we wondered how many weeks we'd all be home because of the COVID-19 pandemic, I couldn't have imagined we would rework the proposal and sell the book, and that I'd write and research it all as the pandemic transformed the lives of families. Jill, you have been a supportive and insightful guide throughout this whole process. I'm also grateful to Denise Page and Sophia Seidner at JGLM.

So grateful to Sara Carder at TarcherPerigee for acquiring this book and seeing its potential, and to Joanna Ng for jumping in and taking it to the finish line with so much enthusiasm and insight.

Ashley Alliano and the marketing and publicity teams at PRH have been so supportive and committed. Thank you to Brittany Bergman and other PRH copyeditors for saving me from myself.

My author friends make this life less lonely and more fun: Thank you to the ends of the day to the Squad: Nefertiti Austin, Michele Borba, Phyllis Fagell, Katie Hurley, Ned Johnson, Christine Koh, Jessica Lahey, Madeline Levine, Julie Lythcott-Haims, Audrey Monke, Tina Payne

Bryson, Debbie Reber, Katherine Reynolds Lewis, and Catherine Steiner-Adair. Being #friendleagues with you is everything. Thank you to Michelle Icard, who is the big sister/writer friend I've always wished for (except she's my age). Conversations with writer friends Katie Flynn, Jo-Ann Finkelstein, Carrie Goldman, Debi Lewis, Deborah Siegel, Judith Warner, Anya Kamenetz, Emily Maloney, Chris Balme, Christine Carter, Melinda Wenner Moyer, Virginia Sole-Smith, Robyn Silverman, Carla Naumburg, Amy McCready, Ron Lieber, Jeff Selingo, Catherine Pearlman, John Duffy, Heidi Stevens, Julie Miner, Lisa Lewis, Stephanie Malia Krauss, Greg Toppo, Jennifer Wallace, Rosalind Wiseman, Julie Bogart, and Emily Popek have enriched my thinking and made me feel like part of a community during a three-year pandemic winter.

I'm grateful for the work and collegiality of scholars like Carrie James, Emily Weinstein, and Katie Davis. Big thanks to all the principled and committed people who make up the digital citizenship and humane tech communities.

Genoveva Llosa saved both the proposal and the chapters from my tendency to want to include *everything*. Someday we will celebrate in person with yummy snacks. Michael Boezi, Allison Lane, and Betsy Thorpe offered crucial insights on various chapters. Jayme Johnson's web design and Adrienne Fontaine's PR brilliance are my secret weapons. Amy Shearn's discussion guide insights were right on. Leah Ongiri and Ryan Bond are some of the wisest parents and readers I know—your insights mean a lot to me. Thank you to Micco Caporale and Emma Feur for research and endnote support, and to Jenn Doyle for not letting me double-book Zoom meetings.

I could not be more grateful to the young people, parents, and educators I interviewed. Thank you for trusting me with your stories. Talking with you made the stakes very clear to me. We need to work with kids to make the world safer, and we need to listen to young people about both the potential upsides and the risks of convening digital communities.

Charlene Margot and Gilda Ross: In addition to inviting me to speak in your programs, both of you helped me find sources that enriched this book. Thank you to Maureen Kelleher and Angelina Liu for helping me find amazing sources. Lennon Torres, you are a treasure, and I loved our conversation. Catlyn Savado and Lilia Scudamore, your activism is inspiring. Sophia and Natalie Pruett, I learned so much from our conversations.

Thank you to all the experts I interviewed. Traci Baxley deserves special mention—for talking to me while her power was out with a hurricane. Thank you: Ken Ginsburg, Anthony Rostain, Jim Jump, Richard Weissbourd, Carrie Goldberg, Robin DeRosa, Henry Turner, Stephanie Reich, Sonja Montiel, Justin Patchin, Jacqueline Nesi, Stephanie Zerwas, Michael Una, Rachel Lotus, Stacey Steinberg, Anne Collier, Alice Moody Jonathan Singer, researchers from Challenge Success, and so many brilliant people who spoke to me for this book.

If you are finishing a book, I recommend a writer's retreat. Thanks to Deborah Grayson Riegel and her family who gave me one by loaning me their home, where I finished this book! As an extra bonus, it was near Robyn Silverman, and we walked, talked, and went live. Crucial early work on this project was completed at the Ragdale Foundation. Thank you for choosing me and offering me the gift of time and space.

My family and friends endured years of hearing about this project and remained encouraging. Thank you for being supportive and loving: Lenore, Howard, Lois (the three best grandparents a kid could have). Thank you to my sister, Sarah, and the other I'm-lucky-to-be-related to you family members like Ethan, Antonia, Jessie, Kate, Sean, Seth, Mei, Glenn, and Mary. Thanks to the young folx in the family for giving me the lowdown on growing up digital: Julia, Emily, Tyler, Emma—any of you are free to take over my TikTok so I can go viral. But you are likely too busy with your own awesome projects.

I feel so lucky to have friendships that can survive a pandemic. Special gratitude for stalwart friendship in these crazy times to Todd, Naomi, Nadia, Liz, Lori, Moira, Tracy, Lara, Susan, Catherine, Chloe, Amy, Sarah, Sunny, Gilit, Michael, Sara, George, Joanie, Jon, Tamar, Elliot, Frida, Roy, Marv, Posey, Stacey, and the entire Lomdim Community. Rebecca, Rachel, Karen, and Rosie: thank you for being the mom friends I didn't know I needed and for raising some excellent teenagers! Amazingly enough, I even made a few new friends during this infernal pandemic and book-writing time. Carmella and Nikole, stick around if this (gestures wildly) isn't too much. Simon's Rock friends, thanks for staying weird. Grateful for recent meetups in Portland, San Francisco, and Los Angeles. Middle and high school friends: maybe it is good that we didn't have Tumblr or Instagram, but I did take a lot of pictures and we wrote lots of letters. Contact me if you want copies or if you prefer that I destroy them.

Most especially, my gratitude and love for Dan and Harold transcend what I can say here. This book is for you. Dan, you literally keep us alive and fed, and more importantly, your love and support as a partner and coparent make everything good in our lives possible. Grateful every day that we're doing this together.

Harold, as hard as it has been not to post pictures of you these last few years, it was worth reducing my short-term goal of likes and adulation to build the trust we have and to explore alternatives to social media to keep our family connected. Talking with you and your friends as you all become teenagers and young adults gives me tremendous hope for the future. I'm not putting it all on you all—us old folks need to get it together on this front and so many others. But hopefully, it is okay to be inspired and a little awed by this new generation of young people—because I am.

notes

chapter 1

1. **a study on parental online monitoring:** Monica Anderson, "Parents, Teens and Digital Monitoring," Pew Research Center, January 7, 2016, https://www.pewresearch.org/internet/2016/01/07/parents-teens-and-digital-monitoring.

2. **a study of 695 public four-year and community college students:** M. Brown, G. Chase, J. Navarro, M. Lippold, K. Wyman, and M. Jensen, "The Role of Parental Digital Tracking on Emerging Adult Perceived Support of Autonomy and Well-Being," Poster, Rio Grande, Puerto Rico: Society for Research on Child Development, Constructing the Other Special Topic Meeting, 2022.

3. **As tenth grader McKenna said:** Sonia Freedman, "Life 360: Friend or Foe?," *M-A Chronicle*, February 14, 2022, https://www.machronicle.com/life-360-friend-or-foe.

4. **A *New York Times* technology reporter:** Kashmir Hill, "I Used Apple AirTags, Tiles and a GPS Tracker to Watch My Husband's Every Move," *New York Times*, February 11, 2022, https://www.nytimes.com/2022/02/11/technology/airtags-gps-surveillance.html.

5. **One college woman spoke to Tulane University's newspaper:** Olivia Barnes, "Life360 Enables Helicopter Parenting of College Students," Opinion, *Tulane Hullabaloo*, November 10, 2021, https://tulanehullabaloo.com/57913/views/opinion-life360-enables-helicopter-parenting-of-college-students/.

6. **After carefully considering her options:** "COMPOSE Yourself!," Culture Reframed, accessed January 11, 2023, https://www.culturereframed.org/compose-yourself/.

chapter 2

1. **appearance-related social media consciousness:** Sophia Choukas-Bradley, Jacqueline Nesi, Laura Widman, and Brian M. Galla, "The Appearance-Related Social Media Consciousness Scale: Development and Validation with Adolescents," *Body Image* 33 (2020): 164–74, https://doi.org/10.1016/j.bodyim.2020.02.017.

2. **"Changes within our bodies":** Nick Morrison, "Negative Impact Of Social Media For Girls, Boys Varies By Age," *Forbes*, March 28, 2022, https://www.forbes

.com/sites/nickmorrison/2022/03/28/negative-impact-of-social-media-for-girls-boys-varies-by-age/.

3. **One study from the UK found:** Sophia Choukas-Bradley, Jacqueline Nesi, Laura Widman, and Brian M. Galla, "The Appearance-Related Social Media Consciousness Scale: Development and Validation with Adolescents."

4. **"pressure to curate positive and well-liked content":** Amanda Lenhart, "Social Media and Friendships," chap. 4 in *Teens, Technology and Friendship*, Pew Research Center, August 6, 2015, https://www.pewresearch.org/internet/2015/08/06/chapter-4-social-media-and-friendships/.

5. **As Dr. Eva Telzer from UNC–Chapel Hill:** "Understanding the Teenage Brain, with Eva Telzer, PhD," American Psychological Association, video, 30:48, August 24, 2022, https://www.youtube.com/watch?v=R1bjYPUkRP8.

6. **Social media has really . . . changed the social landscape:** "Understanding the Teenage Brain," (emphasis mine).

7. **research project with middle schoolers:** Stephanie M. Reich, Allison Starks, Nicholas Santer, and Adriana Manago, "Brief Report—Modeling Media Use: How Parents' and Other Adults' Posting Behaviors Relate to Young Adolescents' Posting Behaviors," *Frontiers in Human Dynamics* 3 (May 2021): 86–90, https://doi.org/10.3389/fhumd.2021.595924.

8. **a European study of kids' susceptibility to being hurt:** Patti Valkenburg, Ine Beyens, J. Loes Pouwels, Irene I. van Driel, and Loes Keijsers, "Social Media Use and Adolescents' Self-Esteem: Heading for a Person-Specific Media Effects Paradigm," *Journal of Communication* 71, no. 1 (2021): 56–78, https://doi.org/10.1093/joc/jqaa039.

9. **Keith N. Hampton and Inyoung Shin found that children:** Keith N. Hampton and Inyoung Shin, "Disconnection More Problematic for Adolescent Self-Esteem than Heavy Social Media Use: Evidence from Access Inequalities and Restrictive Media Parenting in Rural America," *Social Science Computer Review*, August 5, 2022, https://doi.org/10.1177/08944393221117466.

10. **more than 57 percent of kids between thirteen and seventeen:** Amanda Lenhart, "Teens, Technology and Friendships," Pew Research Center, August 6, 2015, https://www.pewresearch.org/internet/2015/08/06/teens-technology-and-friendships/.

11. **an article for the *New York Times*:** Devorah Heitner, "Rules for Social Media, Created by Kids," *New York Times*, January 5, 2017, https://www.nytimes.com/2017/01/05/well/family/the-unspoken-rules-kids-create-for-instagram.html.

12. **TikTok has the potential to make someone famous overnight:** Drew Harwell and Taylor Lorenz, "Sorry You Went Viral," *Washington Post*, October 21, 2022, https://www.washingtonpost.com/technology/interactive/2022/tiktok-viral-fame-harassment/.

13. **she recorded a video performing:** Rebecca Black, "Rebecca Black Is Back," interview with Nora McInerny, *Terrible, Thanks for Asking,* podcast, WNYC Studios, November 10, 2020, https://www.youtube.com/watch?v=5Oca3V EnLT8.

14. **Super Awesome Sylvia, the star of a YouTube STEM channel:** "Super Awesome Sylvia Was a Role Model to Girls in Science. But Then Sylvia Became Someone Else," *Washington Post,* September 28, 2017, https://www.washingtonpost .com/video/national/super-awesome-sylvia-was-a-role-model-to-girls-in-science-but-then-sylvia-became-someone-else/2017/09/29/32105934-a47f -11e7-b573-8ec86cdfe1ed_video.html.

15. **In a Medium article:** Zephyrus Todd, "Closing the Chapter on the Girl I Was, to Be the Man I Am," Medium, January 28, 2019, https://medium.com/@ zeropointzeph/closing-the-chapter-on-the-girl-i-was-to-be-the-man-i-am -da0023292f3c.

16. **he also used Twitter to come out as bisexual:** Neal Broverman, "Parkland Activist Cameron Kasky Comes Out: 'I Wanted to Be Straight.'" *Advocate,* September 13, 2021, https://www.advocate.com/news/2021/9/13/parkland-acti vist-cameron-kasky-comes-out-i-wanted-be-straight.

chapter 3

1. **Annette Lareau calls "concerted cultivation":** Annette Lareau, *Unequal Childhoods: Class, Race, and Family Life,* 2nd ed (Berkeley: University of California Press, 2011), 2.

2. **Christie Tate:** Christie Tate, "Don't Perpetuate the Mean-Girl Myth on Behalf of My Daughter," *Washington Post*, October 24, 2021, https://www.washington-post.com/news/parenting/wp/2016/11/18/dont-perpetuate-the-mean-girl-myth-on-behalf-of-my-daughter/.

3. **"None of them seemed embarrassing to me":** Tate, "Don't Perpetuate the Mean-Girl Myth on Behalf of My Daughter."

4. **Stacey Steinberg:** Author interview with Stacey Steinberg, August 2, 2021. See also Stacey Steinberg, *Growing Up Shared* (Naperville, IL: Sourcebooks, 2020).

5. **college-rejection YouTube:** Chloe Bryan, "YouTube College Rejection Videos Are More Hopeful Than You'd Expect," Mashable, October 29, 2021, https:// mashable.com/article/college-rejection-youtube-videos.

chapter 4

1. **95 percent of elementary schools:** Sophia Kunthara, "Closing The Gap Between Classrooms And Students, ClassDojo Sees Skyrocketing Usage," Crunchbase News, April 1, 2020, https://news.crunchbase.com/startups/closing-the-gap -between-classrooms-and-students-classdojo-sees-skyrocketing-usage/.

2. **Joe Bower:** Joe Bower, "6 Reasons to Reject ClassDojo," *For the Love of Learning* (blog), November 21, 2014, http://joe-bower.blogspot.com/2014/11/6-reasons -to-reject-classdojo.html.

3. **Manoush Zomorodi:** Manoush Zomorodi, "ClassDojo: Do I Want It in My Kid's Class?," interview with Sam Chaudhary and James Steyer, *Note to Self,* podcast, WNYC Studios, March 31, 2015, https://www.wnycstudios.org/podcasts/note- toself/episodes/classdojo-privacy-schools.

4. **empowers teachers to pick tools:** Salvador Rodriguez, "ClassDojo Wants to Do for Education What Netflix Did for Enter," *Inc.,* September 20, 2016, https://www .inc.com/salvador-rodriguez/classdojo-monetization-slack-classrooms.html.

5. **investigative journalists at *The Markup*:** Todd Feathers, "This Private Equity Firm Is Amassing Companies That Collect Data on America's Children," *The Markup,* January 11, 2022, https://themarkup.org/machine-learning/2022/01 /11/this-private-equity-firm-is-amassing-companies-that-collect-data-on -americas-children.

6. **Brad Shear stated to the *Washington Post*:** Heather Kelly, "School Apps Track Students from Classroom to Bathroom, and Parents Are Struggling to Keep Up," *Washington Post,* September 25, 2019, https://www.washingtonpost.com /technology/2019/10/29/school-apps-track-students-classroom-bathroom -parents-are-struggling-keep-up/.

7. **following note to their community:** "Rye Schools Restricts Access to Student Portal, Calling It a Student Distraction and Source of Stress," *MyRye,* August 14, 2019, https://myrye.com/my_weblog/2019/08/rye-schools-restricts-access-to -student-portal-citing-it-a-student-distraction-and-source-of-stress.html.

chapter 5

1. **Biles explained that she was withdrawing:** Daniella Silva, "'We're Human, Too': Simone Biles Highlights Importance of Mental Health in Olympics Withdrawal," NBC News, July 28, 2021, https://www.nbcnews.com/news/olympics/we-re -human-too-simone-biles-highlights-importance-mental-health-n1275224.

2. **Kanye West opens up about his bipolar diagnosis:** Nathan Diller, "Kanye West Calls Bipolar Disorder A 'Superpower' in a New Song & Fans Are Seriously Divided," *Bustle,* June 1, 2018, https://www.bustle.com/p/kanye-west-calls -bipolar-disorder-his-superpower-in-a-new-song-fans-are-seriously-divided -9265131.

3. **Bunny Michael:** Margot Harris, "An Influencer Is Sharing Their Story of Being Strip-Searched at 16 after Shoplifting to Shed Light on the 'Dehumanizing' Be- havior of Law Enforcement," *Insider,* June 12, 2020, https://www.insider.com /influencer-bunny-michael-shared-story-police-strip-search-16-2020-6.

4. **Brittani Boren Leach:** Eric Todisco, "YouTuber Brittani Boren Leach's Infant Son Dies after He Was Found Unresponsive While Napping," *People,* December

30, 2019, https://people.com/parents/youtube-brittani-boren-leach-son-crew-dies/.

5. **In 2020, Lurie Children's Hospital surveyed two thousand parents:** "Parenting Teens in the Age of Social Media," *Lurie Children's Blog*, Lurie Children's Hospital, September 1, 2020, https://www.luriechildrens.org/en/blog/social-media-parenting-statistics/.

6. **"this girl's straight and this girl's not":** Sethuraman S, "Queer Teens Are Using a Jason Derulo Song to Come Out and the Reactions Are Just Priceless," *Upworthy*, June 10, 2021, https://scoop.upworthy.com/queer-teens-using-a-jason-derulo-song-to-come-out-and-the-reactions-are-priceless.

7. **"this server is for people ages 16–24":** "Public Discord Server List," Disboard, accessed June 15, 2022, https://disboard.org/servers/tag/autism.

8. **"During the time of an investigation:** "East High Students Rally for Change about Sexual Assaults in Denver Public Schools," CBS Colorado, September 4, 2020, https://denver.cbslocal.com/2020/09/04/sexual-assault-east-high-school-denver/.

9. **racist behavior they've experienced:** Nicole Brittingham Furlonge and Kenny Graves, "Research Insights: Using the Black@ Instagram Archive to Improve Schools," NAIS, Spring 2022, https://www.nais.org/magazine/independent-school/spring-2022/research-insights-using-the-black@-instagram-archive-to-improve-schools/.

10. **digital self-harm:** Justin W. Patchin and Sameer Hinduja, "Digital Self-Harm among Adolescents," *Journal of Adolescent Health* 61, no. 6 (September 18, 2017): 761–66, https://doi.org/10.1016/j.jadohealth.2017.06.012.

11. **her severe anxiety:** Lindsay Dodgson, "Charli D'Amelio Opened Up about Her Mental Health and How She's Overcoming 'Scary' Panic Attacks in Therapy," *Insider*, December 23, 2020, https://www.insider.com/charli-damelio-tiktok-opened-up-mental-health-panic-attacks-2020-12.

chapter 6

1. **fascinating study:** Anne J. Maheux, Reina Evans, Laura Widman, Jacqueline Nesi, Mitchell J. Prinstein, and Sophia Choukas-Bradley, "Popular Peer Norms and Adolescent Sexting Behavior," *Journal of Adolescence* 78, no. 1 (2019): 62–66, https://doi.org/10.1016/j.adolescence.2019.12.002.

2. **UK study:** Jon Needham, "Sending Nudes: Intent and Risk Associated with 'Sexting' as Understood by Gay Adolescent Boys," *Sexuality and Culture* 25, no. 2 (April 2020): 396–416, https://doi.org/10.1007/s12119-020-09775-9.

3. **"non-pressured" sexting:** Yu Lu, Elizabeth Baumler, and Jeff R. Temple, "Multiple Forms of Sexting and Associations with Psychosocial Health in Early Adolescents," *International Journal of Environmental Research and Public Health* 18, no. 5 (2021): 2760, https://doi.org/10.3390/ijerph18052760.

4. **Channing Smith:** Heidi Stevens, "Column: A 16-Year-Old Boy Died by Suicide after His Intimate Messages to Another Boy Were Made Public. What Some Experts Say Parents Need to Know about Sexting," *Chicago Tribune*, October 1, 2019, https://www.chicagotribune.com/columns/heidi-stevens/ct-heidi-stevens-tuesday-channing-smith-suicide-intimate-texts-1001-20191001-ngtjty6jpfdhxcyiv662ucts2q-story.html.

5. **LGBTQ+ kids are subject to harassment and violence:** "School Climate Survey," GLSEN, accessed June 6, 2022, https://www.glsen.org/school-climate-survey.

6. **Others might send:** Emily Weinstein and Carrie James, *Behind Their Screens: What Teens Are Facing (and Adults Are Missing)* (Cambridge, MA: MIT Press, 2022), 98–103.

7. **between two sixteen-year-olds:** Manoush Zomorodi, "Sext Education: Teens, Photos, and the Law," interview, *Note to Self*, podcast, WNYC Studios, September 6, 2016, https://www.wnycstudios.org/podcasts/notetoself/episodes/consensual-sexting-teenagers-laws.

8. **the ages of those who send and receive sexually explicit photos:** Marybeth Sullivan and Shannon King, "OLR Research Report: Connecticut Teenage Sexting Law," Connecticut General Assembly, accessed June 14, 2022, https://www.cga.ct.gov/2016/rpt/2016-R-0022.htm.

9. **Texas allows an exception for "sexting":** "'Before You Text': Bullying and Sexting Course," Texas School Safety Center, accessed June 14, 2022, https://txssc.txstate.edu/tools/courses/before-you-text/module-3-2.

10. **Elizabeth Englander:** Elizabeth Englander, "Low Risk Associated with Most Teenage Sexting: A Study of 617 18-Year-Olds," July 2012, https://vc.bridgew.edu/marc_reports/6/.

chapter 7

1. **the teenage brain is different:** Daniel J. Siegel, *Brainstorm: The Power and Purpose of the Teenage Brain* (New York: TarcherPerigee, 2014).

2. **she felt "disrespected" by the university's choice:** Danny Emerman and Andrew Crane, "SU Athletes 'Disrespected' by Charlotte de Vries' 2nd Chance after Racist Video," *Daily Orange*, August 13, 2020, https://dailyorange.com/2020/08/su-athletes-disrespected-charlotte-de-vries-2nd-chance/.

3. **Twitter account shared it:** Noah Ovshinsky, "Twitter User Who Posted Controversial Baraboo Photo Yet to Be Identified," Wisconsin Public Radio, November 20, 2018, https://www.wpr.org/twitter-user-who-posted-controversial-baraboo-photo-yet-be-identified.

4. **Instead of reckoning with what they had done:** Brady Carlson, "How Baraboo Continues to Wrestle with a Photo That Shocked the World," Wisconsin Public

Radio, April 9, 2019, https://www.wpr.org/how-baraboo-continues-wrestle-photo-shocked-world.

5. **made individual apologies to Jewish families:** Joseph Bernstein, "The Baraboo Nazi Prom Photo Shocked the World. The City's Response Shocked Its Residents," *BuzzFeed News*, April 2, 2019, https://www.buzzfeednews.com/article/josephbernstein/baraboo-nazi-prom-photo.

6. **"four qualities of our minds":** Siegel, *Brainstorm*, 7–8.

7. **Katie Hurley:** Author interview with Katie Hurley, January 10, 2022.

8. **more likely to support Black Lives Matter:** "Seven-in-ten U.S. teens say they at least somewhat support the Black Lives Matter movement, including 31% of teenagers who strongly support it, according to a survey conducted in April and May among American teens ages 13 to 17. By comparison, a little over half of U.S. adults (56%) said in a March survey that they support the Black Lives Matter movement." Kiley Hurst, "U.S. Teens Are More Likely Than Adults to Support the Black Lives Matter Movement," Pew Research Center, June 15, 2022, https://www.pewresearch.org/fact-tank/2022/06/15/u-s-teens-are-more-likely-than-adults-to-support-the-black-lives-matter-movement/.

9. **The phenomenon of online disinhibition:** John Suler, "The Online Disinhibition Effect," *CyberPsychology & Behavior* 7, no. 3 (July 2004): 321–26, https://doi.org/10.1089/1094931041291295.

10. **Owatonna, Minnesota:** John Eligon and Jenn Ackerman, "Few Talked about Race at This School. Then a Student Posted a Racist Slur," *New York Times*, June 7, 2019, https://www.nytimes.com/2019/06/07/us/school-racism-students.html.

11. **social researcher Brené Brown writes:** Brené Brown, "Shame vs. Guilt," Brené Brown, website, January 15, 2013, https://brenebrown.com/articles/2013/01/15/shame-v-guilt/.

12. **Taya Cohen, an organizational psychologist:** Timothy Meinch, "Shame and the Rise of the Social Media Outrage Machine," *Discover*, February 12, 2021, https://www.discovermagazine.com/the-sciences/shame-and-the-rise-of-the-social-media-outrage-machine.

13. **Christian Picciolini, a former white supremacist leader:** Christian Picciolini, "See the Child, Not the Monster," *Breaking Hate: Confronting the New Culture of Extremism* (New York: Hachette Books, 2022), p. 141.

14. **Hanna Stotland:** Author interview with Hanna Stotland, August 27, 2019.

chapter 8

1. **While slightly more:** Project Zero at Harvard, "PZ Digital Dilemmas Survey—Dilemma Slides," Google Slides, Google, https://docs.google.com/presentation/d/1H2y94DbObjoatzqodRwjnJbmMerARAXwW0Q__XUQmmE/edit#slide=id.g925e037414_0_571.

2. **A 2019 survey conducted by Kaplan:** "Kaplan Survey: Percentage of College Admissions Officers Who Visit Applicants' Social Media Pages on the Rise Again," Kaplan, accessed June 14, 2022, https://www.kaptest.com/blog/press/2020/01/13/kaplan-survey-percentage-of-college-admissions-officers-who-visit-applicants-social-media-pages-on-the-rise-again/.

3. **got a lot of media attention:** Samantha Schmidt, "Harvard Withdraws 10 Acceptances for 'Offensive' Memes in Private Group Chat," *Washington Post*, June 5, 2017, https://www.washingtonpost.com/news/morning-mix/wp/2017/06/05/harvard-withdraws-10-acceptances-for-offensive-memes-in-private-chat/.

4. **a framework for thinking about character:** "Character Assessment in College Admissions," Making Caring Common Project, 2022, https://mcc.gse.harvard.edu/research-initiatives/character-assessment-college-admissions.

5. **Forty percent of American high schools use the program:** Emily Tate Sullivan, "Naviance Wields Much 'Power and Influence' in College Admissions, Harvard Researcher Finds," *EdSurge*, April 18, 2019, https://www.edsurge.com/news/2019-04-18-naviance-wields-much-power-and-influence-in-college-admissions-harvard-researcher-finds.

6. **dampens her expectations:** Mark Kantrowitz, "Undermatching: Why Do Smart Low-Income Students Not Enroll In Selective Colleges?" College Investor, September 26, 2021, https://thecollegeinvestor.com/38195/what-is-under matching/.

7. **align their actions:** Devorah Heitner, "It's Not Just about College Admissions: Teaching Kids to Live Well, Even When No One Is Watching," *Washington Post*, April 3, 2019, https://www.washingtonpost.com/lifestyle/2019/04/03/its-not-just-about-college-admissions-teaching-kids-live-well-even-when-no-one-is-watching/.

chapter 9

1. **Meredith Balogh:** Dan Weissmann, "My Neighbor the Health-Care Ninja," interview with Meredith Balogh, *An Arm and a Leg*, podcast, November 21, 2019, https://armandalegshow.com/episode/my-neighbor-the-health-care-ninja/.

2. **describes how her parents fostered her independence:** "The Best Way My Parents Helped Me Prep for College," T1 Everyday Magic, 2021, https://www.t1everydaymagic.com/the-best-way-my-parents-helped-me-prep-for-college/.

3. **for 40 percent of college students is a *daily* activity:** Michaeline Jensen, Andrea M. Hussong, and Emily Haston, "Digital Parenting of Emerging Adults in the 21st Century," *Social Sciences* 10, no. 12 (2021): 482, https://doi.org/10.3390/socsci10120482.

index

about the author

Devorah Heitner, PhD, has spoken and written widely about parenting and growing up in the digital age. Her work has appeared in the *New York Times,* the *Washington Post,* the *Wall Street Journal,* and CNN. She is the author of the Amazon bestseller *Screenwise: Helping Kids Thrive (and Survive) in Their Digital World.* Dr. Heitner earned a PhD in Media, Technology, and Society from Northwestern University and has taught at DePaul University and Northwestern. She lives with her family in Chicagoland.

VISIT DEVORAH HEITNER ONLINE

devorahheitner.com
DevorahHeitnerPhD
DevorahHeitner

Felix the Fluffy Kitten
and Other Kitten Tales

Jenny Dale

Illustrated by Susan Hellard

A Working Partners Book

MACMILLAN CHILDREN'S BOOKS

'Felix the Fluffy Kitten', 'Star the Snowy Kitten' and 'Nell the Naughty Kitten'
first published 1999, and 'Snuggles the Sleepy Kitten' first published 2001,
in four separate volumes by Macmillan Children's Books

This bind-up edition published 2018 by Macmillan Children's Books
an imprint of Pan Macmillan
20 New Wharf Road, London N1 9RR
Associated companies throughout the world
www.panmacmillan.com

Created by Working Partners Limited
London WC2B 6XF

ISBN 978-1-5098-7126-1

1 3 5 7 9 8 6 4 2

A CIP catalogue record for this book is available from the British Library.

Typeset by Nigel Hazle
Printed and bound by CPI Group (UK) Ltd, Croydon, CR0 4YY